FOUR SEASONS RESORT
Jackson Hole

Dear Guest,

The present-day Grand Teton National Park took decades to create, and would not exist if it were not for the perseverance of inspired and dedicated people such as Horace Albright and John D. Rockefeller, Jr.

Crucible for Conservation is about the making of Grand Teton National Park as one of the greatest conservation success stories in U.S. History. I hope you will take time to read this book during your stay with us as well as visit this amazing natural resource located just minutes from your room.

If you are inspired by your visit and this book, I would encourage you to help support programs and projects in Grand Teton National Park by making a donation to the Grand Teton National Park Foundation.* Four Seasons Resort Jackson Hole has pledged to match these gifts up to $10,000.00. Hopefully together we can help carry on the tradition of philanthropy, local involvement and private-public partnerships that has successfully formed this beautiful National Park.

Sincerely,

Paul Cherrett
General Manager

Donations can be dropped off at the Front Desk. Checks should be made out to Grand Teton National Park Foundation.

For Pat, my mother and my father.

Grand Teton Natural History Association, Moose, WY 83012

Copyright © 1982 by Robert W. Righter
Published 1982, Reprinted 2000
Printed in the United States of America

Cover photography by Paul Frederick Martin

Library of Congress Card Catalog Number 81-69792

Text design by Mary Mendell
Cover design by Backwaters Publications
Printed by Patterson Printing

ISBN 0-931895-54-5

CONTENTS

O_N September 14, 1950, President Harry Truman signed a bill enlarging Grand Teton National Park to its current boundary, "... for the purpose of including in one national park, for public benefit and enjoyment, the lands within the present Grand Teton National Park and a portion of the lands within Jackson Hole National Monument." With the stroke of his pen, Truman enlarged Grand Teton National Park and ended the lengthy battle to protect much of Jackson Hole from future development.

Many of the issues that shaped the original 1929 Grand Teton National Park, the controversial 1943 Jackson Hole National Monument, and the new 1950 Park continue to affect conservation and management of this region. Today the park provides a legacy of grand proportions, with worldwide recognition for dramatic mountain scenery, bountiful wildlife, and diverse recreational opportunities. The scope of Grand Teton National Park is due in no small part to the dedication and perseverance of visionary men and women who believed that the greatest good for Teton landscape was as a "public park or pleasure ground for the benefit and enjoyment of the people of the United States." In *Crucible for Conservation*, Robert Righter captures the definitive hard-won battle for preservation of Jackson Hole. Righter details a remarkable story and gives us a sense of the length and breadth of a conservation dream that prevailed and became reality.

Decades of conflict challenged this conservation effort. While reflecting upon the saga of park creation and enlargement, we dare not rest. We must persistently seek in our hearts and minds a vision that will secure the future of this spectacular Teton Range and Jackson Hole valley.

Jack Neckels
Grand Teton National Park Superintendent
January 2000

PREFACE

Reckoned by geologic time, man's encounter with the land of North America is but an instant. Yet, within that twinkling of time he has transformed his environment, for better or for worse. Armed with vast technological knowledge and few ethical restrictions, Americans have often touched the land with the philosophy of Midas. Wealth, profit and progress were to be derived from the land. Nevertheless, we have managed to spare some of the continent from our drive for personal wealth or national power. This is the story of how one small valley and a noble range of mountains in northwest Wyoming was spared. Certainly most of the millions of Americans who annually visit Grand Teton National Park could not imagine any other fate but preservation for this remarkable country. However, as the story unfolds it will be evident that this national park did not just simply come to be. A fifty-year gestation period indicates that the birth of the park was not without trauma and enduring patience to those who promoted its establishment.

I first viewed the Teton Mountains as a boy. Although I don't recall much of that vacation, I do distinctly remember the mountains. Once seen, they are difficult to erase from the mind. Many years later when I came to the University of Wyoming to teach history, it was natural to renew my acquaintance with the "aesthetic corner" of Wyoming. At first pleasure, my motive soon became professional.

It became evident that the story of Grand Teton National Park had not been completely told. While Yellowstone National

Park to the north required only two years from idea to realization, Grand Teton took fifty-two years! Obviously here was a
story worth telling. Perhaps an article for a historical journal
was in order. However, soon it was apparent that the subject
would require much more. I felt much like Verne Chatelain, the
first chief historian of the National Park Service, who, in 1932,
was assigned to write a memorandum summarizing the history
of the struggle to create Grand Teton National Park. After concluding his 101-page "memo," Chatelain confessed that "since
its organization in 1916 the National Park Service has had to
deal with no special problem which occupies so large a place
in the public record and files of the Washington Office as does
that concerning Jackson Hole, Wyoming. The tremendous
quantity of material," continued Chatelain, "now relating to
the subject is one of the difficulties in the way of concise analysis." How true! Yet, when historian Chatelain made his observation, the Jackson Hole issue was eighteen years and many
reams of paper away from solution.

The subject warranted more than an article. Unmistak-
ably, the creation of Grand Teton National Park was a classic
case in the difficulties of park making, and although the focus
might be local, the subject was national in scope. While the establishment of Yellowstone Park was a case of simplicity, Grand
Teton was one of complexity. Also, it became apparent that the
park was a triumph of man's patience and determination, for
the park was no product of chance, but rather of men acting
deliberately in a noble cause. Broadly speaking, the establishment of Grand Teton National Park and the preservation of
northern Jackson Hole was one of the most notable conservation victories of the twentieth century. Surely, a modest book
was in order.

In preparing this study I owe thanks to the librarians and
archivists who assisted me in locating material. Robert Swen-
ningsen of the Federal Archives and Record Center in Denver
was particularly helpful, as were Gene Gressley, David Crosson,
Emmett Chisum and the late E. B. "Pete" Long, all of the Western History Research Center, University of Wyoming. They, as
well as Curtis Clow of the Rockefeller Archives, provided materials and the physical space to use them. Fred Smith and
George Lamb of the Jackson Hole Preserve, Inc. aided in obtain-

ing access to private materials which were important to this study.

Professors H. Duane Hampton, Theodore Hinckley, Robert Levinson, Werner Marti, and Alfred Runte all read portions or all of the manuscript. Their suggestions were extremely valuable, and saved me from a number of errors of fact or interpretation. Merrill Mattes of the National Park Service and Philip Hocker of Jackson Hole gave insights into certain facets of the story. John Daugherty, park historian at Grand Teton National Park, helped me avoid some errors and worked hard to find and reproduce pertinent photographs. Barbara Long gave the manuscript a close reading and suggested many stylistic changes. My colleague and friend at the University of Wyoming, Peter Iverson, listened and provided helpful criticism when asked. Roger L. Williams, Department of History chairman at the University of Wyoming, gave continual encouragement to this project. Irene Walker and Diane Alexander assisted through their secretarial and typing skills. I wish to acknowledge the financial assistance of the University of Wyoming for two summer research trips, and the Jackson Hole Preserve, Inc. for a generous grant to help with the costs of publication. Parts of Chapter VII appeared in a somewhat different form in *The American West*, to which acknowledgment is due.

Finally, let me extend a hearty thanks to that grand man of the national parks, Horace M. Albright. From the moment I approached him on the subject, this fine gentleman gave more assistance than I could reasonably expect. His constant encouragement kept me working, and his detailed reading of the manuscript prevented a number of errors. Those that remain, of course, are my responsibility.

Robert W. Righter

I

A COUNTRY FOR CONTROVERSY

"... the riches of such a country."
Donald MacKenzie, 1819

THE winter of 1818–1819, like every winter in Jackson Hole, was deep in snow and chilling cold. Yet for Donald MacKenzie, fur entrepreneur for the British North West Company, the seasonal inconvenience did not blind him to the beauty and the promise of the Jackson Hole country. As he snowshoed through the valley, he later recalled, he regretted with every step he made "that we had been so long deprived of the riches of such a country." [1]

Today, the Jackson Hole country is still a rich land. Its riches, however, are not derived from beaver pelts but from the magnificent panorama of beauty that it offers to the viewer. This sublime beauty, which is presently protected as Grand Teton National Park, has inspired many Americans and engendered fierce loyalties in those who call Jackson Hole home. It is, therefore, not surprising that the ownership and use of the Teton mountains and Jackson Hole should have excited the emotions of those directly as well as indirectly involved. A great prize was at stake: one of the picturesque places in the nation. The story to be told in this narrative is how that prize was preserved for the American people. It is a story of patient determination. It is the drama of a significant conservation victory won over a period of some thirty-five years. It is a chronicle of a group of determined individuals who fought to create the gem of the national park system—Grand Teton National Park.

The park is dominated by the needle-like peaks and pinnacles of the Teton Range and the mountain valley known as Jackson Hole. The two complement each other: the level valley and the perpendicular mountains. It is this contrast of the smooth, flattened valley abruptly interrupted by precipitous mountains rising majestically that gives this country its noble beauty. Between the mountains and the valley is nestled a series of exquisite lakes. Jackson Lake dominates in size, yet Leigh, Jenny, Taggart, Bradley, and Phelps Lakes all have their particular charm and alpine appeal.

Flowing through Jackson Hole is the Snake River, which gathers its waters in the highest reaches of Yellowstone National Park, then courses south to empty into Jackson Lake. Exiting from the lake, it transverses the length of Jackson Hole, bisecting the eight-mile-wide, forty-mile-long mountain valley. It is a river of grand proportions, yet decidedly swift and clear running. As it wends its way through the valley the Snake is augmented by Buffalo Fork, the Gros Ventre River, and to the extreme south, the Hoback River, as well as numerous lesser streams flowing from the surrounding mountains.

Although Jackson Hole is well watered by a network of rivers and streams, it is a lush land only in places. Much of the river basin, particularly on the eastern side of the Snake, is barren land, dominated by miles of sagebrush flats. In almost all of Jackson Hole the altitude and severity of climate make agriculture a marginal activity, and cattle grazing a seasonal endeavor. Nor does the region contain significant mineral deposits, although the southern part touches a recently discovered, oil-bearing geologic formation known as the "overthrust belt." Because Jackson Hole, like Yellowstone, contained neither mineral wealth nor outstanding agricultural potential it was largely spared as the northern Rocky Mountain country was settled in the late nineteenth century.

Just when and how the first human inhabitants came to Jackson Hole is a matter of some conjecture. Evidence suggests that they had arrived in the region by at least 11,500 B.C. According to one anthropologist they probably began to visit the Jackson Hole region some 10,000 years ago.[2] These early Indians left clues of their coming and going, such as rings of rocks to anchor their tepees, projectile points, and various handmade tools. They found Jackson Hole a hospitable land in the summer, and small extended-family groups lived well by hunting deer and bighorn sheep and fishing for cutthroat trout. By the sixteenth and seventeenth centuries these early inhabitants were driven off by Shoshonean-speaking peoples expanding from the Great Basin. As nomadic hunters they no doubt appreciated Jackson Hole, but found the land unsuited to a lifestyle of the horse and the hunt. Although the Crows, Blackfeet, Gros Ventres, and the Shoshonis all claimed a loose hegemony to surrounding lands, there is no evidence to suggest that any stayed for extended periods in Jackson Hole.

The first white man to enter Jackson Hole sought to trade with these Indians. John Colter, a Virginia-born veteran of the Lewis and Clark Expedition, traveled extensively in northwest Wyoming in 1807. He sought beaver pelts and trade agreements. Because the record is not perfectly clear, historians have disputed the exact route of Colter's epic travels throughout northwest Wyoming in 1807. Some question whether he actually entered the valley and viewed the Tetons, however the preponderance of evidence indicates that Colter entered Jackson Hole via Togwotee Pass and departed over Teton Pass.[3] During the next three decades the region was often traversed and trapped by mountain men. Some historians would have Jackson Hole as the center or crossroads of the fur trade, although a more logical focal point was the upper Green River basin, where six of the eight fur trade summer rendezvous were held between the years 1833 and 1840.[4] No yearly rendezvous was ever held in Jackson Hole, nor did any fur trade company or the government consider it important enough to warrant establishment of a trading post or a fort. Nevertheless, the Teton Range was a landmark to trappers, and the name given the mountains ("Les Trois Tetons" —The Three Breasts) and the valley were of fur trade origin. While the mountains were given their curious appellation by a group of nostalgic, love-starved Iroquois trappers, the valley was named after David Jackson, partner of William Sublette and Jedediah Smith in the Rocky Mountain Fur Company.[5] For many years authors and residents clung to the grammatically correct Jackson's Hole, but the more contemporary usage drops the possessive to Jackson Hole.

When the beaver were depleted and London dandies no longer fancied beaver top hats, Jackson Hole became virtually unvisited. Although the late 1840s and early 1850s witnessed a mass westward migration unparalleled in the American experience, few if any of these husbandmen or "argonauts" passed through Jackson Hole. The Union Pass-Hoback River trail was a feasible route to Oregon, but not so convenient or as established as South Pass and the Oregon Trail. Off the thoroughfares of the Westward Movement, Jackson Hole from 1840 to 1870 was a blank area on the map, and like Yellowstone, a place of legend and rumor but of which there was little real knowledge. It was a valley where Shoshoni, Gros Ventre, and Blackfeet Indians might hunt and summer with little disturbance from the encroaching white man.

Of course those hearty pioneers of the mining frontier left no stream untried in the second half of the century. During the Civil War the gold strike at Grasshopper Creek and Alder Gulch, Montana Territory, spawned activity in the Greater Yellowstone region. In 1863, Walter DeLacy and Charles Ream headed a prospecting party through Jackson Hole and up the Snake River into Yellowstone.[6] In 1864 and again in 1867 other prospectors sifted and panned the waters of Jackson Hole. None of these miners left a record of their perceptions of the remarkable valley and the Teton Range. No doubt their eyes as well as their thoughts were cast downward in search of gold-bearing soils, not toward the mountains. We do know that they found nothing but a trace of gold, leaving the region virtually unexplored and unpublicized.

It was explorers associated with the "scientific frontier" who initially furnished Americans with accurate information about the region. Captain William F. Raynolds, heading a railroad reconnaissance expedition, entered Jackson Hole in the summer of 1860. His reports were not widely circulated and the nation was soon concerned with problems more crucial than exploration of the American West. After the Civil War America's romance with the West was renewed. In the vanguard came such men as Clarence King, John Wesley Powell and Ferdinand V. Hayden, scientists who viewed this land from a different perspective. As paleontologists, ethnologists, topographers and geologists, they perceived the region as an immense laboratory in which emerging scientific theories, such as that of Charles Darwin, might be tested. In carrying out this task they combined knowledge, training, skill and courage (as attested to by Powell's courageous descent of the Colorado River) heretofore reserved only to those great explorers of Elizabethan England. Supported by congressional appropriations, these men made public their findings to Congress and the American people. Their reports were more than mere formality. Carefully constructed as to both literary and visual appeal, the reports may not have been as colorful or enticing as our current "coffee table" productions, yet they were meant to be widely read in a fashion that government documents today rarely achieve.[7]

Ferdinand V. Hayden first opened the northwest corner of Wyoming to public view. In the late 1860s this prototype of the "gilded age" explorer publicized the beauty and economic possibilities of much of Colorado and Wyoming. In 1871, after reading and hearing of the exciting discoveries made by the Washburn-Doane-Langford expedition of 1870 to the Yellowstone region, Hayden determined to visit the area to give scientific verification to the stories of geysers and other thermal phenomena. His 1871 expedition succeeded, and his scientific findings—made valid in no small part by the remarkable photographs of William Henry Jackson—were presented to the public. Partially as a result of his findings and testimony, the following year Congress established Yellowstone National Park, the first national park in the United States, or in fact, in the world.[8]

In 1872 Hayden returned to Yellowstone. Splitting his survey division, he sent a party headed by James Stevenson to make a brief "geologic-photographic" examination of the Jackson Hole region.[9] While camped in the valley, Stevenson and Nathaniel Langford claimed the first ascent of the Grand Teton. While the heroics of these two men have been discredited by some and never completely verified by others, the famed photographer William H. Jackson nevertheless scrambled about with his cumbersome equipment, recording the beauty of the Teton mountain range for the first time.

In the years immediately following the Hayden Survey, other scientific and military expeditions entered Jackson Hole for various purposes ranging from Indian surveillance, to scientific enlightenment, to sporting-type outings. Certainly the most famous of the latter was the 1883 visit of President Chester A. Arthur. It was a rather grand show, directed by General Philip Sheridan and dedicated to the enjoyment of the president and his fishing cronies. Because the press was not allowed to accompany the party, we have no firsthand accounts of his thoughts, but evidently the president was not of a mind to fully appreciate the beauty of the regions he traversed.[10]

While men of wealth and prestige frequented Jackson Hole to hunt and fish, persons of humbler means settled the valley. When the beaver business ended most of the mountain men returned East or found new livelihoods on the West Coast. However, a small number could not tolerate the thought of relocating to a more sedentary life. They remained in the northern Rocky Mountains eking out an existence through trapping, guiding, and, occasionally, farming. Such a man was "Beaver Dick" Leigh, who with his Indian wife and family knew the northwest corner of Wyoming as well as anyone. However, this somewhat rootless trapper could usually be found on the Idaho side of the Tetons. The first permanent residents of the hole were John Holland and John Carnes, two more survivors of the trapping fraternity reluctantly engaged in farming. Accompanied by Carnes's Indian wife, Millie, in the summer of 1884 the men hauled simple farm equipment down the Gros Ventre River and homesteaded along the bottom land of Flat Creek. They did not prosper, but they did survive. Others followed, so that by 1889 some forty settlers had established themselves throughout the valley. Among them were Dick Turpin, Stephen Leek and Robert Miller—all young men destined to play important roles in the struggle to establish Grand Teton National Park. The following year the tiny population was increased by the arrival of five Mormon families headed by Sylvester Wilson.[11] Homesteaders continued to trickle in during the 1890s so that by the turn of the century discernible settlements had been established at Jackson, Moose, Moran, Wilson and Kelly.

These clusters of pioneers, far removed from the pressures of an increasingly urban-industrialized nation, wrested out a living in a fashion reminiscent of their past rather than portentous of their future. They tried their hands at agriculture, ran a few cattle, guided an occasional hunting party, and generally lived off the land. They were not affluent, yet often the hardy settlers were willing to endure privation to live in this special place. And isolated as they were, they extolled the virtues of independence, self-sufficiency and a life in close communion with nature. It was easy to become attached to this way of life and to the valley that sustained them. Man has always had a possessory inclination toward a particular piece of land or even a whole mountain valley, and perhaps the greater the beauty the more determined that attachment becomes. This is one reason why Jackson Hole in the first half of the twentieth century was destined to be a "valley in discord." [12]

Thus it was that few people who knew of the Tetons and Jackson Hole thought in terms of preservation. Those who came were intent on ownership of a small piece of beautiful land. Fortunately for the national interest, Jackson Hole was indeed stingy in sustaining human endeavor, for profitable mining opportunities did not exist, and the severe climate precluded intensive agriculture and limited ranching opportunities. Lodgepole pine forests were of little value, and those interested in logging were wise to venture farther west to the lofty forests of the Northwest. Thus much of the land in Jackson Hole remained in the public domain, perhaps appreciated but unwanted.

In many respects these pioneers shared their home with wildlife. Jackson Hole, then and now, is world famous for the abundance of big game. Deer, bear, wolves, and antelope flourished. The few remaining bison found a modicum of protection in nearby Yellowstone National Park. However, the elk were both the most noble and numerous of the Jackson Hole wildlife. The Jackson Hole elk herd deserves special mention, for the welfare of the herd was an issue intertwined in the Grand Teton National Park fight from beginning to end.

According to wildlife authority Olaus Murie, when Europeans first arrived on the North American continent, elk were the most widely distributed of the deer family. Except for the extreme East Coast and considerable portions of the arid West, elk ranged throughout the continent.[13] Gradually these noble creatures were dispossessed of their forage and browse by the mounted Plains Indians and the onrushing Americans. It was to the broad forests and lush meadows of the Yellowstone region that the elk retreated, seemingly safe from the molestations of man.

In Yellowstone, however, they encountered a new adversary. Situated on the crest of the continent, Yellowstone was subject to perhaps the severest winter weather in the nation. Few mammals would survive, save through hibernation. Therefore, over the years the elk developed migratory patterns to es-

cape the perils of winter. While the northern herd sought shel-
ter along the Yellowstone River of Montana, the southern herd
journeyed south via Jackson Hole or the crest of the Absaroka
Mountains, many descending into the Green River valley. Some
grazed south to the Red Desert of Wyoming, then turned north
as the first signs of spring appeared. This pattern was followed
throughout the nineteenth century. However, the appearance
in the 1880s of permanent ranchers in both Jackson Hole and
the Green River valley brought disruption. While the presence
of man inhibited these shy creatures, his fences often presented
difficult, if not insurmountable, obstacles. Finally, the rancher's
cattle co-opted the range and pasture land which had formerly
supported elk.

As a result of this set of circumstances, the elk began to
winter in large numbers in Jackson Hole. Yet this was a less
than satisfactory solution, for Jackson Hole winters are long and
severe. Elk, concentrated by the thousands, faced a limited
amount of grass and browse. The result was starvation: hundreds in a mild winter, thousands otherwise.

Compounding the herd's struggle for survival was the
economic value of the bull elk's canine teeth. The handsome
teeth were considered a valued trophy, and were particularly
prized by members of the B.P.O.E., the Elks Lodge. An aged,
well-stained set of bull elk tusks could bring from twenty to
twenty-five dollars.[14] While most Jackson Hole residents col-
lected the tusks legally, there was a group, kindred souls to the
buffalo market hunters, who poached large numbers of elk simply for the canine teeth. These "tuskers" infuriated residents,
for they killed wantonly, taking only the tusks, and leaving the
valuable meat as coyote carrion. It was a waste of a resource
which residents valued not only for meat, but to lure free-
spending hunters. Thus residents fought to end the waste and
to initiate policies of wise use of a valued resource.

While poachers were eventually punished, legally or ex-
tra-legally, for their nefarious occupation, the problem of winter starvation was not so easily solved. When necessary, some
local ranchers provided what hay they could spare from their
own stock. But this individual undertaking, though altruistic,
could not provide relief in such an awesome winter as 1908–
1909. It was a wintertime that was never ending, and through it
all Stephen Leek, a pioneer rancher with a talent for photog-

raphy, recorded on film the agony of the starving elk. His photographs, published in newspapers and magazines, drew national attention to the plight of the animals and, consequently, generated governmental action.

The state of Wyoming first took action by appropriating $5,000 to provide grain. Shortly thereafter, Congress appropriated $20,000 for the purchase of hay. By 1911 both the state of Wyoming and the federal government had committed themselves to a program of artificial feeding. In 1912 Congress authorized the purchase of some 1760 acres of land in the Flat Creek area, the nucleus of the National Elk Refuge. In the years to follow Congress would extend the refuge by further purchases and the withdrawal of public land from private entry. Private land donations by the Izaac Walton League and John D. Rockefeller, Jr., provided further expansion until presently the refuge encompasses over 23,000 acres, bounded by the Gros Ventre River on the north and the town of Jackson to the south.[15] Thus, near the turn of the century, authorities began the necessary steps to safeguard the herd. But the size of the herd (generally between 8,000 and 30,000) and the jurisdiction of the elk would be two sources of ongoing controversy.

Another source of discord has been water. No natural resource provoked more disputes in the arid West than the storage and distribution of water. At the time Jackson Hole was being settled, westerners enjoyed the myth that reclamation through irrigation would transform the arid West into a garden. Such avid irrigationists as William Smythe predicted that with proper development of her water resources Wyoming would eventually "sustain a population as large as that of Ohio and Illinois." [16] Certainly this was attractive to the population-poor state. When the Reclamation Act of 1902 established the Bureau of Reclamation, Wyoming eagerly awaited the benefits. The state was not disappointed, for the bureau completed the Buffalo Bill Dam on the Shoshone River by 1910 and the Pathfinder Dam on the North Platte in the following year. Although neither of these projects fulfilled Smythe's expectations or the bureau's predictions, Wyoming enthusiastically supported the efforts of the Reclamation Service. Thus when the bureau proposed to dam Jackson Lake to store water to irrigate Idaho sugar beets and potatoes (Minidoka Project), nary a word of protest was uttered. To accomplish their purpose, the bureau constructed a rather crude rock-filled, log-crib dam in 1906. Four years later it washed away, to be replaced in 1911 by the concrete dam which still remains today.[17]

The damming of Jackson Lake was an act of environmental desecration second only to the inundation of Yosemite's Hetch Hetchy Valley. Yet while Hetch Hetchy provoked a nationwide outcry, no voices protested the damming of Jackson Lake.[18] Irrigation promised such progress and such a rosy future to struggling western farmers and ranchers that it would have been an act of considerable courage to oppose publicly the project. At that time only a handful of individuals understood the finite nature of scenic lands, or realized their value as a commodity (to use a commercial term). Fewer still had the courage to speak out against this "wise use" of our resources.

The Bureau of Reclamation may have been wrong in sacrificing Jackson Lake, but they were nonetheless well meaning in their conviction that they were accomplishing noble ends. Private irrigationists active in Jackson Hole were not motivated by such lofty ideals. They hoped to profit by fraudulent use of the Carey Irrigation Act of 1894, a complicated piece of legislation designed to promote irrigation by private enterprise with the cooperation of the state on land donated by the federal government.[19] One firm that attempted to use the act was the Teton Irrigation Company, headquartered in Cheyenne. Using the Carey Act, the company filed water claims in 1909 and 1912 for water on the Gros Ventre River, Buffalo Fork and Spread Creek. Ostensibly the company planned to irrigate the sagebrush floor of the valley. Skeptics were numerous, for the flat land was so strewn with stones that agriculture was well-nigh impossible. "Even badgers won't dig in it," quipped Struthers Burt, "and that is saying a good deal." [20] This did not faze the company officials, for they had other ideas. Namely, when failure occurred they would sell their water downstream to Idaho farmers. This they did until 1930 when the state of Wyoming suspended the firm's operation.[21]

Other irrigation schemes threatened the Jackson Hole environment. Two corporations, the Osgood Land and Livestock Company and the Utah-Idaho Sugar Company, succeeded in securing water storage rights on Emma Matilda and Two Ocean Lakes. Although neither firm carried out its original plans, small wooden headgates appeared at the outlet of each lake and were not removed until 1950. The most potentially dangerous was a plan involving the two most exquisite lakes in Jackson Hole: Jenny Lake and Leigh Lake. Following a drought in 1919 the state engineer became convinced that it was proper to impound their waters. The National Park Service, by then deeply committed to Jackson Hole, fought the plan with great determination, thus winning many friends and averting calamity.

Foremost in advocating the welfare of the elk herd and cessation of irrigation schemes was a small group of ranchers with the appellation "dude-wrangler." Some came to this dual occupation through necessity. With a brief growing season, severe winters and a fluctuating market, ranching was a marginal business. In time some of the ranchers began to supplement their incomes by taking in summer guests. At first dude-wrangling, according to Struthers Burt, "didn't seem a real business to the cattlemen. . . ." But soon the economic possibilities overcame whatever hesitancy was harbored by old-time ranchers. Only a few, however, were successful, for their clients were wealthy, and therefore selective. Those who prospered, according to Burt, were educated westerners with an intimate knowledge of the East. In reality, many were easterners, for the refinements of life had of necessity been abandoned by most of the rugged ranchers of the area. But from whatever section of the country, the dude-wrangler had to be a jack-of-all-trades. "The dude-wrangler is a ranch owner, a cowman, a horseman, a guide, a wholesale chambermaid, a cook, and storekeeper rolled into one." [22]

For our purposes Struthers Burt left out an important attribute: the dude-wrangler supported the preservationist cause. Of all the early settlers in Jackson Hole, it was the dude-wrangler who understood the value of the big game and the natural beauty. He realized that scenic mountains, rivers and valleys were business assets that might be marketed, often much more profitably than cattle. He understood that wise game management would guarantee that the big game need never disappear. He knew that wilderness areas were necessary in the scheme of things, and could be considered as economic assets.[23] And in his own mind he already knew that the future of Jackson Hole lay not in livestock, agriculture or timber, but in tourism: tourism not based on gaudy dance halls, gambling or liquor, but one centered on a comfortable but close relationship with nature. Jackson Hole would offer a summer respite from the overcrowded, over-civilized eastern cities. It would offer semi-wilderness to those who could afford a unique, natural experience tempered by the amenities of civilization. To accomplish this end Jackson Hole had to remain natural and unspoiled.

Thus, during these early days it was not the National Park Service or the Sierra Club or the Boone & Crockett Club that fought off the poachers, water-power men and the land schemers. It was the dude ranchers. Often typed as reactionary and opposed to progress, in truth they understood the potential of Jackson Hole. Admittedly, in opposing development they acted in their own self-interest. Fortunately that interest was in accord with the national purpose. In the struggle to come, the National Park Service and John D. Rockefeller, Jr. would find the dude ranchers dedicated, though independent, allies.

I·I
GENESIS OF AN IDEA

"A NATION'S PARK, *containing man and beast,*
in all the wild and freshness of
their nature's beauty!"
George Catlin, 1832

W HILE Jackson Hole struggled to emerge from raw
frontier to settlement, an important idea began to take hold in
the nation. The parks idea dates well before the birth of Christ.
Hunting enclosures were a common feature within the Persian
Empire as were public plazas or assembly places in the Greek
city states.[1] However, the national parks idea perhaps finds
stronger roots in modern rather than ancient history. Parks became fashionable as eighteenth century Romantics questioned
the progress represented by the Industrial Revolution. Primitiv-
ism, an offshoot of Romanticism, extolled the virtues to be
found in nature, while critical of the constraints and corrup-
tions of urban life. However, until the mid-nineteenth century
Europeans believed that these natural, pristine places ought to
be the preserves of the wealthy, where they might cavort, free
from the pressures of their managerial roles. In pastoral settings
they pursued such pastimes as angling, hunting, or simply stroll-
ing through the woodlands. This governing class assumed that
the proletariat class had neither the aesthetic sensitivity nor
the cultural sophistication to benefit from the beauty of nature.

Such an idea could not withstand the liberal political theories of the mid-nineteenth century. The winds of democracy
blew in the parks as well as the streets of Europe, England, and

America. By 1850 parks in England and France were open to the poor as well as the rich. In the United States, with its vigorous egalitarian tradition, there was never any doubt. When in 1832 George Catlin first proposed "A *nation's Park,* containing man and beast, in all the wild and freshness of their nature's beauty," he had in mind a place of refuge for the nation's dispossessed— the Native American.[2] When Henry David Thoreau made a plea in the *Atlantic Monthly* in 1858 for national parks, he observed that America must not follow the monarchial patterns of Europe.[3] Frederick Law Olmsted, the famed designer of New York's Central Park, echoed the democratic impulse when he asserted that Yosemite Valley "should be held, guarded and managed for the free use of the whole body of the people forever . . ."[4]

Whereas there was no doubt parks were for the people, the idea of setting aside sublime areas as public parks ran counter to accepted land use concepts. In the East the land had been parcelled away with little thought of retention of unique features or natural landscapes. Americans assumed that public lands ought to be transferred into private hands just as quickly and as expeditiously as possible.[5] Natural resources and boundless wilderness invited settlement and civilization, not preservation. Scenic lands which offered any productive, economic use were rarely considered for preservation or parks. Even Niagara Falls could not withstand the American proclivity to look upon nature with an eye to profit and progress. By 1860 businesses had located adjacent to the falls to tap its continuous source of power, and private individuals had laid claim to the finest views, exacting a handsome price from tourists. The awesome spectacle of the waterfall was embarrassingly violated by the actions of petty persons intent on commercial gain.[6] Frederick Law Olmsted and others worked hard to extricate Niagara Falls from the hands of the entrepreneurs, but in retrospect it is obvious that in the development of the East natural beauty was secondary to the individuals' drive to acquire property and profit from it.

It was the American West with its broad vistas, startling mountains, and free flowing waters that inspired Americans with thoughts of preservation and creation of national parks. Fortunately, the settlement of much of the West was delayed by a different and often hostile environment. The arid West defied eastern models, hence as emigrants encountered the Great Plains and the Rocky Mountain West in the 1840s they either turned back or quickly crossed to the more inviting lands of Oregon or California.[7] They chose to avoid that strange, wrinkled land of hills and mountains, upthrust pinnacles, flat mesas, and broad sagebrush-covered valleys. To their conditioned eyes it was a forbidding land, shaped by the work of water, yet possessing precious little of its maker. Of course nature had blessed the West here and there with oases of green formed by lakes, streams and moisture-catching mountains, yet to the agrarian-oriented settler, it was not an attractive land.

Until the 1890s the arid West remained largely uninhabited; unwanted except by miners and cattlemen profiting from the public domain. This was fortunate, for during this fifty-year period the movement for preservation of parklands gained momentum so that when it came time for land use decisions in the West, creation of national parks was a viable option. National parks, an "American Invention" as one historian put it, were primarily possible because of the availability of vast stretches of land at a time when a democratic nation could now enjoy the luxury of preservation of spectacular regions for present and future generations.[8]

Not only could the nation afford the luxury of preservation, it would seem that the preservation of the wonders of the West fulfilled a subtle cultural need. Historian Alfred Runte argues convincingly that national parks in the West were not established to glorify or preserve nature, but to act as a substitute for a viable American culture. While Americans found pride in their material progress as well as their political institution, few could question the cultural supremacy of the "Old World." In matters of art, architecture, history and literature nineteenth century America deferred to Europe. In search of a cultural identity many found an answer in the natural wonders of the North American continent. To such Americans as Thomas Jefferson, James Fenimore Cooper, and Washington Irving it was comforting to realize that Europe had no counterpart for the Hudson River Valley, the Potomac River or Niagara Falls. The Thames River paled in significance when matched with the immensity of the Mississippi. Farther west the plains, the vast lofty mountain ranges, the immense trees, and the beauty of the valleys all invited comparison with Europe. The ancient and unspoiled natural wonders of the American West offered an equal to the man-made castles and cathedrals of Europe. We found it convenient to substitute natural history for human history. Hence it became culturally important that natural wonders, whether they were flowing waters, vertical cliffs, big trees older than the civilizations of Greece, or bizarre geysers, be preserved as "monuments" to American culture.[9] When Charles D. Walcott, director of the United States Geological Survey, characterized the Jackson Hole region as "the Switzerland of America" he was not only expressing a recognizable analogy, but making a cultural statement.[10] This natural heritage should not fall into the hands of private individuals who might desecrate or exploit for profit. These were special places, to be protected by the national government and enjoyed by all of the people.

Of course a philosophy and a practice are two different matters. Legislative expression for preservation came in 1864 with the setting aside of Yosemite Valley and the Mariposa Grove of big trees. It was during that time of Civil War chaos and concern that President Lincoln, with little fanfare, affixed his signature to an act granting to the state of California tracts of land embracing Yosemite Valley and the Mariposa Grove of big trees. The act guaranteed that "the said State shall accept this grant upon the express conditions that the premises shall be held for public use, resort, and recreation . . ." and that this public right "shall be unalienable for all time."[11] This may be considered the first legislative step to establish the national park system. Of course, as historian Carl Russell has noted, the act "did not create a national park, but it did give Federal recognition to the importance of natural reservations in our cultural scheme, and charged California with the responsibility of preserving and presenting the natural wonders of the Yosemite."[12]

If the idea was first promulgated with Yosemite, it fell to Yellowstone in 1872, to become the first national park. The action came after the flurry of publicity and scientific discovery in 1870 and 1871. The establishment of Yellowstone National Park did not represent a commitment by Congress to wilderness or preservation of a significant ecosystem. Rather, Yellowstone as a scientific curiosity provided a splendid opportunity to publicize to the nation and the world the uniqueness and variety of our physical environment.[13] On a more prosaic level, congressional debates on Yellowstone indicate that the park was established only after the legislators were quite convinced that the region contained no agricultural, timber, or mining potential.[14]

All of this is to say that neither the Congress nor the American people were deeply committed to national parks or to the preservation idea. This is most evident in the miserly way in which both the Congress of the United States and the state of California cared for their unique possessions. While Yellowstone suffered the indignities of rampant poaching of wildlife and widespread vandalism, Congress turned a deaf ear to the idea of park appropriations.[15] Yosemite Valley fared no better under California's stewardship. Logging was allowed, barbed-wire fences appeared, and the glorious meadows were plowed under and planted with hay to accommodate tourists' horses. In the forthright words of John Muir, whatever improvements were made were "vulgar and mercenary."[16] These examples of the shoddy care of Yosemite Valley and Yellowstone suggest that the day had not yet arrived when preservation of natural beauty would be accepted and supported by a large segment of the populace.

Broad sentiment for preservation of places of exceptional scenic grandeur would not emerge until the turn of the century. By that time an important movement swept the nation. The conservation movement influenced land use decisions throughout the American West, but no more profoundly than in Jackson Hole and the surrounding mountains. The movement is complex and escapes any easy definition. We can see, however, that the American people began to reevaluate their natural resources with a sense of uneasiness. First, it became evident to many thoughtful Americans that the "myth of superabundance" was just that, a myth.[17] Men like Carl Schurz, John Wesley Powell and William John ("WJ") McGee began to realize that our resources were finite, and that we must adopt policies of wise use rather than continued abuse and waste. This did not imply *no* use, but simply that it was time to view our resources as exhaustible, hence to be harvested, distributed and used efficiently.[18] For others the primary thrust of the Progressive conservation movement was to prevent monopoly. Political leaders such as Theodore Roosevelt and Robert LaFollette found it unacceptable that a high percentage of the nation's resources were in the hands of a few. They maintained that continued control of the common heritage by a wealthy minority must end. Many believed that the solution was greater government (i.e., people) participation in the resource management of the nation.[19] Their success was most evident in the public lands policy. While throughout the nineteenth century the policy of the General Land Office was to transfer public lands into private hands as expeditiously as possible, by the turn of the century the government began to think in terms of management rather than marketing. In the terms of the public land authorities Marion Clawson and Burnell Held, the nation's land policy evolved from one of "disposal," to one of "reservation" and "custodial management." [20] This change would cause many a westerner to stamp his foot in rage, for it seemed that he was being denied what every American had come to accept as his birthright—the right to free or cheap land in bountiful amounts.

While the conservation movement was motivated by impulses of democracy and efficiency, other more subtle factors were at work. Post-Civil War America featured rapid, often paroxysmal, change. An agricultural country became an urban-industrial nation. More and more Americans traded a nature-based lifestyle for one dominated by the factory whistle. Wealth and opportunity lay in the city, rather than on the frontier. In fact, by 1890 the United States Census Bureau announced that a distinguishable frontier line no longer existed. This rapidly changing world exhilarated many, but disturbed others. For such historians as Frederick Jackson Turner, the American character at its very marrow was fashioned by the frontier environment.[21] A natural question emerged: If our frontier experience molded American character and virtue, what would happen now that the frontier was gone? No one could answer that, but leaders such as naturalist John Muir and *Century Magazine* editor Robert Underwood Johnson suggested that the retention of some wilderness (frontier) might be a good hedge against the malevolent effects of too much civilization.[22] It was a time when a frontierless nation looked with greater appreciation at what remained.

Given the complexity of the conservation movement, it was natural that in Jackson Hole and elsewhere the idea of conservation would come to mean many different things to different people. On the West Coast John Muir and men of similar sensitivities formed the Sierra Club in 1892, dedicating themselves to the retention of wilderness and natural beauty as a spiritual placebo for over-civilized man. These preservationists soon came into conflict with another prototype of the conservationist, the utilitarian conservationist. Perhaps most typical and influential of the latter group was Gifford Pinchot, America's first professional forester. Pinchot believed that nature should be used, managed and controlled by man in an efficient manner. He opposed wasteful exploitation, but he did not favor wilderness. At one point Pinchot reassured Americans of the non-subversive nature of the conservation movement by insisting that "the first great fact about conservation is that it stands for development." [23]

These two forces first met in battle over the ultimate fate of the spectacular Hetch Hetchy Valley in Yosemite National Park. Should the valley be spared for all time or must it be dammed and inundated to serve the water needs of the burgeoning city of San Francisco? After more than a decade of political maneuvers and heated debate the "temple destroyers" and "devotees of ravaging commercialism," as Muir typed them, won the day.[24] Time and again in the twentieth century the two conservation factions would do battle in nature's arena.

The Jackson Hole writer Struthers Burt caught the enduring aspect of the struggle in his novel, *The Delectable Mountains*. Stephen Londreth, a sensitive, young rancher opposed to the damming of mountain lakes, had just concluded a difficult negotiation with Mr. Welkins, a crass character bent on profit through irrigation projects and development. When Welkins expressed relief that their dickering over property (and ethics) was over, Londreth replied:

Oh, it isn't over . . . it's just beginning. This is a small part of it. The quarrel between men who look at things as you and Duffield do and men who look at things the way I do is as old as the hills and is likely to continue . . . Oh no, it isn't over.[25]

This ongoing struggle between development and preservation is a pervasive theme that spans time in Jackson Hole from the early days of settlement to the present. It has taken many forms, but one of the most important has been the relationship of the United States Forest Service and the National Park Service. Time and again throughout the long struggle over establishment of the park, the two agencies were at loggerheads.

Their differences flowed naturally from differing conservation philosophies, but also because the Forest Service was there first.

Forest Service guardianship over the mountains encircling Jackson Hole has its origins in the nineteenth century. In 1891 the Forest Reserve Act (Article 24 of the Land Act of 1891) slipped by Congress with scarcely any debate. Perhaps the most important act in the history of American conservation passed with virtually no opposition.[26] As a result of this legislation in the next sixteen years four presidents would set aside close to 150 million acres of timberland as forest reserves. Most of the undisposed trees of the American West became federal trees, often to the chagrin of westerners. The initial reserve, set aside by President Benjamin Harrison on March 30, 1891, was the Yellowstone Park Timber Reserve, a 1,239,040-acre expanse surrounding the national park to the south and the east. The southern section of the reserve reached to the northern end of the Jackson Hole-Teton Range country.

As is so often the case, Congress found it easy to create but difficult to appropriate. There was no money for protection or management of the Yellowstone reserve or any other of the newly created forest reserves. Caretaking was non-existent, although the Yellowstone Reserve was nominally under the supervision of the military. Yet the reserves continued to be created. President Grover Cleveland, shortly before leaving office, established Teton Forest Reserve on February 22, 1897. This 829,440-acre reserve extended federal control well to the south of the Yellowstone Reserve, and included most of the land which today comprises Grand Teton National Park.[27] These forest reserve withdrawals assured that the vast forests, craggy peaks and sparkling lakes of the Jackson Hole country would substantially remain in public hands, although poorly managed.

Under President Theodore Roosevelt the forest reserves were greatly expanded. Furthermore, Gifford Pinchot, a close confidant of the president, provided the dynamic leadership needed as he consolidated the disparate reserves into the United States Forest Service, under the Department of Agriculture. Pinchot's enthusiasm was infectious as he built a ranger force unequalled in its loyalty and devotion to its task.[28] Again, the Forest Service would increase its holdings in the Jackson Hole area by the creation of Teton National Forest on July 1, 1908, a 1,991,200-acre domain carved out of the Yellowstone and Teton reserves, and reaching far south to include all of the Teton Range as well as the timber lands surrounding Jackson Hole.[29]

With Pinchot at the helm, the Forest Service not only multiplied its holdings, but took the lead in conservation thought. Pinchot would fashion policies of multiple use and sustained yield, which translated into varied programs of forest use but always with a concern to future as well as present productivity. In Teton National Forest these policies would evolve into a sympathetic interest in cattle leases but not necessarily sheep, empathy for water projects, a certain fascination with the region's timber potential, and a commitment to develop recreational resources, particularly through campground construction and summer home leases.

At the turn of the century the possibility of a national park in Jackson Hole was simply an idea shared by a handful of persons in administrative positions and rather detached from local feeling. On the other hand, the Forest Service controlled the Teton Range as well as the Rendezvous Mountains, the Thorofare County, the Togwotee Pass region, and the Gros Ventre Mountains. All of the forested hills and mountains that enclosed Jackson Hole came under the jurisdiction of the Forest Service, and the rangers, usually members of the community, understood and catered to the economic concerns of the community. It was natural that an alliance of Forest Service officials and local leaders would form a strong cabal of opposition to the invading National Park Service.

I·I·I

ANOTHER WAY—
ENTER THE NATIONAL PARK SERVICE

"This region will find its highest use as a playground."
Petition of Jackson Hole landowners, 1925.

ALTHOUGH exploitive use seemed in the ascendancy in the early days, there were those who believed that Jackson Hole was meant for a higher purpose than providing water for potatoes, lumber for two-by-fours or beef for tables. These persons first considered protection of Jackson Hole by tying it to Yellowstone National Park. This "Greater Yellowstone" concept found expression through General Philip Sheridan. In 1882, just ten years after the establishment of Yellowstone, the general visited the park and expressed his concern for the condition of the wildlife. He recommended that Yellowstone be extended some forty miles eastward and south to the forty-fourth degree of latitude, taking in land to the northern tip of Jackson Lake. Jackson Hole was not included in his recommendation.[1]

In the 1890s the idea of Grand Teton National Park surfaced with that burst of conservation energy that resulted in the establishment of such national parks as Yosemite (1890), Sequoia and General Grant (1890), and Mount Rainier (1899). In 1897 Colonel S. B. M. Young, acting superintendent of Yellowstone, recommended that the Yellowstone National Park authority be extended into Jackson Hole. Colonel Young was a military man with the sensitivity of a conservationist. In his report to the secretary of the interior he deplored the poaching of elk outside his jurisdiction. Young suggested that protection be given to the migratory paths of the elk, and that his troopers might do the job.[2]

The following year Charles D. Walcott, director of the United States Geological Survey, visited the Jackson Hole region. He reiterated Young's concern. It seemed incongruous for the government to protect the elk in their Yellowstone summer range while exposing them to slaughter during the winter migration. Walcott had little if any faith that the state of Wyoming or the forest reserve employees would provide the necessary protection. Extermination was inevitable. The solution, suggested Walcott, incorporated the Tetons and Jackson Hole as either an extension of Yellowstone National Park, or "as a separate park, to be known as the Teton National Park."[3] In recommending national park status, Walcott's interest extended beyond protection of the elk herd. The Tetons, combined with the beauty of Jackson Lake, were deserving of preservation for all time. The area constituted a "Switzerland of America," and he predicted that tourists would find the trip along the Tetons to Jackson Lake and on to Yellowstone Park "the grandest trip ... to be found anywhere in the world."[4] While Walcott surely portended the future, his recommendations were ignored and Congress took no action.

The matter of extension was again brought before Congress in 1902, but with the same result.[5] Indeed, in the years to follow there was scarcely a time when the idea of park extension was not discussed. But while there was concern over the area, there was little consensus. In the meantime, as the world moved toward war, more and more homesteaders found the valley attractive. They took out land in the southern end of Jackson Hole, either with the purpose of speculation or bona fide settlement. Many of these family ranchers were firmly opposed to development. But good intentions are easily subdued by economic necessity. Furthermore, it would take the greed of only a few to play havoc with the beauty of the valley for the many. If Jackson Hole was to maintain its pristine condition it would take strong leadership. This would be provided by the National Park Service.

The establishment of the National Park Service need not be detailed here.[6] It is necessary, however, to understand that from 1872 to 1916 the national parks had been the "administrative stepchildren within the federal establishment."[7] While the

Department of the Interior had legal jurisdiction over the parks, the War Department (U.S. Army) was assigned the task of protecting and administering some of the finest mountain scenery in the world. As custodians, the military played an important protective role, for often a trooper commanded greater respect than a ranger.[8] Yet the parks suffered from the lack of appropriations and a clear purpose, and from the domination of the utilitarian conservation philosophy. It became evident to dedicated park advocates such as J. Horace McFarland that the national parks would thrive only under a new and dedicated agency. By 1912 their arguments had convinced President William Howard Taft, who recommended the establishment of a "Bureau of National Parks." Four years later his recommendation became law through the National Park Service Act. A new agency was established, one that would bring order and direction out of the chaos of the national park system, and one dedicated to preserving the scenery, historic objects and the wildlife of the parks "in such manner and by such means as will leave them unimpaired for the enjoyment of future generations."[9]

Even before the passage of the act two men were quietly taking over the reins of the disparate park system. Stephen Mather was sworn in as assistant to Secretary of the Interior Franklin K. Lane in January, 1915. He was to be in charge of the national parks. To aid Mather, Secretary Lane appointed Horace M. Albright. Both men were Californians, graduates of the University of California, who loved the wilderness of the West, and took pride in their administrative ability and dedication. However, while Albright was a mere youth of twenty-five, Mather had already made a fortune in the borax business and was now prepared to meet new challenges through public service. The two formed a friendship which would end only with Mather's death in January, 1930.[10] Certainly it was fortuitous for the national parks movement that Secretary Lane brought together two men who would soon become central figures in the American conservation movement of the first half of the twentieth century.

The initial year of their association was devoted to publicizing the national parks and drumming up support for the establishment of a National Park Service. The highlight of their efforts to capture the interest of influential people was a High Sierra pack trip in which such well known writers and conser-

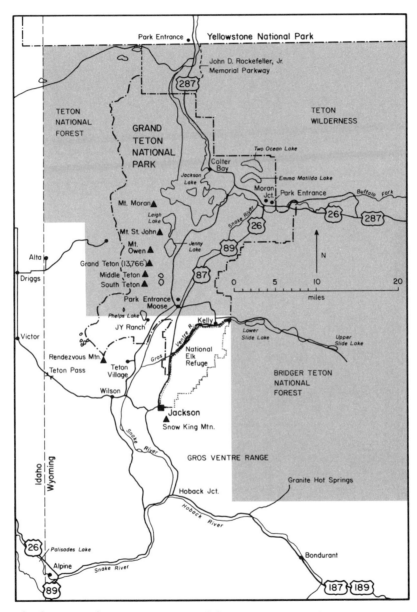

Charles D. Walcott's 1898 Proposal for Teton National Park

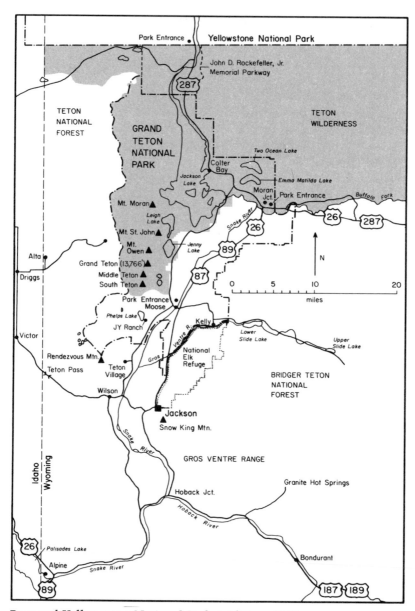

Proposed Yellowstone National Park Addition, 1919

vationists as Gilbert Grosvenor, editor of the *National Geographic Magazine,* Henry Fairfield Osborn, head of the American Museum of Natural History, writer Emerson Hough, and a covey of prominent Washington politicians were all introduced to the splendor of the Sierra Nevada without any of the hardships.[11] After this successful outing Mather and Albright traveled north to Mount Rainier and then east to Colorado to take part in the dedication of Rocky Mountain National Park. Then it was on to Yellowstone, two energetic men proselytizing for the parks wherever they went.

It was during this 1915 visit to Yellowstone National Park that Stephen Mather and his tall, slim assistant, Horace Albright, first viewed the Grand Teton range. While touring the southern reaches of Yellowstone the two men decided to journey south to Moran over what Albright described as "terrible roads." [12] Whatever the inconvenience suffered, it was forgotten with the sight of the Teton range. Like so many before and after, Mather and Albright were entranced by the sublime magnificence of the Jackson Hole country. But it was young Albright who would perceive the prospect of the panorama before him. He was at once determined that this area of unexcelled grandeur should be preserved for all time as part of the national parks system. Transforming an idea into reality would prove more difficult, and Albright would feel endless frustration, give countless speeches and absorb innumerable insults before, thirty-five years later, he would realize this vision.

During the following winter one of Albright's tasks was to research the history of the Jackson Hole-Teton Range area with an eye to future park status. The results seemed promising, and the next summer again found Mather and Albright motoring south from Yellowstone to the Jackson Hole country. This time they were accompanied by Alexander T. Vogelsang, first assistant secretary of the interior, and Huston Thompson, assistant attorney general and a close friend of President Woodrow Wilson. The group spent an afternoon boating on Jackson Lake and then dined on thick steaks at Ben Sheffield's lodge at Moran. In the evening they slipped outside to watch the twilight steal over the mountains and "the night finally shut out all details." [13] To this group of high ranking government officials it seemed inevitable that this stunning country must become part of the national heritage. While enthusiastic over the park possibilities, the men were conversely appalled by the activities of the Bureau of Reclamation, particularly the flooding of the road from Jackson Lake dam north to Lizard Creek. When Mather returned to Washington he prevailed upon the Bureau of Reclamation to appropriate $10,000 for a new road skirting the flooded area.[14] It was the first effort by the National Park Service in behalf of the Jackson Hole country.

In the next two years considerable work was done to formulate a feasible park plan. Land titles were checked, contacts were made in Jackson Hole, and the Wyoming congressional delegation (Senators Francis E. Warren and Clarence D. Clark, and Congressman Frank Mondell) was consulted.[15] Generally all quarters registered sympathy if not enthusiasm. The state of Wyoming signaled agreement, providing encroachments would not be made on their right to control hunting in the area.

As a result of these consultations, Mather, Albright and Congressman Frank Mondell fashioned a bill (H.R. 11661) that was introduced on April 24, 1918.[16] Succinctly, the bill extended the boundaries of Yellowstone National Park to include the Teton Range, Jackson Lake and the series of lakes at the foot of the Teton Range, and the Thorofare area (headwaters of the Yellowstone River-Two Ocean Pass region) south to Buffalo Fork. It was a well-conceived bill that would secure most of the National Park Service objectives. During the summer of 1918 Albright and others lobbied in Washington and solicited support in Jackson Hole. When Chief Forester Henry S. Graves bestowed United States Forest Service approval, the bill seemed likely to pass.[17]

In December Mondell introduced a slightly revised bill (H.R. 13350) which, in February, 1919, unanimously passed the House. It seemed almost time to break out the champagne, but, unfortunately, in the Senate John Nugent of Idaho objected to the bill. His action was effective, for the Senate was in filibuster and a bill required unanimity to move it along to a final vote. The senator from Idaho killed the bill—at least for that session of Congress. After their initial shock, park advocates discovered that at the eleventh hour a few Idaho sheepmen, who feared loss of grazing privileges, prevailed upon Nugent to oppose the bill. It mattered not that their fears were unfounded. An opportunity had been lost. Never again would park extension be so non-controversial.

At the time, of course, it seemed to Congressman Mondell that he need only reintroduce the bill, mollify Nugent's objections, and the desired objective would be achieved. However, this was not to be. The momentum for passage had been curbed, and the pendulum of feeling had swung against the National Park Service. When Mondell reintroduced the bill in May, 1919 (H.R. 1412), it was never reported out of committee.[18] Opposition to park extension had begun to coalesce within three primary groups: the Forest Service, the livestock interests, and the dude ranchers. The opposition of the Forest Service in 1919 was never overt, but the record indicates that administrative and field personnel may well have worked toward disruption of the extended park idea. While Chief Forester Graves was restrained in public, it was known that in private he often spoke against park expansion at Forest Service expense.[19] On the local level it seemed more than mere coincidence that in 1919 the livestock grazing quota was cut in much of the proposed park extension land. Ranchers mistakenly suspected that this move was dictated by the National Park Service. When Congressman Mondell inquired of Graves the meaning of the reduction, the chief forester claimed that readjustment of grazing privileges was simply to safeguard the elk herd rather than to influence the extension question.[20] This may have been the case, but in the field local rangers opportunistically connected these grazing cutbacks with park extension.[21] It was a subtle move, but one surely designed to increase the apprehension of the ranchers and drive them to action.

Jackson Hole ranchers were further encouraged by the success of the small number of Idaho sheepmen in killing the 1918 Mondell bill. They noted that it was possible to force their collective will through political action. Whatever the facts of the park extension regarding grazing rights, the livestock interests opposed in principle further federal control. Ever since the beginning of government restrictions on the public domain in the 1880s, cattlemen and sheepmen felt hounded by Washington administrators who knew little and cared less about their problems. After defeat of the Mondell bill, F. J. Hagenharth, president of the National Wool Growers Association, confessed

to Stephen Mather that their opposition was based on the attitude of national parks *in general* regarding sheep, and the fact
that livestock grazing privileges had been curtailed "from
twenty-five to thirty-five percent during the past three years." [22]
Clearly it was distrust and hostility toward the federal government in general and the National Park Service in particular that
prompted much of the ranchers' opposition.

While the purpose and position of the livestock interests
were easily understood, the dude ranchers' motives were more
complex. Usually they supported the National Park Service, but
not always. In 1919, they did not. In that year spokesman
Struthers Burt condemned the aspirations of the National Park
Service in terms well understood by the fiercely independent
local people. Readers of the Jackson Hole *Courier* found Burt's
venom-dipped pen lashing out at the monopolistic practices of
the National Park Service with regard to concessionaires. It was
a policy detrimental to private enterprise and initiative. Perhaps more telling was Burt's conviction that the new federal
agency placed far too many restrictions on personal freedom in
the appreciation of nature. Burt was opposed to the proliferation of "Do Not Touch" and "Stay On The Path" signs in Yellowstone National Park. He believed that most Americans who
visited Yellowstone underwent "disagreeable experiences" and
generally preferred to camp elsewhere—quite often in Jackson
Hole. The dude rancher and author charged that the park service now proposed "to drive them out of this last refuge." [23] Burt
reflected the feeling of many persons who were not prepared to
submit to the environmental restrictions which the park service
found necessary to carry out its charge to preserve nature unimpaired for future generations. For many, Jackson Hole represented one of the last bastions of individual freedom, and in
some respects their attitude toward government control was not
unlike their nineteenth century frontier counterparts.

Further alienation of the dude ranchers came through an
innocent error. It was almost axiomatic that westerners favored
an improved and expanded road system. The promise of highway construction was a ploy that the National Park Service rou-
tinely utilized in gaining local support. It was natural for
Horace Albright to assume that hinting at an expanded road
system in Jackson Hole would be warmly received in the valley.
Conversations with Wyoming Governor Robert D. Carey rein-

forced that assumption, for Carey believed that an efficient, high speed highway system was the key to Wyoming's agricultural and industrial development.[24] Thus, when Albright was asked in late summer, 1919, to address a Jackson meeting, he assumed a pro-road position, suggesting a new route up Pacific Creek, over the Thorofare country, then down to the eastern edge of Yellowstone Lake. The well-known dude rancher, Howard Eaton, had suggested the idea. However, as Albright soon realized, Eaton had no idea of the sentiment of local ranchers. The majority in attendance did not want the proposed highway or any other road. They feared the National Park Service would "over-civilize" the country and proceeded to harangue Albright unmercifully. That August evening was a serious setback to Albright's aspirations. Later he recalled: "I just took a beating that night. Every time I made a move I was talked down, sometimes shouted at and the men that made the most telling arguments against me were these dude ranchers, among them Struthers Burt and Horace Carncross who sat right in the front row."[25]

Discouraged, Albright retreated to Yellowstone, there to take up the challenging duties as superintendent of the vast park. For ten years he would hold this position, earning himself the rather factitious title, the "Duke" of Yellowstone.[26] Continually on his mind was the Teton country. Certainly a temporary setback only hardened his determination, for in those early, buoyant days defeat was not in the National Park Service lexicon, and surely must have been anathema to Superintendent Albright. Soon he was engaged in proselytizing prominent people to his cause. George H. Lorimer, editor of the *Saturday Evening Post*, as well as writers Emerson Hough, Elizabeth Fraser, and Hal Evarts were introduced to the grandeur of the Teton country in 1920. Men in political power found the young superintendent eager to share his vision. John Barton Payne, secretary of the interior, and Josephus Daniels, secretary of the navy, as well as Senators C. B. Henderson of Nevada and Thomas J. Walsh of Montana were all circuitously or directly conducted to the Teton region.[27] Although Albright's responsibilities included fairly broad powers of supervision over all national parks of the West, aside from managing Yellowstone, he considered park extension to the Jackson Hole country his most important assignment.[28]

The activities of the National Park Service were not confined to conducting prominent guests to Jackson Hole. When it had been assumed that the Mondell bill would pass, President Wilson issued an Executive Order of July 8, 1918, withdrawing from all forms of entry or disposal over 600,000 acres within Teton National Forest. Although the bill failed to pass, the executive order was not rescinded.[29] The tangible effect of this withdrawal was to give the National Park Service "veto power" over any Forest Service plans for the area. By 1922, Acting Chief Forester L. F. Kneipp was vigorously protesting this "divided responsibility," and calling for Forest Service autonomy in decision making. In response, Arno Cammerer, then assistant director of the National Park Service, acknowledged that it was "a difficult system for both services," but the National Park Service would not relinquish its right of review.[30] In the next few years conflicts of interest between the two agencies would become more inflamed until finally a third party would be asked to intervene.

It is understandable that Arno Cammerer responded as he did to Kneipp's request that the National Park Service get out of Jackson Hole. The review power gave the National Park Service their only weapon with which to combat unwanted development. The most immediate issue was a concerted attempt by irrigationists between 1919 and 1921 to raise the level of Jenny Lake twenty feet and Leigh Lake ten feet through the construction of a dam at the outlet of Jenny Lake.[31] While the Forest Service was quiescent on the matter the National Park Service was downright pugnacious. The state of Wyoming and the Department of the Interior finally abandoned the scheme, licking their respective wounds.[32]

No sooner had a reprieve been won for the Jenny-String-Leigh Lakes then another irrigationist plan emerged for Two Ocean Lake and Emma Matilda Lake. These two lakes were not of comparable beauty, but the Park Service again leaped to their defense as a matter of principle, for they would fall within the proposed park extension. To Wyoming State Engineer, later governor, Frank Emerson and many others, the park service position was untenable. In a letter to Albright, Emerson disputed the scenic value of the lakes in question, then reasoned that since the state had relinquished plans for Jenny and Leigh Lakes, "it seems a matter of fair play" that the Park Service respond positively to his request. Albright replied that he wasn't terribly interested in "fair play" and "there will be no chance of my agreeing with you." [33] In this case Albright's position was in direct conflict with that of the Forest Service, which had approved the water storage project. District Forester R. H. Rutledge reluctantly conceded the veto power of the Park Service and the project was shelved.[34] Yet the question of water storage and irrigation in Jackson Hole would remain, and there is little question that such officials as Teton National Forest Supervisor A. C. McCain often dangled the carrot of compliance with irrigation plans to enemies of national park extension.

While the "hard line" position of Albright and the National Park Service incurred the wrath of many, it did win the respect and loyalty of the dude ranchers. It became clear that the misunderstanding in 1919 regarding roads was just that—a misunderstanding. It had become apparent that neither the Forest Service, the townspeople, nor the cattlemen could be counted on to preserve the country. Although Burt and others were apprehensive, the unequivocal defense of the Jackson Hole lakes convinced them that the National Park Service offered the best hope to quell the onslaught of postwar development. Thus by 1922 Burt would write Congressman Frank Mondell that "Mr. Albright's ideas coincide absolutely with ours." [35]

This joining of interests was formalized in 1923. Informal discussions among concerned parties resulted in an invitation to Horace Albright to meet at Maud Noble's cabin, located along the banks of the Snake River at Moose. Thus on July 26, 1923 Albright, Struthers Burt and Horace Carncross, representing the dude ranchers, rancher Jack Eynon, businessman Joe Jones, newspaper owner Dick Winger, and Maud Noble pulled their chairs around the fireplace (for Maud enjoyed a fire even in the summer) to discuss the fate of the pristine valley they all loved.

Surely this meeting was motivated by fear—fear of the loss of a unique region to development. The close of World War I had witnessed the proliferation of the automobile, wealth and leisure time, a combination which could play havoc with the atmopshere of Jackson Hole. The group was most interested in proper zoning to guard against unsightly development.[36] Just how this could be accomplished was unclear. However, the majority believed that Struthers Burt's proposal that the Hole should be a "museum on the hoof" was a good one. Under this

plan indigenous wild animals would be fostered and/or reintroduced, houses would be uniformly log, roads would be unpaved,
and the town of Jackson would retain a strong frontier flavor.
To the north of Jackson, private land would be purchased and
then administered somewhat along national park lines as a
recreational area. Opting for a "recreational area" reflected the
feeling of those present that they wanted protection but not
preservation. Traditional activities such as hunting, grazing and
dude ranching would continue.[37]

Perhaps Horace Albright could have wished for more,
but at least there was a common ground with which to work.
If the meeting did not support national park principles, at least
it recognized the benefits of Albright's involvement in the fate
of the valley. Furthermore, the recognition of the need for federal involvement indicated a severe dent in the armor of
"rugged individualism" which had long dominated the attitude
of residents. Albright encouraged the group.

Of course many an idea has died aborning for lack of
funds. This fate seemed to await the plan advanced at Maud
Noble's cabin. The plan of action called for one or more
wealthy men to quietly purchase private land north of Jackson,
then hold it until Congress would see fit to reimburse the individual, take over the land and add it to the national park system.[38] But where to find an interested philanthropist? Albright
and Burt wrote numerous letters to conservationist friends so-
liciting funds to send Dick Winger and Jack Eynon to the east
coast. Eventually some $2000 was raised and the two men
headed east with the hope of interesting such prominent families as the Whitneys, Morgans, or the Vanderbilts. The trip was
an abysmal failure. Winger and Eynon were effective in Jackson
Hole, but the two westerners failed to attract eastern money.
Where they needed thousands they received hundreds—or
nothing.[39] It became evident that a plan was one thing, but
bringing it to fruition was quite another.

In the meantime Yellowstone Park was enjoying a post-
war tourist boom. Visitors increased from 98,223 in 1922 to
138,352 the following year. By modern park statistics these figures are hardly startling, but they did represent a heightened
awareness of the national parks that must be partially credited
to Director Stephen Mather and his young Yellowstone superintendent, Horace Albright. Neither ever missed an opportunity

to publicize the parks. Prominent writers were invariably given the red carpet treatment and this hospitality was handsomely repaid through a number of articles on the Yellowstone-Teton region in popular magazines. The most prestigious visitor during the summer of 1923 was President Warren Harding. While touring the southern vicinity of Yellowstone, the president beheld the Teton Range, some forty miles away. Taken by their snow-capped grandeur, he asked Albright about the Jackson Hole country. Within a short time Harding was committed to the park extension plan.[40] This commitment went for naught, for within a month the president, after an exhausting Alaskan tour, would suffer a cardiac malfunction and die in his San Francisco hotel.

Had Harding lived it is unlikely that he would have honored his commitment once he had been advised of the growing friction between the National Park Service and the Forest Service regarding adjacent boundaries. In Arizona, California, Oregon, Washington and Colorado disputes over boundary lines festered, demanding to be resolved. In Wyoming the National Park Service sought to adjust Yellowstone's 1872 artificial boundaries to more natural, definable lines. To the east they argued for a boundary following the crest of the Absaroka Range. To the south the Park Service continued to press for the land sessions contained in the 1918 Mondell bill. The two agencies were at loggerheads. Finally it seemed propitious to arbitrate their differences. To this end President Calvin Coolidge authorized the Coordinating Commission on National Parks and Forests, created by the President's Committee on Outdoor Recreation in February, 1925.[41]

During the summer of 1925 the commission (or their appropriate representatives) examined a number of controversial boundaries in the West. Much of August was spent with local hearings at Cody, Moran, and Jackson, and on-site inspections of the proposed Yellowstone boundary changes. Agreement was rather easily accomplished with regard to the eastern natural boundary for Yellowstone, but extension into Jackson Hole was vigorously opposed by the Forest Service. Contrary to their 1918 position, Forest Service officials now argued that the forested land surrounding Jackson Lake was of significant economic value.[42] Forest Service studies in the early 1920s proposed a sawmill at Moran to be supplied by logs floated across Jackson

Lake. Furthermore, the Snake River, below Jackson Lake, could be utilized for driving logs, provided proper wing dams, piers and booms were constructed to channel the river. The Coordinating Commission on National Parks and Forests also read reports and heard testimony on the potentially valuable coal, phosphate and asbestos deposits contained within the proposed extension. The Forest Service, however, indicated a sensitivity to the scenic and recreational importance of the country. Although they consistently advocated summer home development on the shores of Jackson Lake, they pledged that the Leigh-String-Jenny Lake area would remain undeveloped and free of any irrigation projects.[43]

The Forest Service position was enunciated in a letter from Chief Forester William Greeley to Stephen Mather and in a memorandum from L. F. Kneipp to the Coordinating Commission. In these two statements the highest Forest Service officials claimed that certain economic resources should and could be developed without impairment of the high scenic value of the Grand Teton area. They were prepared to offer the public "popular and simple forms of outdoor recreation not compatible with National Park principles of administration." More specifically, the area should be managed "for the accommodation of mass recreation, with public camping grounds, store and hotel facilities, and summer home areas . . . ."[44] Thus the Forest Service pledged that they could allow limited economic activities and provide for masses of vacationing Americans, both without disturbing the natural pristine beauty of Jackson Hole.

One may wonder at such an audacious claim to be all things to all people—and not to disturb the ecology of the country. Yet, Pinchot's old organization was arguing tenaciously for retention of their domain. They seemed to regard anything that might appeal to local support and/or national interests as fair. Their position, was, however, reflective of a changing philosophy and purpose within the Forest Service. The dedication to utilitarian use of the nation's forests was giving way to recognition of the importance of aesthetic and cultural values. In the 1920s three men spearheaded the change. Aldo Leopold, an ecologist who gained posthumous fame with the publication of *A Sand County Almanac* (1946), was in the vanguard of those service employees opposed to development at the sacrifice of scientific or aesthetic values. He found a kindred spirit in Arthur Carhart, an aggressive Denver-based Forest Service employee working as a "recreational planner." In later years Carhart would lend his talented pen in defense of Jackson Hole, but in the 1920s he was engaged in convincing his superiors that many areas ought to remain roadless and primitive, and that scenery and recreational possibilities ought to be major "products" of the Forest Service.[45] While Carhart resigned his Forest Service position in frustration in 1923, the following year another man destined to gain recognition as an eloquent defender of wilderness joined the Forest Service. Bob Marshall worked out of Missoula, Montana from 1924 to 1928 and within that brief time the future founder of the Wilderness Society began to think in terms of preservation rather than utilization of Forest Service lands.[46]

Surely this budding awareness of aesthetic values was a practical stance for the Forest Service to adopt. They were loath to see the National Park Service continually preempt their most scenic lands, and if promising a new sensitivity to nature were necessary, it would be done. Of course the National Park Service contended that the Forest Service could not be trusted with Jackson Hole. A chameleon can change its color but not its skin. In a letter to William Greeley, Stephen Mather noted that had it not been for the National Park Service, the Forest Service would have allowed the most scenic lakes in Jackson Hole to suffer aesthetic ruin through irrigation projects. He believed that "only a permanent withdrawal under park status will permanently protect this magnificent scenic territory." In arguing his case Mather noted that the Forest Service had seen fit to criticize the Park Service for allowing livestock grazing in Sequoia National Park, hence really conducting a national forest under the guise of a national park. Now the reverse would be true if the Forest Service attempted to enter the domain of preservation in Jackson Hole, adding further public confusion regarding the respective roles of the Forest Service and the National Park Service.[47] For obvious reasons, Mather strenuously opposed any presumption that the Forest Service could enter the fields of preservation or recreation.

As might be anticipated, the Coordinating Commission on National Parks and Forests compromised on the question of Jackson Hole. They recommended that the lion's share of the land desired by the Park Service remain in Forest Service control, but that approximately 100,000 acres of land embracing the Grand Teton range be added to Yellowstone National Park as a separate unit.[48]

This recommendation satisfied neither agency but since there was no appeal, Mather and Albright reasoned that half a cake is better than none. When legislation (S. 3427) was introduced in 1926 to carry out the recommendation of the commission, the Park Service supported it. However, the Forest Service did not. The key politician was Senator John Kendrick of Wyoming. An ex-cowboy who had read while others caroused, Kendrick married the boss's daughter and eventually became a wealthy rancher in Sheridan. Late in life he turned to new challenges, and, as one newspaper editor put it, became "the craftiest politician the state has ever produced."[49] Elected to the Senate in 1916, Kendrick had served Wyoming well, avoiding partisan politics at home while pursuing Wyoming interests in Washington. Like all western senators, he favored economic development, but he was not necessarily a foe of the National Park Service. Thus, when the Yellowstone Extension bill came before the Senate Committee on Public Lands in 1926, he did not kill it, but rather asked for time to assess the sentiments of his constituency. For the moment his only request was that the new park not be an extension of Yellowstone National Park. He reasoned that many tourists believed that Yellowstone Park was in Montana, whereas in fact it was almost totally within the state of Wyoming. The new park, which he suggested should be designated as Teton National Park of Wyoming, should be exclusively within his state.[50]

The following year Senator Peter Norbeck of South Dakota, a firm friend of the National Park Service, suggested that the Park Service again prepare a bill to establish Grand Teton National Park. Norbeck was uncertain what the name of the new park should be, but stated that for the moment he would introduce it as "Kendrick National Park."[51] This rather blatant attempt to firm up the support of the senator from Wyoming was unsuccessful. In hearings Kendrick professed to appreciate the compliment but quipped that "it is my conviction that it is unsafe to name anything after a cattle man until he has been dead at least 50 years."[52] Furthermore, Kendrick indicated that he was not yet prepared to see the bill voted out of committee.

Like his western colleagues, Kendrick was reluctant to lend support to more federal control of land. In the case of the proposed park the land was merely being transferred from one federal agency to another, yet he could not ignore resolutions such as that of the Wyoming State Legislature (1927 session) requesting that Congress authorize the Teton Range as a state park.[53] Unlike Senator Norbeck, who believed that the parks ought to be viewed from a national rather than a state perspective, Kendrick was determined to proceed slowly and with his ear closely attuned to local attitudes. He asked that the bill be deferred for another session.

In keeping with Kendrick's desire, the Senate Committee on Public Lands held public hearings during the summer of 1928 in Cody, Jackson and on the JY Ranch in Jackson Hole. The July 22nd hearing in Jackson was considered crucial. Albright, Richard Winger, Struthers Burt and other park advocates had rounded up support so that when Committee Chairman Gerald Nye called for a show of hands of those favoring the park, seventy-six of seventy-seven persons present indicated their approval. Rising to the occasion, Senator Kendrick declared that ever since he had viewed the Tetons in all their grandeur he "realized that some day they would become a park dedicated to the Nation and posterity. . . ."[54]

The harmony of the afternoon, however, was disrupted by the evening. After the committee had retired to the JY Ranch accommodations a small group of ranchers and businessmen called on them and demanded a hearing. Although the afternoon meeting had been widely advertised, they insisted that they had not been informed. Now they wished to be heard. After some discussion, Senator Kendrick finally consented to a meeting the following morning.

At that small assemblage, Stephen Leek argued for continued Forest Service control since they would allow limited lumbering of beetle-infested trees. State Senator R. C. Lundy made a plea that the senators recommend state park status for the Tetons. Senator Henry Ashurst of Arizona gave his opinion that Lundy's proposal could never be enacted. When it was evident that the senators could not be dissuaded from recommending national park status for the Tetons, the local group exacted some concessions. Led by state Senator William C. Deloney of Jackson, the most influential resident in attendance, the group pressed for a rather unusual provision. Since the park seemed inevitable, Deloney and others requested that no new hotels or camps be allowed within the new national park. Struthers Burt and Horace Albright supported the idea, and it was unanimously agreed that the park bill would include a provision banning the construction of new roads, hotels or permanent camps.[55] This was no concession to preservation. Deloney wished to protect Jackson merchants from increased competition and the dude ranchers wished to protect their monopoly. Nevertheless, when this provision was included in the 1929 bill (S. 5543) it was the first time non-development and *de facto* wilderness protection was written into the law.

Later it was claimed that at the JY Ranch discussions Horace Albright promised Senator Kendrick and others that if the legislation establishing the park was approved, no further attempts at expansion would be contemplated by the National Park Service. A few years later Albright vigorously denied ever having made the promise, and in any case he "could not have bound" his successors.[56] Perhaps at that meeting Albright may have given certain assurances that efforts to extend Yellowstone National Park southward would be abandoned, but there is no substantive evidence to that effect. With the evidence at hand, we can only conclude that Albright gave no indication to Kendrick, Deloney or anyone else that the ambitions of the park service for Jackson Hole would be called to a halt with the park bill. In fact at the very period of the JY Ranch meeting the National Park Service was fully cooperating with Rockefeller's Snake River Land Company in buying up private land within Jackson Hole.

In view of the lack of opposition to the Commission's recommendation for a new park, Senator Kendrick introduced a bill (S. 5543) to establish Grand Teton National Park. Although Kendrick wished "of Wyoming" as an appendage, most felt that no other national park had been identified by state and the precedent should not be allowed. Senator Kendrick's bill cleared the Congress handily in February, 1929, and on the 26th of the month President Calvin Coolidge signed the bill establishing Grand Teton National Park.[57]

Although establishing the park was no small political accomplishment, it was only half a park. In the words of historian John Ise, the 1929 park "was a stingy, skimpy, niggardly little

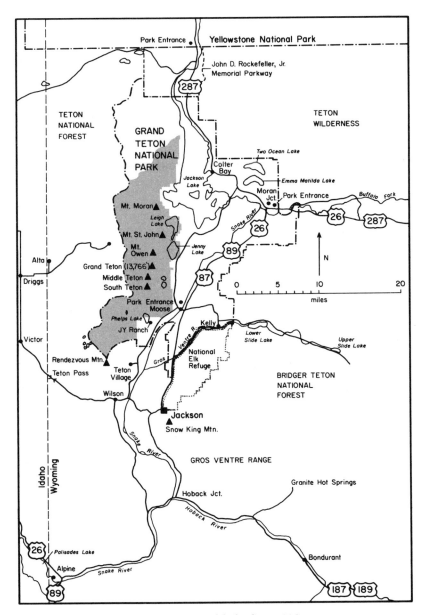

Grand Teton National Park as established in 1929

park of only about 150 square miles, from three to nine miles wide and twenty-seven miles long . . ."[58] It was a Pyrrhic victory. The mountains by their very ruggedness were protected from exploitation. Furthermore, since the Teton Range contained no significant mineral or forest resources, little incentive existed for private ownership. True, the new park included the exquisite piedmont lakes, but the park lines skirted so close to the shoreline that adjacent development was inevitable. In a sense the new park was a victory for tourism and commercialism, for it simply confirmed the obvious: the Teton Range's "highest use" would be to attract tourists. Nothing should impair that economic value. Although the new park was surely a political as well as psychological victory, it was no preservationist triumph.

Many residents believed that the 1929 park settlement portended a new era of stability. They were wrong. Neither the National Park Service nor those conservationists clustered about the leadership of John D. Rockefeller, Jr., were satisfied. The grim specter of development haunted them. Jackson Lake, the Snake River and thousands of acres of sagebrush and wooded lands remained unprotected. The land in the foreground of the mountains which afforded the majestic and incomparable view must not be marred. For those devoted to saving the valley, the 1929 park was a beginning, not an end. Nature molded, shaped, and preserved the region over the many centuries; it would be man's responsibility to assume that stewardship.

I·V

PHILANTHROPY AND PROPERTY

"...I suppose you'll try to get the whole valley."
Will Deloney, 1929

IT required a certain messianic zeal to be an ardent conservationist in the 1920s. In taking a stance against private enterprise and development, the preservationist lashed out against institutions as American as motherhood, apple pie and the flag combined. He was out of step with his times. The concept that some of the land should be off limits to man's manipulations resided in only a handful of individuals of his day, and no one could conceive of Aldo Leopold's rather bizarre notion that man had an ethical responsibility to natural communities, "to include soils, water, plants, and animals, or collectively: the land." [1] Furthermore, as an advocate of planning and prediction, the preservationist received little sympathy in the West, a region that often honored the "belief that progress is accidental and miraculous and unplanned." [2] For the westerner his close relationship with nature was to his liking, but it ought not to get in the way of making a living. He loved his streams, valleys and mountains, but he did not feel restrained in the use or abuse of these resources. On the other hand, a handful of preservationists saw the danger inherent in this attitude. In their minds appeared horrific scenarios of masses of people and concommitant commercialism snuffing out nature and a quality of life that demanded that an intimate experience with nature ought to be every American's birthright.

Surely these fantasies were held by those who fought to preserve Jackson Hole. The persons who met at Maud Noble's cabin in 1923 were motivated by idealism, but also by fear. Fear that the pristine valley they knew and loved would be overrun in a rapidly changing world dominated by urbanization and industrialization. They were determined that some of nineteenth century frontier America should remain inviolate, and this objective was, in some indefinable way, important. Their convictions were such that they seemed intransigent to those who did not agree with their position. And, indeed, like any zealots, they were.

One who exemplified this passion for preservation of the past was Horace Albright. Raised in the Owens Valley of California at the base of the eastern slope of the Sierra Nevada, he spent his youth in close association with nature and wilderness. The small town of Bishop, with its grand Sierra peaks just to the west, was a good place to live, and the valley of the Owens River offered agricultural possibilities — until it went dry. It was during Albright's youth that the city of Los Angeles successfully fought local interests to divert the Owens River by aquaduct over two hundred miles southwest. As Albright later lamented, his boyhood valley came "completely under the influence and control of modern civilization."[3] Clearly the Benthamite-Progressive dictum of "the greatest good for the greatest numbers," the rationale with which Los Angeles moralized its insatiable thirst, could work to the disadvantage of the minority—and nature was not considered in the formula.

Perhaps the loss of the Owens Valley made Albright all the more determined to guard Jackson Hole. Whatever the cause, the creation of the Teton mountains and Jackson Hole as a unit of the National Park Service became a lifelong project in which he would bring to task all his considerable administrative abilities and his persuasive nature. He would never write or speak with the eloquence of a Henry David Thoreau or a John Muir, but his abilities were, perhaps, more in tune with the twentieth century. He was a superb administrator who knew how to get things done. He was both adept and aggressive in accomplishing his purpose. For some Jackson Hole residents he was too aggressive. Albright always seemed to be one step ahead of them, ready with a sedative for their doubts, a placebo for their fears, and an answer for their objections.

The wellspring of his determination was commitment. For Albright it was simply a matter of time: the inclusion of the Teton range and the Jackson Hole region into the national park system was inevitable and tantamount to a national trust. He once characterized the national park system as the "Nation's Gallery of its finest works of Nature," and leaving the Teton-Jackson Hole expanse out would be like denying access of a Rembrandt to the National Gallery of Art.[4]

Just as philanthropy has brought Rembrandt paintings to the National Art Gallery, it was the charitable instincts of the wealthy that would materialize Albright's dream. John D. Rockefeller, Jr. visited Yellowstone National Park in 1924 with his sons John, Nelson and Laurance. Superintendent Albright met the millionaire in Gardiner, Montana, arranged for him and his family to tour the park quietly for three days, then saw to their departure via Cody, Wyoming.[5] It was the beginning of a lifelong friendship.

This was not the first trip to Yellowstone for John D. Rockefeller, Jr. In 1886, as a youth of twelve, he had accompanied his family to the semi-civilized park in the West. Although we have no record of his impressions, he must have enjoyed the wonders of Yellowstone and the Rocky Mountain West.[6] In time he would give from his great wealth so that some of this mountain splendor would be preserved.

In 1924, however, Albright's instructions were that the scion of wealth from the East was not to be burdened with the financial problems of the Park Service in general and Yellowstone in particular. Albright scrupulously observed these instructions, allowing Rockefeller and his family to enjoy the park with special considerations but with no distractions. Evidently, however, Rockefeller was annoyed by one environmental eyesore in the park. Not long after his return to New York he wrote a warm letter to Albright thanking him for his hospitality but noting that the heavy brush and debris alongside the roads detracted from the beauty of the area.[7] This litter was the result of a road construction budget which did not allow for any cleanup. The upshot was that during the next five years Rockefeller contributed some $50,000 toward the beautification of roads in Yellowstone. Under Albright's direction the results were impressive, and roadside cleanup became a policy in the national parks as well as with many state road projects.[8]

The summer of 1926 found John D. Rockefeller, Jr., his

wife and three children, again journeying to the West. After a visit to the Southwest and California, in July they arrived at Yellowstone for a twelve day stay. Soon Albright was motoring his guests south to the Teton country. The first day they picnicked on a hill (now "Lunch Tree Hill" adjacent to Jackson Lake Lodge) overlooking Jackson Lake. Five moose browsed contentedly in the marsh below them. Across the lake spread the majestic Teton Range. It was a day and a view destined to have a lasting impression on Rockefeller. The following morning they continued south toward Jackson, visiting the Bar BC and the JY ranches; dude ranches owned by Struthers Burt, Horace Carncross and Henry Stewart, all avid supporters of the plan to make Jackson Hole a national recreational area. Rockefeller and his wife were profoundly impressed by the Leigh-String-Jenny Lake region, but were appalled by the encroaching commercialism. A rather tawdry dancehall seemed inappropriate, "unsightly structures" marred the road, and telephone wires bisected the Teton view. Jackson Hole seemed destined for the ubiquitous uglification coincidental with unplanned tourist development. Mrs. Rockefeller was particularly irate and asked if anything could be done. Visual abuse led to verbal communication and soon Albright was sharing his ideas. Returning to Yellowstone, they stopped at Hedricks Point, a bluff overlooking the Snake River which afforded a magnificent view in all directions. It was here that Albright revealed the concerns of the Maud Noble cabin meeting three years earlier, and the plan to save not only the mountains but much of the valley spread out before them.[9]

Although Rockefeller was noncommittal, he listened intently to Horace Albright's account of the efforts to save the valley. In truth, it may not have been the first time he had heard of the project. In March of 1926, Struthers Burt had written an article for the prestigious magazine, *The Nation,* in which he outlined the history of the valley and the efforts to save it, with particular emphasis on the Maud Noble cabin meeting.[10] However, well before publication of the article Burt met with Kenneth Chorley, a member of Rockefeller's inner circle of confidants, and the man who would direct most of John D. Rockefeller, Jr's. conservation and park efforts. On December 21, 1925, Chorley joined Burt for lunch at a New York City coffee house. The conversation centered on the Jackson

Hole issue. On March 9, 1926, the two men met again. Chorley noted in his diary that Burt "talked to me a long time about the question of Yellowstone and acquiring some additional land." This was Jackson Hole land, and could be purchased, according to Burt, "for a little over $1,000,000." Chorley's diary entry concluded that Burt "is very anxious for me to see Albright... while I am out West this summer and talk the matter over with him." [11]

Shortly after their second meeting, Chorley wrote Burt congratulating him on his article, stating that "you have so aroused my interest that I am going to try terribly hard to see Albright and possibly get if only a glimpse of something of the Jackson Hole country." [12] Since Rockefeller would soon be vacationing in the region, it would seem most probable that Chorley brought the article to the attention of his superior and reported on his conversations with Burt. Thus, it is likely that Albright's explanations were elaborations on a theme with which Rockefeller was already familiar.

If this was the case, Rockefeller gave no indication. At Hedricks Point he gave no sign of approval or disapproval, leaving Albright in a state of anxiety. However, concern changed to guarded optimism when Rockefeller wrote from New York requesting that maps be prepared and sent to him indicating the private holdings south of Jenny Lake and west of the Snake River. He also invited cost estimates for purchasing some of the roadside properties on which stood the most offensive structures. Albright was delighted, writing his friend Burt that Rockefeller was "very much interested in our big Jackson Hole plan." [13] Perhaps the philanthropist they had sought in 1923 had now been found?

The following winter Albright called on Rockefeller in New York, well-laden with maps prepared by Dick Winger. These maps detailed the information Albright had thought Rockefeller requested.[14] After spreading them out it was clear that Mr. Rockefeller was not pleased. Later, Albright recalled that Rockefeller exclaimed, "Mr. Albright, this isn't what I wanted from you." A discussion ensued in which Rockefeller made it clear that he was only interested in an ideal and complete project—namely, the big Jackson Hole project which Albright had outlined at Hedricks Point. When the Yellowstone superintendent responded that the project might cost from a million to a million and a half dollars, Rockefeller assured him that money was not the major consideration. If he was to undertake a project he did not want to do a halfway job. The young Yellowstone park superintendent was instructed to return with new maps and revised estimates which would reflect Rockefeller's intent to purchase all the private land in Jackson Hole.[15]

Euphoric could only describe Albright's state of mind as he left Rockefeller's office. He had come to New York with hopes that Rockefeller could be persuaded to purchase some 14,170 acres at an estimated cost of $397,000, land all on the west side of the Snake River. When Rockefeller signalled his desire to purchase the whole northern valley, it was a remarkable turn of fortune. Shortly thereafter, William A. Welsh, general manager of Palisades Interstate Park, New York, wrote Albright that he had heard that an ambitious young park service employee had "called on a certain gentleman with the idea of selling him a proposition of about a .22 caliber and found this gentleman willing to consider nothing less than a 16 inch cannon . . . ."[16]

Immediately after the interview Albright posted a letter to Richard Winger requesting the necessary information. He was sorely tempted to telephone or wire Winger of the good news, but the latter methods of communication offered little privacy in Jackson in the 1920s.[17] Nevertheless, within a month Albright had the additional maps and estimates and was once again on his way to New York.

Within a few days after receiving the material, Rockefeller gave his approval in a letter to his principal advisor and trusted executive, Colonel Arthur Woods. The letter pledged John D. Rockefeller, Jr., to purchase "the entire Jackson Hole Valley with a view to its being ultimately turned over to the Government for joint or partial operation by the Department of Parks and the Forestry Department." Specifically, he wished to preserve the big game and the outstanding scenery by eventually having the land added to Yellowstone National Park. On the west side of the Snake River Rockefeller empowered Woods to purchase 14,170 acres at $397,000, an average of $28 per acre. On the east side he authorized the purchase of some 100,000 acres at a cost of $1,000,000 or $10 per acre. In typical fashion, Rockefeller then turned over the entire project to Arthur

Woods. "I desire to place this entire matter in your hands," wrote Woods' employer, "to plan, organize and carry out." [18] As with so many of his projects, John D. Rockefeller, Jr., now considered his direct association at an end, and that his capable subordinates would carry out his wishes expeditiously. However, this was not to be, for, as Rockefeller's biographer stated, before this project was completed it "would bring him many perplexing hours." [19] Ironically, it would cause him much more consternation than another concurrent project of much more vast proportions: the restoration of Williamsburg, Virginia. [20]

As with Williamsburg, it was thought wise for Rockefeller's association with the Jackson Hole project to remain secret. The primary intent was to prevent inflation of property. The idea of secrecy was first suggested by Albright in a letter outlining the method by which the purchases might be made. In this letter Albright presented some of the possible pitfalls of the project, including an analysis of the problem of congressional acceptance of the land. He concluded that even if the gift was rejected, the land would surely appreciate in value; thus there would be no loss. As to the method of purchase, Albright advised not only secrecy, but suggested a recreation and hunting club as a "front organization" with the Salt Lake City law firm of Fabian and Clendenin to handle the day-to-day negotiations and legal work. In regard to the priority of land purchases, Albright passed on the suggestions of Struthers Burt: namely, that the land on the west side of the Snake River should be purchased first, then slowly and quietly land on the east side should be incorporated into the purchase program. [21]

Albright's suggestions were adopted without debate, for it was fully understood by Rockefeller's staff that the superintendent of Yellowstone would play a dominant part in decision making. Reporting on the project in late March, Arthur Woods assured Rockefeller that "we have been careful to do nothing that would take the leadership and responsibility in the matter from Albright." [22] The first step was the establishment and incorporation of the Snake River Land Company in Salt Lake City under Utah law. Vanderbilt Webb, a New York attorney, was chosen as president of the company. Webb was an ideal man for the post for he was known by both Chorley and Arthur Woods as a competent executive, his name was associated with Vanderbilt family wealth through his mother, and yet he was not directly connected with the Rockefeller organization. Webb accepted the position, and in the years to follow Webb and Chorley would not only become close business associates, but the best of friends.[23]

Harold Fabian was designated as vice-president. When Albright had suggested that the law firm of Fabian and Clendenin handle the purchases, he had in mind that his old University of California classmate, Beverly Clendenin, would take on the task. This was not to be. The attorney soon to be deeply involved in the project was Harold Fabian, a native of Utah, educated at Yale University, who eventually graduated from Harvard Law School in 1910. During a stint with the military in World War I Fabian and Beverly Clendenin befriended each other and at the conclusion of the conflict they returned to open a law office in Salt Lake City. When Albright approached Clendenin, it was Fabian, with his love of the out-of-doors, the mountains and the West, who responded positively.[24] Of course he could not imagine in 1927 that the project would consume much of his energy for over twenty-five years.

It was decided that the man to act as land purchasing agent should be Robert E. Miller. Miller was, perhaps, the most influential person in Jackson Hole. He was a pioneer, having first settled in 1885. Besides being a rancher, for a time he had been supervisor of Teton National Forest. By the 1920s he had risen to the position of president of the Jackson State Bank. He could not be ignored, and much as Albright would have preferred that his friend Richard Winger handle purchasing, he had to bow to practical realities. He had slighted Miller in 1919 with negative results. He would not make that mistake again. However, Albright could not approach Miller directly, for the past Forest Service supervisor was bitterly opposed to Albright and the National Park Service designs on the Teton Range-Jackson Hole area. Therefore Miller was contacted through Lawrence Larom, a Cody dude rancher whom Albright had taken into his confidence. Both Miller and Larom were in Washington, D.C. in March, 1927, attending a meeting of the Elk Commission when Larom explained the Snake River Land Company project to Miller. However, the Jackson banker refused to take the plan seriously, believing that Larom was proposing a dream rather than reality backed with available cash. Vanderbilt Webb was called down from New York, and by the time Miller departed for Jackson, it was understood that he would prepare a plan to include a list of properties to be purchased with a schedule of prices.[25] As with Harold Fabian, Miller had no idea who the "anonymous donors" were, although he was assured that the land purchased by the company would be used for recreation and conservation purposes.

In truth, Miller was never trusted by the Rockefeller associates and it was felt the less he knew the better. From the beginning his involvement was understood as a necessary evil, primarily because he vigorously opposed the very aims of the project. Not only did he oppose park extension from an ex-Forest Service executive point of view, but as a businessman he believed that park extension portended economic disaster: the real estate and the cattle raising businesses would be crippled, and the country "locked up" from all development. Later Miller would charge that at one of his first meetings with Webb, in June, 1927, he asked the New York attorney if the land purchases were connected with park creation or park extension, and received assurances that they were not.[26]

Whatever his suspicions the Jackson banker was willing to act as land agent for the company, provided equitable prices would be paid and that the near-destitute small ranchers and homesteaders would be treated fairly. This was always the intent of Vanderbilt Webb and "my clients," as he referred to John D. Rockefeller, Jr. Thus in June, 1927, the two parties entered into contract regarding a specific land purchase schedule and compensation for Miller's services.[27] This document is both interesting and revealing. The realtor-banker was to be paid by a rather complicated schedule which emphasized an increased remuneration for shrewd bargaining. Hence it was possible for Miller to realize a total of $43,000 in commissions should he be extremely effective and efficient in his purchases. Specifically, the schedule called for a total purchase of 38,526 acres of land at a price of $1,364,325. Should, however, Robert Miller succeed in obtaining title to this land "for the sum of $1,000,000 or less" prior to July 1, 1929, he would receive an extra compensation of $15,000.[28] Often there is a deep chasm between the ideal and the practical. While Rockefeller, Fabian, Miller and others were intent on offering a fair price for the land, their agreement spoke the language of hardfisted business dealings—namely, that if Miller could purchase the land at $364,325 less than they believed it was worth, the Jackson banker would receive a substantial bonus.

Certainly the seeds of distrust and controversy were sown in the tactics determined in 1927. Rockefeller was motivated by both a desire to do good works and a commitment to accomplish these good works fairly and without injury. However, his subordinates knew their boss was also committed to sound business practices, which, translated, meant driving a hard bargain. Miller, on the other hand, was a banker who had not earned the nickname "old 12 percent" for nothing. Thus it was that the combination of "sound business practices" and a certain penchant for corporate orderliness was bound to make enemies among those who would deal with this mysterious new corporation. In the same vein, the decision for secrecy regarding ownership of the Snake River Land Company cannot be disputed from a business perspective. However, from a political vantage point, it would prove to be the cornerstone in a foundation of mistrust constructed by Jackson Hole residents. When, in April 1930, the ownership and intent of the company was revealed, this vague distrust would turn to resentment and fear that decisions were no longer in their hands. With the benefit of hindsight, it seems possible that had Rockefeller, Woods, Chorley, and Albright committed themselves to openness with regard to purpose, an investment of a few hundred thousand dollars more, and a more compassionate attitude toward petty matters, they might have avoided the incessant charges of wrongdoing which would haunt the project in future years.

In the meantime, before actual purchase could commence the policy of those public agencies owning land in the proposed purchase area had to be ascertained: namely the state of Wyoming and the General Land Office. If either contemplated releasing public lands into private hands the project could be endangered. Although full satisfaction regarding the state of Wyoming's public lands was not forthcoming, it was decided that they did not present a serious threat to the integrity of the project.[29]

The success of the undertaking, however, was most dependent upon the General Land Office withdrawing public domain lands from private entry. Considerable land within the proposed purchase area was still available under such acts as the Homestead Act of 1862, the Timber and Stone Act of 1878, the Desert Land Act of 1877 and the Stock Raising Homestead Act of 1916. If these lands remained open to entry at the same time the Snake River Land Company commenced purchasing adjacent and nearby private lands, the results would be predictable. It was imperative that speculation be suppressed. A visit by Kenneth Chorley to Secretary of the Interior Hubert Work resulted in Executive Order No. 4685, issued July 7, 1927 by President Calvin Coolidge, a land withdrawal which largely accomplished their purpose.[30]

Ironically, while this July 7th withdrawal order served the Rockefeller project well, it stirred up a hornets' nest of activity among those who were wrestling with the long-standing problem of the Jackson Hole elk herd. As heretofore mentioned, much had already been done to safeguard the herd, but in the early 1920s the management of the elk was in a state of confusion. Who was responsible for the herd, the federal government or the state of Wyoming? And which federal agency should have ultimate jurisdiction: the Biological Survey, the Forest Service, or the National Park Service? Just how many elk were there, and how many should there be? How much land should be reserved for their use? How much artificial feeding of hay should take place? And what should be the annual harvest? These were hard questions, not easily answered.

In an attempt to resolve some of them, President Coolidge's Commission on Outdoor Recreation created the Elk Commission, an *ad hoc* commission that accomplished much in establishing a wise elk management policy before it disbanded in 1934. The commission was comprised of representatives of the National Park Service, the Forest Service, the Biological Survey, the governor of Wyoming, the Wyoming Game and Fish Commission, and various conservation and local interests.[31] In its initial recommendations the Elk Commission urged that certain public lands adjacent or near the National Elk Refuge be removed from public entry and ultimately added to the refuge. This was quickly accomplished when President Coolidge signed an executive order on April 15, 1927. However, what was not understood by Charles Sheldon, chairman of the Elk Commission, or Arthur Ringland, the secretary, was that concurrently with their land recommendations, the Snake River Land Company and the National Park Service were requesting that the secretary of the interior recommend land withdrawals in support of their land purchase program. Considerable confusion resulted when, on July 7, 1927, President Coolidge put his signature to another executive order withdrawing from public entry a considerably larger area in Jackson Hole.

Chairman Sheldon was at his wit's end, for the commission had only been able to secure the April 15th withdrawal after assuring the Wyoming members of the Elk Commission that the commission would not seek further withdrawals in upper Jackson Hole. The announcement of the July 7th withdrawal (23,617 acres) seemed an act of bad faith and soon "aroused suspicion throughout the state." [32] Sheldon was so embarrassed and mystified by the action that he expressed his surprise to Secretary of the Interior Work that any action should be taken contrary to the Elk Commission's recommendation, thus undercutting its credibility. Secretary Work responded that the withdrawal had been made at the "suggestion of Mr. Chorley of New York." [33] It required only a little detective work to ferret out the connection between Chorley and Rockefeller. Whether Sheldon pursued the clue is unknown. The same opportunity was open to Jackson Hole residents, when on August 25, 1927, the Jackson Hole *Courier* revealed that "the late withdrawal was brought about by one 'Mr. Chorley of New York' representing a group interested in some new program of elk conservation." [34] The report implied that the New York group hoped to supercede and expand on the Elk Commission plan.

It was evident that the Rockefeller people were in serious trouble, and unless something was done quickly it was likely that the Elk Commission and the state of Wyoming would prevail upon the president to revoke his July 7th executive order. In August, Sheldon had formally requested that the order be rescinded. His appeal was resoundingly seconded by Arthur Ringland, the Forest Service representative on the Elk Commission, when he published a scathing letter in the Jackson Hole *Courier*. [35] As fall approached the mountain valley, Will Deloney joined the chorus calling for rescission and it appeared that he would soon enlist the support of Congressman Charles Winter and Senators Francis Warren and John Kendrick.

The Snake River Land Company officials struggled for a way to escape the dilemma the July 7th withdrawal posed. The main hope of Harold Fabian, Horace Albright and Vanderbilt

Webb was that the excitement would simply die down, the withdrawal would be allowed to stand, and they could get on with the business of purchasing land. However, this was too optimistic. By the middle of October it was evident that the circle of those privy to their plans would have to be enlarged. On October 18th Miller was ordered to halt any land purchase negotiations.[36] Then in late November and early December, 1927, a number of conferences were held in Washington to inform Charles Sheldon, Congressman Winter, Governor Frank Emerson, Senator John Kendrick, and former Congressman Frank Mondell of the intent of the Snake River Land Company. The plan was revealed in some detail, but the Rockefeller connection was withheld. As expected, Vanderbilt Webb was quizzed with regard to the ultimate disposition of the property. Webb responded that the land would not be used for private purposes, and that it would be dedicated to the use of the people. The decision of what public agency would administer the land was undecided.[37] Vague as this explanation was, it sufficed to win over those in attendance, and the threat of revocation of the July 7th order ended.

Once the withdrawal was assured, land purchasing was renewed. By December 5, 1927, new schedules had been worked out in which a few parcels in the northern part of the valley were included and considerable land in the southwestern corner was eliminated. Acreage was cut, but the purchase price remained approximately the same. Like so many estimated costs, the first one presented to Rockefeller was unrealistically low; thus a new, more sensible projection was necessary.[38]

As Miller commenced purchasing land in earnest, he faced the unenviable task of attempting to please conflicting interests. On the one hand he faced the land price schedule he had set up for his clients, on the other was the hard reality of dealing with homesteaders and small ranchers, many of whom were his neighbors and friends. It is generally agreed that Miller purchased land at very fair prices, but there was bound to be animosity in such an inclusive purchase program. A "fair price" is certainly a relative term, and ranchers and homesteaders who were quite satisfied at the time of the sale could easily become bitter a few years later as land prices appreciated and the millionaire behind the project was revealed. Furthermore, as in so many scenic regions, the price of land in Jackson Hole has risen

to such astronomical heights in recent years that the land prices
of the late 1920s, averaging about forty dollars per acre, seem
almost incomprehensible. Later, some early settlers tended to
fantasize about the wealth that would be theirs had they not
sold. Interviewed in 1966, W. C. "Slim" Lawrence, a long time
Jackson Hole resident, believed that the ranchers were not
treated fairly, noting that "a lot of this land that's going for 5
and 6 thousand dollars an acre now, the original ranchers got
$100 an acre for it." [39] Certainly much of the opposition that
would coalesce in the 1930s and 1940s centered about the feeling that somehow landowners had not received full value.

In reality, Miller had paid premium prices. The cattle
business, on which land values were based, had plummeted in
the 1920s, after a high immediately following World War I.
There were hard times in Wyoming, forcing some one hundred
banks in the state to close their doors. While the more urban
and industrial sections of the nation enjoyed the bubble of
prosperity, the great depression was already present in much of
the arid West, particularly in the livestock industry. [40] Thus
many Jackson Hole homesteaders were mightily pleased to get
out from under the debt imposed by the depressed cattle industry and move on to more profitable activities. Yet, time had a
way of distorting their predicament, especially as their dis-
posed-of land appreciated.

In 1928 Robert Miller successfully purchased Ben Sheffield's extensive property at Moran. This was a key acquisition,
for Sheffield, an early guide and pioneer in upper Jackson Hole,
had acquired not only some 343 acres of land but all the buildings at Moran, a town hastily thrown up to house construction
workers on the Jackson Lake dam. For the amount of $106,425
the Snake River Land Company acquired the town of Moran,
consisting of Teton Lodge and 107 structures of varying quality
and worth, plus Sheffield's acreage. The old pioneer retained
only "a case of guns and his clothes," although he remained as
temporary lessee. [41] This was an important purchase for the
project, for Sheffield's property was indispensable to a successful restoration of the natural environment. By the 1950s the
company would completely eliminate the town of Moran,
either destroying the buildings or removing them to other sites.
Later some older residents would criticize the lack of historic
interest on the part of Harold Fabian and the Snake River Land

Company, but in truth Moran was a ramshackle little construction town that deserved its fate. Today grass and willows have reclaimed the site.

Purchase of Sheffield's Teton Lodge posed a new problem for the Rockefeller people. The lodge was one of two places of any size in the northern Jackson Hole area where tourists could purchase meals and find sleeping accommodations. To discontinue its operation would cause inconvenience for both residents and tourists alike. The lodge would have to remain open. Yet Rockefeller never envisioned entering the tourist business, and the Snake River Land Company was a landholding company with a very limited function. The solution agreed upon was to seek private investors to lease the lodge and continue its operation. Harold Fabian sought financial capital where he knew he could find it; in Salt Lake City. There he met with J. H. Rayburn, an acquaintance and the manager of the Newhouse Hotel, proposing to him that he organize a company to take a lease on Teton Lodge. After a trip to Moran to view the operation, Rayburn politely declined the proposal, reasoning that it would not be worth the time and effort necessary for a successful operation. Fabian persisted, and finally Rayburn agreed to operate Teton Lodge with the understanding that the Snake River Land Company would advance $35,000 for renovation and agree to a ten-year lease. Rayburn was able to entice ten Salt Lake City businessmen, including Fabian and his law partner, Beverly Clendenin, to invest an additional $35,000, the minimum capital required. At that point, according to Rayburn, the corporation sought capital from investors in Idaho and particularly in Wyoming. Payton W. Spaulding, an Evanston, Wyoming attorney associated with the land purchase program, invested $1,500 and Richard Winger subscribed and paid $1,000. Bruce Porter, a Jackson druggist and rancher, invested $3,000 and became the Wyoming resident agent for the Teton Lodge.[42]

Other Wyoming residents expressed interest in the business venture. C. R. Van Vleck, a Jackson businessman, took an active part in discussing the plans and organization of the corporation. Van Vleck agreed to take some $3,500 in stock, but he never took up this option. Two Kemmerer, Wyoming, businessmen, Lester G. Baker and John McDermott, each pledged $1,000, but like Van Vleck, they never made good on their notes.[43] These actions by Van Vleck, Baker and McDermott would probably have gone unnoticed were it not for the fact that all three became bitter, determined opponents to park extension. One historian, Verne Chatelain, has charged that Baker and McDermott never expected to pay for their stock: that essentially their support would be "bought off" through a gift of stock. Eventually, when they found out they were expected to pay like other investors, "they defaulted and began a bitter and unjustified attack upon what they knew to be a legitimate enterprise." [44]

The Snake River Land Company found their involvement inextricably extended to not only food and lodging, but to transportation. A local resident, Howard Hout, had been operating a bus between Victor, Idaho, and Moran, but he had sold out to the Union Pacific Railroad Company, which soon abandoned the line. Rayburn and his associates were determined to reestablish the bus route to promote the Teton Lodge and the tourist business in northern Jackson Hole. When Rayburn approached Hout with the idea of renewing the line with first-class equipment, Hout showed little interest. With no good prospects, Rayburn and his Teton Lodge Company associates entered the transportation business, incorporating the Teton Transportation Company and eventually securing a concession to operate in Grand Teton National Park. Within a short time these two corporations merged into the Teton Investment Company. [45]

Perhaps the Teton Investment Company was an unavoidable extension of the land purchase program, but the purchase of Jackson Lake Lodge was not, and indicated a desire on the part of company executives to monopolize not only the land but all the services in upper Jackson Hole. The Jackson Lake Lodge, not to be confused with the present-day lodge, was located approximately one-half mile from Moran. It was built on Forest Service land and was not within the Snake River Land Company's original schedule of purchases. Yet when the owners of the lodge, a group of Casper, Wyoming, businessmen, indicated their desire to sell out, Rayburn and Harold Fabian were quite willing to listen. Negotiations were held in Casper, and eventually it was agreed that the owners of the lodge would receive $40,000 in Teton Investment Company stock as well as $35,000 in cash. The $35,000 was advanced by the Snake River Land Company. [46] In this fashion the Teton Investment Company controlled the tourist business in upper Jackson Hole, and, in turn, the Teton Investment Company was subordinate to the Rockefeller-owned Snake River Land Company.

Surely the entrance of John D. Rockefeller, Jr., into the tourist business was by chance rather than design, and unavoidable rather than intentional. Yet, in the years to come those enemies of park extension would find good arrows for their bows of censure against Rockefeller, for, inadvertently or not, he had established a monopoly not only of land but of services in upper Jackson Hole.

In the meantime the land purchase program proceeded, but not necessarily to the satisfaction of Robert Miller or the Snake River Land Company officials. Miller brooded over the ultimate use of the land he was purchasing, for he was suspicious that somehow his land purchases were related to the expansion plans of the National Park Service: plans which he opposed with all his energy and influence. In February, 1928, after the bill was introduced in Congress to expand Yellowstone National Park southward, Miller again demanded and received assurance that the land purchase program was not related to the park extension effort. Vanderbilt Webb wrote emphatically that the "clients" had "nothing to do with the proposed legislation." [47] Technically this was true, but when Webb divorced Rockefeller from National Park Service goals, it was like separating butter from bread.

Whatever subterfuge Webb had engaged in, no doubt he felt it was justified. Miller had not lived up to expectations. Most galling was the Jackson banker's lack of communication. At one point, after Miller had failed to communicate for over a month when important matters were pending, Webb wired Miller: "Have received no word from you since putting you on subway, December 6th and am beginning to wonder if you are still underground." [48] A number of letters from Webb, Kenneth Chorley and Harold Fabian express their frustration at not being kept up-to-date with the situation in Jackson Hole. Once, in September, 1929, Webb was reduced to listing eleven questions which Miller was directed to answer. [49]

When Miller did answer, he usually did little to alleviate the frustration of Webb, Chorley and Fabian. The strategy agreed upon was that Miller should concentrate on purchasing the more desirable and aesthetic lands on the west side of the

Snake River, then in due time, Miller could acquire the sage-brush flats and grazing land on the east side. Much to their consternation, Miller did just the opposite. In the eyes of his employers Miller seemed to be purposefully buying land only on the east side, much of which was mortgaged to his own Jackson State Bank. Miller, on the other hand, maintained that prices on the west side had become unreasonably inflated. On a number of occasions he counselled patience for the ranch owners were "temporarily out of their heads with no sense or reason, as to values." He would not "be a party to such unreasonable values." [50]

In truth, by mid-1929 Miller had lost his effectiveness. Like any banker in any small community, his use of economic power had won him friends, but also a number of enemies. Struthers Burt was particularly irked by Miller's treatment of some of the property owners. Burt charged that Miller was "about as vindictive a man, in his quiet fashion, as I have ever met." Friends and originators of the Maud Noble cabin plan such as Joe Jones, Dick Winger and Jack Eynon were prepared to sell, but Miller would not offer them true value.[51] Kenneth Chorley responded to Burt's accusations by stating that the Snake River Land Company would not "stand by and knowingly see injustice done to anyone." Chorley suggested that Burt advise his friends to "sit tight," "offering their property from time to time ... but not selling until they receive a price which they consider fair and reasonable." [52]

In justice to Miller it should be noted that some of the individuals close to the project were not above taking a more than reasonable profit. At one point, Horace Albright warned that Dick Winger must come down on his $20,000 selling price for a Timber and Stone Act homestead that he paid $800 for a year before! [53] Surely there were many others bent on preposterous profits, giving validity to Miller's claims. Finally the Snake River Land Company land agent was placed in a terribly disadvantageous position when such company officials as Kenneth Chorley advised ranchers to "sit tight" until Miller offered a "fair and reasonable" price.

By the summer of 1929 the Snake River Land Company officials' patience with Miller was exhausted. Horace Albright visited Jackson Hole, and came away with the conclusion that Miller must be replaced. He recommended that Dick Winger be given the task, but warned that the spunky Winger "better get his price for his own property down the scale a long ways."[54] Both Vanderbilt Webb and Harold Fabian spent considerable time in Jackson Hole that summer, reaching the same conclusion as Albright: Miller's monopoly must be ended and the new agents must move aggressively on the west side of the Snake River.[55] Dick Winger was invited to join the land purchase team, and he accepted, provided that final authority would rest with Fabian rather than Miller. It was also agreed that Mrs. Harold Harrison, well respected with west side settlers, would assist Winger.[56]

After so much frustration and so many plans gone awry, it was with genuine pleasure that Fabian informed Webb that "the Miller-Winger-Harrison combination is working out. I cannot say smoothly because it is a most unruly team, but I can say effectively because we are getting results."[57] Joe Jones's place was quickly purchased by Winger, for Jones had been willing to sell for many months, but not to Miller. Then the Gebo Ranch purchase broke the west side, followed by purchase of the Elbo Ranch, the Ferry Ranch, Harold Brown's place as well as the Altenreid land.[58]

As the land purchase program progressed, the Rockefeller people worked closely with the National Park Service. In Washington, Kenneth Chorley kept the tiny Park Service staff busy with a multitude of research questions regarding land claims and titles in Jackson Hole. It seemed understood that the Rockefeller staff could call on the Park Service personnel to perform many tasks. In the numerous correspondence extant, primarily between Kenneth Chorley and Assistant Director Arno Cammerer, the relationship was amiable, but not altogether equal. Chorley's letters were courteous, yet commanding. Occasionally, Cammerer found the work load irritating to the point of reminding Chorley of their limited staff:

I want to say at this time that a tremendous amount of work was involved in getting out this material for you, and a delay was unavoidable despite the fact that every person in this office who could be used, including the Superintendent of Glacier National Park who happened to be here on a visit, was put on it to get it out, and working nights and Sundays.[59]

Although Sunday and evening efforts might sound slavish today, it was not unusual with the National Park Service.

The service under Stephen Mather had established an *esprit de corps* and purpose which few federal agencies or private corporations possessed. Conrad Wirth, later to be Director, once told of his first years in the Albright administration (1929–1933). Wrestling with problems in Jackson Hole and the Blue Ridge Parkway, landscape architect Wirth often spent his weekends crawling about maps strewn down the hall of the Interior Building. There, with Albright, Arno Cammerer, and a couple of draftsmen they pondered and altered the map of their project park—a map of Jackson Hole some twenty-five to thirty feet in length! [60]

In the field there was also extensive cooperation between the National Park Service and the Rockefeller people. Sam Woodring, the first superintendent of Grand Teton National Park, made his home and headquarters at the Elbo Ranch, owned by the Snake River Land Company. On a more serious note, there is evidence to suggest that at times the Snake River Land Company enlisted the support of the National Park Service to shake the confidence of land owners who were reluctant to sell. Such was the case with Homer Richards, a homesteader who had taken out land on the shores of Jenny Lake and then erected some cabins. It was prime land and Richard Winger offered $25,000, but Richards held out for $35,000. At this point Harold Fabian entered the picture. The "persuader" was revealed to Kenneth Chorley in a confidential letter:

I suggested to Sam Woodring that a change in the road at Jenny Lake would be very effective. Consequently, yesterday he went over there and tentatively selected a line for a new road which would throw the present collection of cabins and stores off the highway. He dropped just enough information so that it would become public gossip.

This, combined with other circumstances, he believed, "should help us get this problem solved." [61]

There is little evidence to suggest that this type of cooperative subterfuge was widely used, yet it does help to explain why the Snake River Land Company and the National Park Service made enemies in Jackson Hole. And for every documented incident there were ten unsubstantiated rumors. Ironically, the recipient of the subterfuge, Homer Richards, became one of the strongest supporters of the park extension idea. He soon sold and moved to Jackson where he prospered in the motel business. [62]

Federal agencies and the Snake River Land Company also cooperated on the perplexing problem of homesteads. Many settlers had not "proved up" on their land within the allotted five years, thus they had no patent to the land. Yet the General Land Office, which was far behind in its work, had not moved to cancel these homesteads. In fact, the policy of the GLO was one of leniency, and often seven or eight years might pass before any action would be taken. Of course it was to the advantage of the Snake River Land Company if these elapsed entries could be cancelled, with the land reverting to the public domain. Correspondence indicated that Kenneth Chorley strongly suggested that Arno Cammerer notify the General Land Office's Board of Equitable Adjudication of the national park plans, with the intent that the board should not consider patents for homesteads which had passed the five-year period. Cammerer complied with this request, and in turn the Assistant Commissioner of the General Land Office promised that although they were behind in their work, they would immediately begin a special study of the area in consideration.[63] This collusion between the Snake River Land Company, the National Park Service and the General Land Office was, of course, totally within the letter, but perhaps not the spirit, of the law. Their actions were legal, but not always just or equitable.

In those cases where it appeared that the homesteader would receive a patent to his land, the Snake River Land Company purchased the homestead. However, rather than completing the patent process, the company would allow the land to revert to the public domain. This was logical, but again it incited considerable local concern, for the effect was to remove potential lands from taxation.[64] This might seem a small matter, but in Teton County, where well over ninety percent of the land was in federal ownership, the very survival of the county as a political entity was dependent on maintenance of a tax base. Providing this tax base while allowing for an expanded national park would become a most difficult problem to resolve.

Another ingredient was added to the complicated mix when the governor of Wyoming, Frank Emerson, became involved. Emerson had crossed swords almost a decade earlier with Albright and the dude ranchers when, as state engineer, he favored damming a number of the lakes in Jackson Hole for irrigation purposes. He lost his fight, but still harbored resentment. When he was approached in 1929 by Roy Van Vleck and a few other Jackson businessmen, he listened attentively. Their complaint was that the Snake River Land Company project was taking valuable agricultural land out of production. Specifically, they deplored the loss of "Mormon Row," an area to the east of Blacktail Butte and along the Gros Ventre River. Here a number of homesteaders had taken up good bottom land and, if not prospering, were existing. The evidence suggests that most wished to sell, but a few did not. Van Vleck and the commercial interests feared the departure of the Mormon Row settlers would hurt their Jackson businesses. They prevailed upon the governor to oppose inclusion of Mormon Row in the project on the basis that it was valuable agricultural land. Although the Snake River Land Company did not necessarily agree with Emerson's analysis, Webb deferred to the governor's wishes, announcing that no further purchases would be made in the area.[65] Ironically, shortly after this decision, a number of Mormon Row settlers who were eager to sell wrote the governor to the effect that with friends like him they needed no enemies. By late 1930 Emerson had recanted, and the Mormon Row lands were reinstated in the purchase program.[66]

With all these problems, inequities, and opposition groups it was surprising that Rockefeller's land purchase program made any headway. Yet it did. Over 25,000 acres of private land had been purchased, and as the decade closed and the nation slipped into the first effects of the great depression, Horace Albright and John D. Rockefeller, Jr., could feel some sense of accomplishment in their joint effort to save Jackson Hole from the excesses of commercialism. The land purchase program was not complete, but it had made such progress that it was now possible to seek federal legislation to expand greatly the newly established Grand Teton National Park.

Furthermore, it was time to lift the veil of secrecy from the project. Although every effort had been made to conceal the identity of the "clients," rumors had become commonplace that John D. Rockefeller, Jr., was providing the financial backing for the Snake River Land Company. In June, 1929, Walter Sheppard, a newspaperman and self-styled defender of the Jackson Hole elk herd, informed Albright that he knew Rockefeller was associated with the land purchases.[67] Harold Fabian had not been informed of the identity of his clients, but was close to the truth. Writing Vanderbilt Webb in January, 1930, Fabian concluded that "the donor of the funds is the Laura Spelmann Rockefeller Institute," and "if that is the case, the name of the donor should be made known." [68] Even such a detached person as W. H. Gray, President of the National Association of Independent Oil Producers, had written Secretary of the Interior Ray Lyman Wilbur, mentioning that he understood the Snake River Land Company was "backed by numerous philanthropists such as the Rockefeller Foundation and others." [69]

It was time to end the secrecy. Thus on April 6, 1930, the full story of John D. Rockefeller, Jr.'s, involvement as well as that of Horace Albright and the National Park Service was revealed through a press release issued to a number of Western newspapers.[70] It was hoped that by making a clean breast of it the way would be cleared to move ahead and quickly consummate the plan.

V

THE BREW BOILS—

INNUENDO AND INVESTIGATION

It has "all the elements of another nationwide scandal,
similar in some degree to the Teapot Dome affair . . . ."
Senator Robert D. Carey, 1933

HE decision to make public the plan of John D.
Rockefeller, Jr., and the National Park Service may have been a
positive step, but it did not quell local opposition. In a sense, it
did just the opposite. Since 1927 local residents were aware that
an unknown company had been purchasing land for a nebulous
purpose. The announcement that the money was provided by
an eastern millionaire and that the beneficiary was to be the
National Park Service exacerbated the latent mistrust and suspicion which had been germinating for over two and one half
years. In the next three years charges of wrongdoing would es-
calate to the point where the conservation purpose of the project would be submerged under a flood of accusations.

Certainly no combination could be more open to local
criticism than the Park Service in collusion with eastern private
wealth. Many of the residents had opposed government incur-
sions on the land for as long as they cared to remember. Tradi-
tionally westerners welcomed government subsidies of stage
routes and railroads, government explorations from Lewis &
Clark to Ferdinand Hayden, military protection, and land grant
colleges. Yet they denied that the government might in any way
dictate policy on their domain, which as often as not, was the
public domain. Through necessity they had learned to live with

the multiple-use policies of the Forest Service, but the "no use" philosophy of the Park Service was anathema to all that they understood about individualism and opportunity in America. Furthermore, revelation of Rockefeller's relationship with the project brought into sharp focus the economic conflict between one of America's most wealthy and influential families and the struggling homesteaders and ranchers of Jackson Hole: a clear case of great wealth amassed against the little man. As of 1930 Rockefeller's involvement had resulted in the withdrawal of considerable land from settlement as well as creation of a monopoly of transportation and tourist facilities, neither of which seemed terribly beneficial to the "expectant capitalists" of Jackson Hole.[1]

While many railed against the lost opportunities, some, such as Struthers Burt, assumed a more realistic stance. In June, 1930, the author dude-rancher published a long letter in the Jackson Hole *Courier*, explaining the project less in idealism than in hard business realities. Burt contended that three-quarters of the land purchased was not "worth one cent to its owners, the county or the state." The northern part of Jackson Hole was practically worthless, he insisted, and viable ranches were located south of Jackson. Tourism, and especially dude ranching, was the key to prosperity in northern Jackson Hole— and the dude ranchers supported the National Park Service and the activities of the Snake River Land Company.[2]

While Burt wrote of economics and livelihood for residents, on the national level he maintained higher ground. In an article for *The Nation* he espoused the idea that "space, solitude, and fresh air, at least for part of the time, are necessary to produce men and women somewhere near his [God's] ideal." Burt maintained that there were two ways of preserving these amenities: democratically or aristocratically. Echoing the arguments of Frederick Law Olmsted's defense of Yosemite Valley's preservation some sixty years earlier, Burt defended public ownership of Jackson Hole in democratic terms. In Europe primitive parklands were the playgrounds of the wealthy, the result being the dehumanization of the lower classes. This could be avoided in America and Burt believed that all eyes would turn to Jackson Hole where "one of the first decisive battles of conservation will be fought out."[3]

Ironically, Burt's democratic appeal made little sense to

those struggling to make a living in Jackson Hole. As before
mentioned, they saw the curtailment of economic possibilities
as an attempt to snuff out individual rights. Furthermore, they
wanted to continue to do what they wanted when they wanted
in their enjoyment of nature. Jackson Hole residents continually complained that the Yellowstone area had become a maze
of negative signposts and restrictions which made an enjoyable
vacation an impossibility. They liked to think that a holiday in
Jackson Hole was a unique experience which would be lost
through the rules and regulations of the National Park Service.
In many ways the land use conflict represented the clash of
nineteenth century values and twentieth century realities.

The Forest Service ideology was much more in accord
with the attitudes of a majority of residents. Local rangers used
their advantage, stressing that their multiple-use policies would
preserve the economic opportunity and the individual freedom
which local residents cherished. Perhaps no one was more adept
at enmuerating the advantages of Forest Service control than
Teton National Forest Supervisor A. C. McCain. He took his
task seriously, for since assuming the supervisor position in
1919, he viewed his position much as a leader of a small nation
surrounded by a Germany bent on *lebensraum*. His most effective weapon was the economic projection ploy, intended to
excite the materialistic instinct. And certainly Jackson Hole,
like the United States, did not lack genuine devotees of the al-
mighty dollar. In a "Summary of Resources" of Teton County,
made public in 1933, McCain estimated that 140 million board
feet of lumber might be harvested annually, yet only 2 million
were being cut. McCain's report stressed that other resources,
including water, coal, phosphate, petroleum and copper ought
to be administered with a policy that allowed for utilization.[4]
McCain's *tour de force* was summer home leases. Often, in both
his public addresses and written reports he stressed that the
Forest Service favored a policy of summer home leases, particularly along the shores of Jackson Lake. In fact, had it not been
for the "veto power" of the National Park Service, they would
have been issued in the 1920s.

The appeal of the Forest Service summer home lease was
twofold: first, it presented an attractive investment. Yearly lease
fees were rock-bottom and a modest but tasteful summer cabin
was bound to appreciate in value. Many of the lease applicants

were local people, perhaps looking with favor on a weekend place, but also mindful of a sound real estate investment. Second, summer places built in northern Jackson Hole could bring in many extra dollars to support land-poor Teton County. In one perhaps rash moment, McCain estimated that some 6,000 summer cottages in northern Jackson Hole, paying an average property tax of $14.00 a year, would enrich the county by some $84,000 each year.[5] It was clear that only the National Park Service stood in the way of realizing this economic bonanza.

Compared to these arguments, the Park Service rhetoric was feeble. Idealistic statements about preserving beauty and attracting tourists paled before the specifics of the Forest Service vision of Jackson Hole. Indeed, it was suprising that there were any converts to the idea of park extension. And yet there were. Perhaps the most important was William C. Deloney. As a member of the state senate and the governor's representative on the Elk Commission, Deloney had built a reputation for his defense of local rights and his sharp temper. He often threatened to walk out and, in fact, did abruptly leave meetings when he felt his views were slighted. In the 1920s Horace Albright and the National Park Service recognized Deloney as one of their most influential and eloquent enemies. Therefore, it came as a surprise when in September, 1930, Will Deloney joined J. L. Eynon, J. D. Ferrin and Richard Winger in sponsoring a plan that represented the wishes of John D. Rockefeller, Jr., and the National Park Service.

This Jackson Hole plan came in the form of a letter signed by the above four men, which was presented to Senators Frederick Walcott of Connecticut, Peter Norbeck of South Dakota, and Key Pittman of Nevada. Junketing in Jackson as members of the Senate Special Committee on Wild Life Resources, the senators were seeking to resolve amicably differences of opinion. The Jackson Hole plan contained five basic provisions: that Grand Teton National Park be expanded to include *both* the east and west sides of the Snake River; that the upper Gros Ventre River range be open to summer cattle grazing; that suitable crossings for cattle be provided within the expanded park; that Teton County be compensated for the loss of its taxable lands for ten years; and that $500,000 be appropriated to purchase private lands for the park not within the Snake River Land Company area of interest. The purpose of the

Jackson Hole Plan was nicely expressed in the following paragraph:

The predominant thought in our minds is that this region be kept in its primitive state as nearly as possible with no more improved roads than are required to provide trunk highways through the area, and with only such accommodations for the traveling public as are necessary to meet that demand and as are in keeping, in location and design, with the general character of this country.[6]

Of course the concept, if not the details, had been agreed upon in the meeting in 1923 at Maud Noble's cabin. By 1927 John D. Rockefeller, Jr. and Horace Albright had a reasonably clear idea of a plan for Jackson Hole. Yet, as Albright would write, the letter "was the first time an effort was made to give definite lines to the project."[7]

Will Deloney's metamorphosis of position deserves further explanation. Contemplating the future of the valley and the elk herd, he concluded that some public agency must be responsible. In his opinion the state of Wyoming was too stingy in its appropriations and too unreliable in its commitment. The Forest Service had at times angered him, but he ruled out their jurisdiction on the basis that most of the land in question was not classifed as forest land. Therefore it was unlikely that Congress would turn over sagebrush and pasture lands to the Forest Service. Deloney ruled out the Biological Survey, a poorly funded federal agency, which he felt would never obtain the needed appropriations to attract tourist travel. Therefore, by a process of elimination, Deloney concluded that there "was no other place to suggest that these lands should go for administration, except to the National Park Service."[8] Thus, with tax provisions for the county and grazing rights for the cattlemen, Deloney joined the park extension team.

Another important defection was that of Walter Perry, editor-owner of the Jackson Hole *Courier*. Perry had judiciously maintained neutrality, but by April, 1931, he had found this position untenable. Readers of the April 30th edition found the following announcement:

We've been asked by both sides to climb on their particular bandwagon. We've tried to maintain a one-man bandwagon and ride the fence. In so doing the editor got so confounded dizzy that he took a tumble and now finds himself on that side of the fence known as Park Extension.[9]

Following this announcement, Perry editorialized continually for park extension, reasoning that prosperity for Jackson Hole would come from recreation and tourism, not cattle. He urged that northern Jackson Hole be returned to a primitive state, making "northwestern Wyoming the Mecca of the recreation seeker . . ." The prime force in restoring northern Jackson Hole was the Snake River Land Company, and Perry urged cooperation with their project, "for the men behind it are our friends." [10]

Perry's stand was indeed courageous in a small town where the weekly newspaper counted heavily on business advertising and every subscription. He quickly felt the impact of his judgment as he was the recipient of a disheartening number of letters cancelling advertisements and subscriptions to the *Courier*. Soon Perry was losing money and found himself facing foreclosure on his mortgage. To keep the paper in the pro-park camp, Wilford Neilson and Henry Stewart found the resources to purchase the weekly. [11]

Whatever problems visited Walter Perry, they did little to alleviate the frustration of the anti-extension forces. They had no medium by which to express their position. They were reduced to sending scathing letters to the editor of the *Courier* or reading Lester Baker's anti-park paper, the Kemmerer *Gazette* —neither of which was particularly acceptable to them. At the Jackson Lion's Club, headquarters for the anti-park forces, leaders such as William Simpson circulated plans for a new newspaper. The fact that Jackson Hole could barely support one weekly paper did not discourage them. They had a cause which they felt must be espoused at any cost.

The Grand Teton appeared on December 29, 1931. From the first edition it was evident that this new weekly would not give full coverage to national or world events, nor would it be dedicated to an objective presentation of local news. Perhaps reminiscent of earlier frontier newspapers, *The Grand Teton* was a vindictive, spunky, devil-may-care, master-of-insult newspaper. Intensely local with nary an iota of national interest, the new tabloid considered everything and everyone outside of the geographic proximity of Jackson Hole as against its cause. As the year 1932 unfolded, *The Grand Teton* used every journalistic tool at its disposal to appeal to that segment of the population which feared monopoly, eastern capital and the federal government. Analogy, character distortion and half-truth were the journalistic devices that the little weekly perfected.[12]

The newspaper delighted in describing Rockefeller as a feudal lord holding "thirty-five thousand acres of our valuable farming lands in the Jackson Hole Valley," and requiring "gratuitous donations" as part of the "fealty." [13] The feudalistic analogy was extended to Horace Albright who, according to the weekly, made Henry I of England appear an unsophisticated novice in the arts of suppression and autocratic rule. "No king in medieval times was more avaricious in his dynasty than is Horace M. Albright," clamored *The Grand Teton*. This dynasty was supported by "the Rockefeller crowd," which included Harold Fabian, Richard Winger, dubbed "Dickie Bird," J. H. Rayburn and a number of investors in the Teton Investment Company. The company, Rockefeller-owned and Salt Lake City-based, was an easy target for slander and insinuation. The incorporators, according to the tabloid, were intent on monopolizing the tourist business in Jackson Hole. Like most "foreign corporations," the Teton Investment Company was profit oriented and cared little for the welfare of Jackson Hole.[14]

Residents who supported park extension incurred particular wrath and were considered *personae non gratae* in the pages of *The Grand Teton*. Will Deloney probably had cause for a libel suit should he have so desired. He was labelled a "traitor" to Jackson Hole who had been elected state senator by "a power more subtle in efficiency than Stalin of Soviet Russia . . ." [15] Those landowners who had sold out to the Snake River Land Company were characterized as "wandering in the desert of their agony, without hope of establishing property or standing, in the short life that remains them." [16]

Especially annoying to park supporters was the fact that the little paper had gained access to confidential letters, particularly those of Horace Albright. The paper regularly printed Albright's personal correspondence, which often contained frank assessments of political realities in Jackson Hole. The source of these letters was traced to Julius Greer, a disconsolate former employee on the ranger force at Yellowstone, who had rifled Albright's files before leaving the service.[17] The letters were embarrassing, but not devastating, for, as Albright wrote Teton Park Superintendent Sam Woodring: "I am not ashamed of anything I wrote . . ." [18] He had no reason to be. However, when set within the colorful journalistic tapestry of *The Grand Teton* the letters gave readers pause in evaluating the nature and purpose of the whole Rockefeller-Albright plan.

Continued slanderous attacks by *The Grand Teton* would seem to demand a response from the pro-park faction. However, it was thought best to simply ignore the charges, lest heated exchanges would fan smoke to fire. Dick Winger, in correspondence with Fabian, argued that the wisest strategy was to refuse to acknowledge the paper's existence. "The more they are ignored," reasoned Winger, ". . . the more violent they will become. . . . These men cannot do anything conservatively. . . . I think they should be allowed to run wild." Fabian agreed, noting that to reply to the "vicious and reckless" charges of such men as William Simpson and Lester Baker would simply place the Snake River Land Company on the defensive, constantly expending energy in a charade in which the opposition would have every advantage.[19]

As *The Grand Teton* rained journalistic blows on the project it was bound to attract the attention of Robert D. Carey, a Wyoming rancher seeking to fill the senatorial vacancy caused by the death of Francis E. Warren in 1929. Carey was the son of one of Wyoming's pioneer politicians, Joseph C. Carey. He had served as governor of the state from 1919–1923. Like most western politicians, Carey felt obligated to criticize the federal government's activities by calling attention to the fact that laws enacted on the Potomac River often did not serve the needs of persons living on the Platte River.[20] Specifically, he argued that the state of Wyoming should have a greater hand in the management of the natural resources of the state. He was a firm believer in states' rights and local control. The aggressive policy of the National Park Service and the implied suppression of livestock grazing rights in Jackson Hole could not but excite Carey's bias.

Although Carey had privately assured Harold Fabian that he "was heartily in favor" of the project, shortly after his election to the Senate in November, 1930, the junior senator moved to the camp of the opposition.[21] Carey evidently perceived that it was to his political advantage to oppose Rockefeller and park extension, and more and more the views of such extremists as Lester Baker and William Simpson dominated his attitude. When in December, 1930, Harold Fabian and

Vanderbilt Webb testified before a Senate committee, Carey drew the two men aside to inform them that he was satisfied with their testimony and approved of what they were doing, but he would never recede from his position against park extension.[22]

The following year Carey kept his promise. The senator accepted malicious gossip as truth, claiming that the Snake River Land Company never informed the Wyoming congressional delegation of their plans, that farmers were being run off their land in Mormon Row, and that the Snake River Land Company failed to cooperate in locating a power line across their property.[23] In public meetings he proclaimed his unalterable opposition. He would only support the extension plan if the people of Wyoming voted for it in a special election, at which time he would campaign vigorously against passage.[24] As he condemned Will Deloney's Jackson Hole plan, he unveiled what he called the "state park plan," which would turn over federal land and Rockefeller-purchased land to the state of Wyoming to be managed in such a manner as the state saw fit.[25]

Senator Carey found considerable support among his political colleagues. While Senator Kendrick assumed a moderate stance, Governor Frank Emerson and Congressional Representative Vincent Carter were willing to believe the worst. Carter was particularly susceptible to his two Kemmerer friends, John McDermott and Lester Baker, unprincipled men who would sell their influence to the highest bidder. As we have seen, McDermott and Baker had attempted to obtain stock in the Teton Investment Company in exchange for their support. This modest form of bribery had been rejected. Undaunted, in April, 1930, they suggested that they would support the Snake River Land Company, but that public opinion must be modified by a heavy advertising campaign in Baker's Kemmerer Gazette.[26] This suggestion was dismissed without comment. Frustrated by their lack of success in partaking of financial gain, the two redoubled their opposition. Unfortunately, Carter chose to listen. In Harold Fabian's judgment, both Carter and Carey fell under the influence of men "who are trying to 'shake us down,' and either punish us or make us pay toll."[27]

Whereas by the close of 1931 the Rockefeller people fully understood the nature of the opposition, the reverse was not evident. Somehow, Carey believed that by bluff and bluster he could win, forcing a compromise of his choosing. Unfortunately, the Wyoming senator did not accurately gage the determination of John D. Rockefeller, Jr. From the beginning, as Albright learned, he was interested in an "ideal" project, and this did not include diluting the plan with such solutions as Carey was likely to propose. Beyond his calm, composed exterior, John D. Rockefeller, Jr., was stubborn in a way that only a man of great wealth could be. He was also patient. Visiting Jackson Hole only a month after one of Carey's public outbursts, Rockefeller wrote Albright of his conviction regarding the project:

I came away [from Jackson Hole] increasingly convinced of the far reaching importance of [our] scheme and confident that nothing short of the most comprehensive and complete program should be followed, fully believing that whether the program is carried out now or ten years later, it will ultimately be carried out, and for myself, quite willing to wait and let time do its work of adjusting and mollifying, rather than to seek an early settlement of the question, through unwise compromise that would for all time mean a less ideal and worthwhile program.[28]

If he could maintain this high ground, the advantage lay with Rockefeller. While politicians might grovel for votes by advocating the economics of the short view, Rockefeller was in the enviable position of being impervious to time and immediate pressures. Furthermore, he seemed to understand and accept the fact that he could expect little praise from the present generation, and that "his thanks must come from posterity when wild life and primitive areas will be less abundant." [29]

While Rockefeller bided his time, Carey became impatient. As 1931 gave way to the election year of 1932, the Wyoming senator reached a point of frustration and vindictiveness that left him quite closed to rational argument. Particularly evident was his loathing of Horace Albright, which dated from Carey's tenure as governor of Wyoming, from 1919–1923. During that period Carey evidently felt neglected in Yellowstone decision making, nor had he ever been consulted regarding the proposed Teton extension. Furthermore, Carey was convinced that Rockefeller would not meet with him because of misrepresentation of his position by Albright. If he could obtain a fair hearing with Rockefeller, free from Albright's bureaucratic meddling, he was certain the eastern millionaire would be amenable to compromise.[30]

By the summer of 1932, Carey's frustration brought him to the point of playing his political trump card — the threat of a congressional investigation of the activities of the Snake River Land Company and the National Park Service. On June 10th, Senator Carey, with the support of Senator Kendrick, introduced Senate Resolution #226 to effect this purpose. The move was strategic. Senator Carey expected that a threat of a congressional investigation would act as a lever to force compromises through discussion with John D. Rockefeller, Jr. He miscalculated. So maligned had the project and its participants become through the bombastic journalism of *The Grand Teton* and publicity-seeking politicians that the Snake River Land Company officials did not fear an investigation. It could do no harm, for as Fabian wrote Vanderbilt Webb, he doubted "if there has ever been an undertaking that has been more lacerated by the claws of personal interests and ulterior motives than this Snake River Land Company project." [31]

Still Carey pressed his perceived advantage. In December, 1932, with the support of Senator Kendrick and Representative Carter, Carey again proposed his state park idea. In reply, Arthur Woods wrote a brief note to Secretary of the Interior Ray Lyman Wilbur saying that Mr. Rockefeller had given the plan careful study and was not interested in it.[32] Undaunted, both Carey and Kendrick sought a meeting with Rockefeller, reasoning that if they could only reach the source of power, their views would prevail. The interchange of letters between the two parties indicates a good deal of strategy and one-upmanship. Arthur Woods informed Carey that Rockefeller would be in Washington, D. C., in late January, 1933, and they could arrange a meeting at that time. Carey responded immediately that they wished to see Rockefeller no later than early January, for, while they preferred settling the controversy by means other than a congressional investigation, if they delayed until early February, the Senate might not act on their resolution. Woods's return letter surprisingly proposed that it would be best not to consider a conference until after the completion of the proposed investigation. In denying Carey's request, Rockefeller gave the Wyoming senator no choice but to proceed with that which he threatened. In a bellicose letter, Carey informed Woods that under the circumstances he must proceed to ask for the investigation. "We are not willing," exclaimed Carey, "to see this section of Wyoming exploited or its citizens driven out to gratify Mr. Albright's ambition or to establish a monopoly for the benefit of Mr. Rockefeller's agents." [33] Much later Kenneth Chorley summarized this exchange of letters in a more lighthearted vein: "Mr. Rockefeller wanted the senator [Carey] to know that he could not investigate him and have lunch with him. He could do one or the other, but not both." [34]

While Carey fumed and fulminated, Senator Kendrick acted independently. The seventy-six-year-old master politician kept an open mind on the issue, rejecting the dictums of his headstrong junior colleague. Twice he met with Albright in January, 1933, and on February 1st he lunched with John D. Rockefeller, Jr. in the apartment of Interior Secretary Wilbur. The meeting accomplished little. Kendrick was somewhat embarrassed in attempting to reestablish Carey's reputation—an idea that Rockefeller did not accept. Rockefeller merely reaffirmed that he would hold out for the ideal project, and that he would not yield to pressure or pleas of compromise.[35] Whether Kendrick reported the results of this meeting to Carey is unknown.

Perhaps Rockefeller's determination was buttressed by the elections of November, 1932. Into the White House came Franklin Delano Roosevelt with an enthusiasm and confidence that were sorely needed for a nation deep in the throes of depression, both economic and psychological. Just what the new chief of state would do with regard to conservation issues was uncertain, but there was reason for confidence. Most would agree with Struthers Burt's appraisal that in Roosevelt conservationists "will find the most sympathetic president they have had since Theodore of the same name." [36]

In Cheyenne, the capital of Wyoming, there was also cause for optimism. The new governor, Leslie Miller, surprisingly favored the project. As early as 1925, Miller had watched his rancher brother, Don, try to scratch out a living in Jackson Hole. He came to the conclusion that the future of the valley was with recreation.[37] Harold Fabian soon called on Miller and was delighted with his reception. "I was with Governor Miller until 10:30 p.m.," Fabian wrote Vanderbilt Webb, "and the three hours were the most pleasant I have spent in Wyoming with officials in the past six years." [38] This initial meeting was the beginning of a long and close relationship between Governor Miller and those who fought so long to establish present-day Grand Teton National Park. Miller was the only prominent Wyoming politician to argue consistently for the Jackson Hole plan, and his determination may have been one of the reasons for his defeat in his bid for reelection in 1938.

Once it was certain that the congressional investigation would take place in the summer of 1933, Snake River Land Company officials and the National Park Service lost no time in making preparations. They considered the investigation as an open forum, and they planned to make the most of it. There was a flurry of activity, prompting Albright to confess to Harold Fabian that "your letters to me and carbon copies of letters to Van [Vanderbilt Webb] and Kenneth [Chorley] have been coming so fast that I am not sure I have acknowledged them all." [39] Most of this activity concerned the upcoming investigation. How should they prepare? Should they draft written statements for publication? What newspaper columnists should be enlisted for their cause? Who should be encouraged to testify at the hearings? What evidence would Carey and the opposition present? And how might they defend themselves from adverse testimony?

It was decided that an effective defense would be a factual, well-written history of the involvement of Albright, Rockefeller, the Snake River Land Company and the National Park Service. To this end Harold Fabian, with the assistance of Josephine Cunningham, compiled a 135-page document detailing the Snake River Land Company's activities from March, 1927, to December, 1932. [40] From this compilation Fabian composed a long letter addressed to Wilford Neilson, editor of the Jackson Hole *Courier*. The letter was carefully composed and the contents subject to considerable editing, as witnessed by a four-page Memorandum from Rockefeller to Fabian suggesting revisions in the draft. [41] Horace Albright undertook the same task as Fabian, concentrating his account on the pre-1927 period. He was assisted by Verne Chatelain, the first chief historian for the National Park Service. [42] The brief history of the Teton Investment Company was told in a letter from the president of the corporation, J. H. Rayburn.

First printed in the Jackson Hole *Courier*, the letters were then published as a ninety-one-page booklet, entitled *Mr. John D. Rockefeller, Jr.'s Proposed Gift of Land for the National Park System in Wyoming.* Five hundred copies were privately printed by the Snake River Land Company and distributed shortly before the Senate investigation commenced. Fabian distributed the work in Jackson Hole and to conservation friends in the western states, while Albright undertook the same task in Washington, D. C. Ivy Lee, a newspaper columnist, was responsible for distributing the tract to influential newspaper editors.[43] The pamphlet was important in swaying public opinion, for its reasoned, factual appeal was in stark contrast to the histrionics of *The Grand Teton.*

In Wyoming the National Park Service and the Rockefeller people searched for friends. They could count on support from Governor Leslie Miller and perhaps on neutrality from Senator Kendrick. Lawrence Larom, a Cody, Wyoming, dude rancher, was working hard in both Washington, D. C., and Jackson Hole to win support for the pro-park forces. Charles C. Moore, a Dubois, Wyoming, dude rancher, conservationist, member of the state legislature, and vice president of the Dude Ranchers' Association, was indefatigable in his support. While Carey's political ambitions were the object of Moore's scorn, he bolstered Albright's morale with letters assuring him that "a great many of us recognize in you a great friend of the State of Wyoming." [44] At times those who fought for preservation thought Wyoming was all enemy ground, but such men as Charles Moore and a sizable minority understood that preservation of the northwest corner of the state was essential to their aesthetic and economic well-being.

In Washington, Albright worked to see that the Senate investigating committee would be impartial, if not favorable, to the National Park Service cause. He particularly feared the possibility that Senator Carey would be appointed chairman of the committee. He voiced his concerns to Senator Gerald Nye of North Dakota, and his longtime friend and congressional supported informed him that Carey would have to be on the committee, but that he positively would not be chairman.[45] Once the committee was composed, Senator Nye served as its chairman. Senator Kendrick refused to allow himself to be placed on the committee. The elderly senator's health was failing, and perhaps he realized that he had much work to complete before death would overtake him on November 3, 1933.[46]

As the summer hearings in Jackson approached, two events served to heighten interest. The first was the unexpected announcement of the resignation of Horace Albright as director of the National Park Service, effective August 10, 1933. It was natural that Albright's enemies would associate this June announcement with wrongdoing on the part of the director. *The Grand Teton* lost no time in proclaiming in bold capital letters: "NO HONEST PUBLIC OFFICIAL EVER RESIGNS UNDER FIRE: THAT IS CERTAIN." [47]

Certainly the timing of Albright's announcement was not propitious, although the evidence indicated that the Jackson Hole controversy did not play a part in his decision. Much later Albright asserted that his association with Interior Secretary Harold Ickes convinced him that sooner or later he would cross swords with the "old curmudgeon," and that he ought to resign to an advantageous position rather than be fired to join the soup lines of the unemployed.[48] Other evidence suggests that Ickes's mercurial personality played little part in Albright's decision. He had never been totally satisfied with public service. Almost from the beginning of his association with the National Park Service, Stephen Mather had to keep assuring Albright of the importance of their work and occasionally supplement his assistant's meager salary from his own personal funds.[49] When in November, 1932, the United States Potash Company offered him the position of executive vice-president and general manager at a salary of $20,000 a year, more than twice his income as director, Albright promised to think it over.[50] By mid-January, 1933, he had evidently made up his mind, writing confidentially to Arthur Woods that "I have an offer from outside the Government Service which seems to make it necessary for me to resign before January 31st [1933] . . . Please think about my going from the standpoint of my connection with the Jackson Hole and other projects in which Mr. Rockefeller is interested, and also from the standpoint of the investigation proposed." [51] Albright received an extension on the job offering, but by February, 1933, he had accepted the post with the understanding that he would take up his new position as soon as it was convenient to leave the National Park Service.[52] When on June 10, 1933, President Roosevelt transferred jurisdiction of all historic battlefields and monuments to the National Park Service, Albright won a major objective. Assured that the National Park Service would administer all federal parks and monuments, the second director could leave, confident that he had helped create a strong and enduring agency.

Albright's resignation may be viewed in two ways. Certainly the Jackson Hole project would lose its most dynamic champion. Albright's ambition was, as William Herndon referred to Abraham Lincoln's, "a little engine that knew no rest." [53] He was indefatigable, and the volume of his correspondence gives evidence of his total dedication to the realization of the dream he and Rockefeller conceived. On the other hand the virtues of vision and determination made strong enemies. A number of important persons were fighting Albright's ambition and assertiveness as much as the idea of park extension. He was the personification of the efficient, enterprising Washington bureau· crat that many westerners had little use for. Perhaps it was time for National Park Service leadership to pass to a less visible, lower keyed personality, such as Albright's successor, Arno Cammerer.

Although Horace Albright's resignation signalled the end of his official involvement with the project, it did not lessen his interest. As he assured F. S. Burrage, editor of the Laramie *Boomerang*, he was leaving the service but was "not dropping the Jackson Hole Project. I am going to be on the firing line on that project until it is consummated." [54] Nor would he sever his close association with John D. Rockefeller, Jr., and his sons. Although never in the employment of the Rockefeller family, he often gave advice on conservation matters, and served on the Board of Directors of the Snake River Land Company and the Jackson Hole Preserve, Inc., until his resignation in 1977. For Horace Albright, Grand Teton National Park was an idea that transcended mere employment.

The second event that lent interest to the forthcoming hearings was the inflammatory remarks made by Senator Robert Carey in an interview with Francis Wayne, a reporter with the Denver *Post*. In a July 14, 1933, article, Carey was quoted as stating: "Settlers were induced, one way or another, to sell their property or dispose of their leases. Refusal found fences burned, [and] houses destroyed by fire." [55] Three days later the New York *Herald Tribune* picked up the story, quoting Carey that the Jackson Hole investigation had "all the elements of another nationwide scandal, similar in some degree to the Teapot Dome affair . . ." [56] Whatever Carey's motivation for such provocative rhetoric, he did succeed in exasperating his committee colleagues, Senators Peter Norbeck and Gerald Nye, both of whom considered the statements unwarranted and perhaps a "show of desperation." [57] Furthermore, he made certain that the investigation in Jackson could not be ignored by the national press. Certainly it would be no Scopes Trial, but the possibility of a scandal mandated that the major newspapers and presses must send reporters to the little-known town nestled within the mountains of northwestern Wyoming.

The hearings before a Senate Subcommittee of the Committee on Public Lands and Surveys were held from August 7th through August 10th. It was a major event for the town, and as the time approached it was difficult to find a serious conversation in Jackson on another subject. Later Harold Fabian quipped that during the four days of the investigation "there wasn't a dish washed in Jackson. . . . They were all in the hearing hall." [58] Adding to the excitement was the presence of reporters from the *Christian Science Monitor*, the New York *Times*, the Denver *Post*, the Salt Lake City *Tribune*, the wire services, and a host of small local newspapers. They anxiously awaited some newsworthy story, particularly if it would implicate John D. Rockefeller, Jr. in wrongdoing.[59] Many expected a squall every bit as violent as that which sent five people to their deaths on Jackson Lake the day before the hearings commenced.[60]

On the afternoon of August 7th Senator Gerald Nye, Chairman of the Subcommittee, rapped his gavel, calling the committee to order. After the usual formalities, Senator Nye introduced John C. Pickett, a young Cheyenne attorney employed as the investigating officer for the committee. However, before Pickett could take over, an altercation between Senators Nye and Carey immediately indicated their particular bias. Nye wished to introduced as evidence the letters of Albright, Fabian and Rayburn to Wilford Neilson. Carey was piqued that Albright was not there in person, protesting that a mere statement was not satisfactory. Nye withdrew his request, and, although later in the hearings the letters were made part of the record, they were never printed.[61]

After some confusion and interruptions from the audience, perhaps as a result of the high emotion of the moment,

Pickett took control and explained his general plan of presenting evidence. His intent was to explore the beginnings of the plan to preserve Jackson Hole, and then proceed to show the connection with John D. Rockefeller, Jr., and the Snake River Land Company. He would then call witnesses who had sold land to the company or who had been approached but did not sell their land. He intended to seek testimony from some of the concessionaires within Grand Teton National Park and lessees of Snake River Land Company property. The hearings would conclude with witnesses who had complaints against the Snake River Land Company or the National Park Service.[62]

From the beginning it was evident that Pickett was Senator Carey's man and that his primary purpose was to prosecute rather than investigate. He often interpreted statements in a manner of a cross-examiner, eliciting excited protests that *that* was not what the witness had meant. His methods often prompted Senators Nye or Norbeck to come to the aid of witnesses or to take issue with the drift of Pickett's questioning. Senator Norbeck often engaged in heated exchanges with Pickett. At one point of frustration, Norbeck exclaimed: "Won't you be frank with the Committee? There are five members of the committee, and you have only consulted one [Carey]." Pickett, equally piqued, retorted: "At least, I have the courtesy of four." Norbeck then reminded counsel that he was an employee of the committee, charged with the task of assisting the committee in ascertaining the truth.[63]

This charge, of course, was not easy, but as the hearings entered the third day it was evident that the national reporters could pack their bags or perhaps do a little trout fishing, for no sensational scandal was going to surface. The best Pickett could offer was that there had been questionable collusion between the National Park Service and the General Land Office, the result being that General Land Office investigators in the field were advised to "go hard" on homesteaders seeking patents for their land.[64] It was also revealed that Albright and National Park Service officials had directly influenced the denial of Albert Gabbey's Stock Raising homestead patent on Jenny Lake, although Gabbey was in compliance with the law.[65]

However, this was not the stuff of a national scandal. Pickett and Senator Carey were unsuccessful in their efforts to show that Rockefeller and the Snake River Land Company used improper methods in their land purchase program. The evidence given by many witnesses indicated just the opposite. Specifically, Pickett attempted to establish that Dick Winger forced sale of land by threatening the owner with condemnation proceedings. While Winger admitted to discussing condemnation in casual conversations, the evidence indicated that he never used this threat to the advantage of the Snake River Land Company.[66]

As the hearings concluded on August 10th, few could deny that the National Park Service and the Snake River Land Company had been exonerated. They had won an important public relations victory. The few improprieties exposed were the fault of individuals rather than policy, and many now understood that much of the furor was generated by a small number of recalcitrant ranchers, businessmen, and ex-Forest Service employees. The Denver *Post* summarized sarcastically but accurately when it reported that the hearings revealed the Jackson Hole story was not a tempest in a teapot, as heralded. It was not even a "squall in a thimble."[67]

As the senators departed Jackson, they differed in their analysis. Senator Carey insisted the hearings showed that the Park Service had used arrogant and unfair methods, but Senator Nye denied that conclusion. Senator Norbeck was most verbal, proclaiming the $5,000 spent on the hearings as "an outrageous expenditure of funds."[68] Senator Nye agreed, and in support he cancelled further hearings on the matter which were scheduled for Washington, D. C. Writing to Horace Albright, the North Dakota senator expressed his conviction that the hearings "have virtually written finish to the squabble..." He was returning to Washington with his family. Once there, he would "strightway [sic] see Ickes and the president with the primary thought in mind of settling down on the Forest Service. They still block the way to proper settlement."[69] Surely Senator Nye's hope that the question could be resolved was shared by many others, no matter where they stood on the issue.

Jackson was a small, struggling frontier town in 1924. Western History
Research Center, University of Wyoming.

William Owen, credited with the first ascent of the Grand Teton, is introduced to the Crown Prince of Sweden by Stephen Mather, Director of the National Park Service. Horace Albright stands to the right while in the background is Robert Miller's Jackson State Bank. Western History Research Center, University of Wyoming.

◄*Above*. At Maud Noble's cabin in July, 1923 a group of Jackson Hole ranchers, dude ranchers, and businessmen met with Horace Albright to make plans to save the valley from development. Western History Research Center, University of Wyoming.
Below. The fate of the Jackson Hole elk herd played a continual role in the struggle to establish the park. Here Mrs. Stephen Leek feeds two favorites. Western History Research Center, University of Wyoming.

Following the completion of Jackson Lake Dam, rising waters inundated over 7,000 acres of lodgepole pine forest, creating what one observer called a "grim graveyard of derelict trees." The Civilian Conservation Corps (CCC) cleaned up the lake shore in the early 1930s. The National Archives, Washington, D.C.

Above. Mr. and Mrs. John D. Rockefeller, Jr. enjoy a cookout with Superintendent Sam Woodring. Grand Teton National Park.

Below. Olaus Murie (front, left) and party on Jackson Lake in 1933. Grand Teton National Park.

Above, left. Leslie Miller, governor of Wyoming from 1933–1939, was one of only a handful of state leaders to favor enlargement of the park. Courtesy of Josephine Fabian.

Above, right. Vanderbilt Webb, a New York attorney, played an important role in land acquisition as president of the Snake River Land Company. Courtesy of Josephine Fabian.

Below. Struthers Burt—author, dude rancher, conservationist—relaxing in Jackson Hole in the early 1950s. Courtesy of Josephine Fabian.

A number of government committees visited Jackson Hole in the late 1920s and 1930s. Shown here is the Senate Special Committee on Wildlife Resources assembled at Moran in September, 1930. Grand Teton National Park.

Senator Gerald Nye (third from right) and other members of the 1933 Senate Public Lands Committee view Jackson Hole from Hedricks Point. Grand Teton National Park.

Vanderbilt Webb, Harold Fabian, and Imer Pitt show off a nice string of Jackson Hole trout. Courtesy of Josephine Fabian.

Horace M. Albright speaking at the dedication of Grand Teton National Park in 1929. Although this was surely a satisfying day for him, the real struggle had just begun. Grand Teton National Park.

Above. Ranger Roger Toll acted as chauffeur for Secretary of the Interior Ray Lyman Wilbur and Kenneth Chorley. Harold Fabian and Horace Albright stand to the right. Courtesy of Josephine Fabian.
Below. Harold Fabian, Wyoming Governor Leslie Miller, Dick Winger, and Charles Huff enjoy Two Ocean Pass where Pacific and Atlantic Creeks separate. It is September, 1933 and they look confident, for just a month earlier the Senate Subcommittee on Public Lands had exonerated the Snake River Land Company of any wrongdoing, and the enlarged park seemed imminent. Courtesy of Josephine Fabian.

Horace Albright (standing) and Wyoming Governor Nellie Taylor Ross and friend stop for a photograph before the Cathedral Group 1926. Courtesy of Josephine Fabian.

Above. The JY Ranch on the shores of Phelps Lake became a favorite haven for both John D. Rockefeller and his son, Laurance. Courtesy of Josephine Fabian.

Below. Angered by President Roosevelt's proclamation that created Jackson Hole National Monument, local ranchers protected their herds with rifles on a spring drive across the area in 1943; their right to cross was not contested. Shown here are Clifford Hansen (later U.S. Senator from Wyoming), Amass James, screen actor Wallace Beery, Rod Lucas, L. G. Hill, and P. C. Hansen. Wide World Photos.

V·I

A DECADE WITHOUT A SOLUTION

"There was no such thing as getting
together and talking it over."
Olaus Murie, Wapiti Wilderness, 1966

T HERE is a time when conflicting forces finally are prepared to meet and attempt to compromise their differences. The period immediately following the 1933 hearings was such a time. As Senator Nye, Senator Carey and other subcommittee members returned to Washington there was room for cautious optimism. Strong differences of opinion existed, yet all agreed that the issue had gone unresolved far too long and that the unsettled state of affairs in Jackson must be ended. In the statehouse in Cheyenne the governor, Leslie Miller, enthusiastically endorsed the project and vowed to work toward a settlement.[1] Perhaps symbolic of this temporary hiatus was the resignation of William Simpson as editor of *The Grand Teton* and the quiet demise of the one-issue oriented tabloid in May, 1934.[2]

As a first step to resolution the federal agencies involved had to end their squabbling and begin cooperating. Senator Nye took the lead in suggesting that the three agencies come together and discuss a plan to effect the enlargement of Grand Teton National Park. In April, 1934, Arno Cammerer met with J. N. Darling, chief of the Biological Survey, and Ferdinand Silcox, the newly appointed chief of the Forest Service. By the conclusion of their talk an atmosphere of compromise was most evident.[3] Perhaps Ferdinand Silcox was most instrumental in this, for the new Forest Service chief was a man of relatively unconventional views who represented a departure from the past just as surely as did the president who had appointed him.[4]

Once the federal agencies had agreed to cooperate, the next step was to call together the other interested parties. On May 2, 1934, a conference was held in Senator Carey's office, attended by Carey, Senator Joseph O'Mahoney (appointed on the death of Senator Kendrick), Governor Leslie Miller, Arno Cammerer and Hillory Tolson from the National Park Service, and Vanderbilt Webb representing the Snake River Land Company. In a rather rare show of give-and-take the parties reached a general accord on all issues.[5] For two weeks following the meeting, Harold Fabian, Kenneth Chorley and Vanderbilt Webb worked on the final bill to be thrown into the legislative hopper.

On May 28, 1934, Senator Robert Carey introduced S. 3705, a bill to extend the boundaries of Grand Teton National Park. As written, it represented a bundle of compromises. The tourist business in Jackson was protected by a provision prohibiting construction of tourist facilities within almost all of the park addition. Ranchers were guaranteed a right of way for cattle in transit to summer pasture, and those few persons having Forest Service or Bureau of Reclamation summer home leases were guaranteed twenty-five year's continuance. Teton County was to be reimbursed for twenty years for the loss of the Rockefeller lands from the tax rolls. Finally, in a major concession by the Rockefeller interests, the bill designated that the new addition of land west of the Snake River would be administered by the National Park Service, but that the lands east of the river and south of Buffalo Fork would be under the jurisdiction of the Biological Survey. Under this rather complicated arrangement the Park Service would retain some control of Biological Survey land, for any plans for construction would have to gain their approval. The last section of the bill directed the secretary of the interior to issue Albert Gabbey a patent on his Jenny Lake land, a tacit admission that the Park Service, the Geological Survey, and the General Land Office had conspired to prevent Gabbey from "proving up" on his stock-raising homestead.[6]

An analysis of the bill indicated that Rockefeller deviated from his ideal project by agreeing to deed over his land to Biological Survey jurisdiction. Evidently he felt that the Park

Service veto on the construction of buildings would assure adequate protection against the pressures of commercial interests. Certainly Rockefeller and the National Park Service compromised much to gain support for an enlarged park, for the bill was, in the words of the Jackson Hole *Courier*, "drawn to the last word for the protection of local industry." [7]

With the support of almost all interested parties, it was hoped that S. 3705 would breeze through Congress. However, as the 1918 Yellowstone extension bill met the unexpected opposition of Idaho's Senator John Nugent, S. 3705 was ambushed by the Bureau of the Budget. After passing the Senate handily, the House Committee on Public Lands approved S. 3705 with an amendment, at the request of the Bureau of the Budget, that Teton County be compensated for the loss of taxable lands by means other than with federal funds. This was a serious setback, and Congress adjourned without taking action on the bill. [8]

Frustrated in defeat, it was evident to the supporters of S. 3705 that in their efforts to win approval of all interested parties they had overlooked the views of a crucial government bureau. For years both sides had recognized the justice of reimbursing Teton County for the loss of the Rockefeller land from property taxes. However, while the Bureau of the Budget was sympathetic, it was also aware that compensating the county for ten years based on full assessment and the following decade at an annually declining rate of 10 percent, as allowed under S. 3705, would open a pandora's box. Many counties throughout the western states would seize the opportunity to demand their share of payments in lieu of taxes on their federal lands. The bureau wanted no such precedent established as was proposed under S. 3705. [9]

In explaining his position to Vanderbilt Webb, Lewis W. Douglas, Director of the Bureau of the Budget, closed his letter with the suggestion that some other method be found to compensate Teton County. [10] The inference was that John D. Rockefeller, Jr.'s philanthropy ought to be extended to the payment of a total of $150,000 in taxes to the county. However, to the Rockefeller interests this seemed an unfair imposition and the hint was simply ignored. This additional investment might have meant the prompt passage of S. 3705. In time John D.

Rockefeller, Jr., and his son, Laurance, would invest far more than $150,000 in time, salaries, taxes, and effort before they would turn over responsibility for the land in 1949.

Considering the strong support for S. 3705, it was reasonable to assume that Senators Carey and O'Mahoney would introduce an identical bill in the next session of Congress. However, when, on June 3, 1935, Carey introduced S. 2972, the bill was similar but hardly identical. The northern part of the proposed park addition, to include Jackson Lake and all the land and the lakes north of Buffalo Fork, had been eliminated, and the review power over construction of buildings within the elk refuge had been stripped from the Park Service and vested in the Department of Agriculture! Both the Rockefeller interests and the National Park Service quickly withdrew their support.[11] S. 2972 never emerged from committee status.

Even without these rather blatant changes, it is doubtful that S. 2972 could have passed. The fragile coalition formed in May, 1934, was rapidly disintegrating. Most evident was the change of attitude in the Department of Agriculture. While Ferdinand Silcox had reluctantly agreed to Forest Service support of S. 3705, we find his boss, Secretary of Agriculture Henry A. Wallace, opposing the passage of S. 2972 on the basis that the land east of the Snake River was not of national park caliber.[12] By mid-1936 it was evident that the second opportunity to establish an outstanding national park had been lost.

Not only had the delicate coalition formed in 1934 fallen apart, but there was a serious division among conservationists with regard to Jackson Hole. This dispute centered on national park standards. For many years the question of inferior parks had plagued the National Park Service. Struggling communities understood the economic benefits of a nearby national park. Continually they pressured their congressmen to sponsor for national park status any patch of soil that might serve as a camping place or recreational area.[13] These proposals for commonplace parks had to be squelched, but in a diplomatic manner that would not offend the particular congressman or his constituents. Assisting the National Park Service in this ticklish task was the National Parks Association. This private organization, formed in 1918 by Charles D. Walcott and Robert Sterling Yard, was dedicated to defending "the National Parks and Monuments fearlessly against assaults of private interests and aggressive commercialism." [14] Quickly it became evident that not only would the National Parks Association defend existing parks, but they would vigorously oppose proposed parks which were not within national park "standards."

Usually the National Park Service and their supporting association agreed on that nebulous term "national park standards," but the association did not fear to disagree with the Park Service. In the case of the proposed expansion of Grand Teton National Park the federal service and the private association were at loggerheads. Specifically, the National Parks Association was opposed to the inclusion of Jackson Lake and the large areas of sagebrush lands east of the Snake River.

The case against Jackson Lake was easily understood. Since it had been dammed by the Bureau of Reclamation it had become an artificial body of water. The association considered reservoirs of water as incompatible with national parks. This idea surely came when ardent conservationists lost a heated battle to save the Hetch Hetchy Valley within Yosemite National Park. By 1913 the decision had been made to replace a valley with a reservoir. Although they lost, preservationists had waged a national campaign, arguing that a reservoir was a violation of the sanctity of a national park. It now seemed incongruous to voluntarily allow inclusion of Jackson Reservoir into the National Park System. It would establish a dangerous, perhaps disastrous, precedent.[15] Yellowstone National Park was under constant attack by Idaho and Montana irrigationists, demanding that dams be built to provide water storage for downstream users. Particularly threatened was the beautiful Bechler Valley and the immense Yellowstone Lake. If Jackson Reservoir could be "lived with" by the National Park Service, surely they could be flexible to the needs of farmers dependent upon Yellowstone waters. The National Parks Association was convinced that defense of the national parks would be strengthened by the exclusion of Jackson Reservoir from the system.

The logic of this argument was enhanced by the appearance of Jackson Reservoir. When the dam was constructed the Bureau of Reclamation made no effort to prepare the shoreline. As the waters rose, some 7,234 acres of lodgepole pine forest were inundated and died. By the 1920s the waters were ringed by an inextricable mass of tangled and snarled tree trunks and branches. At the northern end some six square miles of debris marred the former beauty of the lake. It was, perhaps, accurately described as "a grim graveyard of derelict trees." [16] The lake served as a visible reminder of man's capacity to destroy the beauty of nature. The National Parks Association was determined that the park system needed no such reminders within its borders.

And yet by the mid-1930s the shoreline tragedy of Jackson Lake had been removed. The work began in 1929 when the National Park Service and the Bureau of Reclamation received a $100,000 appropriation earmarked for the task. In the spring of 1933 the work was turned over to the Civilian Conservation Corps (CCC), a New Deal agency established to create jobs, and, incidentally, to provide labor for conservation projects. Over 100 young men spent the summer of 1934 cutting and piling some 17,000 cords of wood to be burned during the winter months. [17] By 1936 it was possible to walk to the water anywhere on the perimeter of the reservoir, although fluctuations in the water level still made it evident that this reservoir was subservient to the agricultural needs of Idaho.

Other interested organizations joined in opposition not only to Jackson Reservoir, but to the inclusion of the land east of the Snake River. Henry B. Ward, representing the American Association for the Advancement of Science, recorded his reservations in a letter to Director Arno Cammerer. Ward questioned the advisability of taking in Jackson Reservoir and "a lot of sagebrush east of the river." [18] Certainly few could question this opinion, for sagebrush is hardly unique in Wyoming or the West. However, the National Park Service position was that the Teton mountains and Jackson Hole were one, inseparable. The character of the region could only be preserved by protection of the total area. This fact had been recognized from the very beginning by all who feared the dangers of encroaching commercialism.

Henry Ward's letter provided an opportunity for Arno Cammerer to reply to the "purists" within conservation circles. This he did in a long, carefully written letter sent to forty-one prominent conservationists throughout the nation. Director Cammerer reasoned that the time had passed when the Park Service could save areas of absolute naturalness, untouched by man. It was no longer possible to establish parks such as Yellowstone, for by the 1930s every scenic area had been commercially exploited or tied up with economic claims of some kind. "Because civilization has moved into the choicest areas faster than they could be established as national parks," wrote Cammerer, "some parks must now be carved out of developed areas." To allow an existing commercial use to thwart the establishment of parks would mean the loss of all remaining areas of national park quality. In a mild critique of the "purist" faction, Cammerer asserted that "an ideal is something toward which to work; it should not be something which prohibits us from working." [19]

To those opposed to the inclusion of Jackson Reservoir, Cammerer reaffirmed the opposition of the National Park Service to the creation of reservoirs within the parks. But the director maintained that "the construction of a new reservoir which means violation of another great scenic area, is a very different thing from the attempt to save a previously violated area from further exploitation!" Reversing the logic of the purists, Cammerer maintained that rejection of Jackson Reservoir on the basis of commercial exploitation would set a dangerous precedent, for in contemporary times it would mean the end of the establishment of large park units.[20]

Continuing his offensive, Director Cammerer wrote to William Wharton of the National Parks Association, reminding him that in the past "it was necessary to accept Mesa Verde, Mount McKinley and Grand Canyon National Parks with mining privileges; to accept Glacier and Lassen with summer homes; to accept Glacier and Mount Rainier with electric railway privileges, and in some instances with rights for tramways. Many of the parks were accepted with grazing and logging rights..." Most of these parks had been freed of these threats, but nevertheless the Park Service had received these lands with less than perfect aesthetic conditions. History, the director asserted, showed "that I am not wavering in my stand on principles..." [21]

Perhaps Cammerer's most sensible argument was that Jackson Reservoir and the sagebrush flats must be included to provide a "natural or biotic unit... which can be preserved intact." This unit should have been created in 1872, but it was not. Now the opportunity was manifest to *restore* and preserve this biotic unit "under one agency of Government with one definite and constant objective." This objective would be to reestablish "the teeming wilderness which the early fur traders discovered over a hundred years ago." "Should we forego this opportunity for constructive conservation," asked Cammerer, "simply because the natural character of Jackson Lake has been modified?" [22]

The answer was yes. At least the response of Ward and Wharton was to the effect that they appreciated Cammerer's reasoned arguments, but they could not agree with him. In fact, Wharton no doubt infuriated Park Service officials when he suggested that protection of Jackson Lake "can be attained under the jurisdiction of the Forest Service as effectively as under that of the Park Service." [23]

At the heart of the rift were not only standards but a basic disagreement of the concept of the national park system. The National Parks Association and the fledgling Wilderness Society (1935) envisioned the Park Service as the caretaker of "primeval parks"; that is, parks with a minimum of roads and commercialism and a maximum of naturalness and wilderness. The National Park Service, on the other hand, was busy expanding its power and domain with little thought to an exclusive function. Under Horace Albright the Park Service had greatly increased its province by assuming the management of many eastern historic battlefield sites, previously under control of the War Department. Furthermore, under the Roosevelt Reorganization Order of 1933, the National Park Service had not been reluctant to take over many national monuments, preserved more for their historic and scientific interest than their aesthetic appeal.[24] It was an unfortunate schism between two supportive organizations, for both sides were sincere and informed. In Jackson Hole it was particularly ruinous, for those who opposed park extension for less idealistic reasons were able to exploit this preservationist disagreement to their advantage.

With so many factions and schisms, the situation looked dismal indeed. Three years of hearings, debates, compromises and legislative attempts had netted nothing. To those most directly concerned the chasm they could not bridge was the tax reimbursement problem. Teton County would not give up the demand, and neither Rockefeller, the National Park Service, nor the Bureau of the Budget seemed able to resolve the dilemma. In private Kenneth Chorley and Governor Leslie Miller discussed the possibility of the elimination of Teton County through amalgamation with adjacent Lincoln County. However, this was a desperation move, and the governor warned Chorley that "no word about the possible elimination of Teton County be given to anyone whomsoever," for the consequences could be "utterly disastrous." [25] Fortunately, Miller's stern warning was heeded.

One person not easily discouraged was Interior Secretary Harold Ickes. The crusty "New Dealer" thrived on controversy and possessed the determination and forthrightness that made loyal friends and treacherous enemies. While Cammerer and the Park Service staff had turned their attention to creation of Olympic National Park (1938) and Kings Canyon National Park (1940), Ickes still had his mind on Jackson Hole. In July, 1937, he sent Cammerer a brief memo which once more centered Park Service efforts in northwest Wyoming:

This proposed extension of Grand Teton National Park has been a troublesome matter but I wonder if we haven't allowed ourselves to become unduly discouraged. I want this whole matter vigorously and persistently urged until we get affirmative action.[26]

So back to the battlefield of Jackson Hole came the troops of the National Park Service, armed with a sixteen-page pamphlet, entitled "A Report by the National Park Service on the Proposal to Extend the Boundaries of Grand Teton National Park, Wyoming." [27] The slim tract argued the benefits of tourism, pointing out that visitors to Yellowstone and Teton National Parks spent some $4,500,000 yearly, and that business was on the rise. Analysis of other economic activities such as grazing, hunting and logging accentuated the predominance of the tourist trade in Jackson Hole. In a bold move, the pamphlet contained specific legislation to accomplish the enlargement of Grand Teton National Park.

If the Park Service expected that residents would rush to embrace their new proposal, they were sadly mistaken. Public opposition formed immediately.[28] Even though the new editor of the Jackson Hole *Courier*, Charles Kratzer, promised a "full discussion of the issue," there was no effort at objectivity. Throughout December, 1937, and January and February, 1938, it was quite evident that the *Courier* had picked up where *The Grand Teton* had left off. Hardly an issue of the weekly was published without an editorial on the evils of park extension and a lengthy satirical letter in opposition by the "Sage of Antelope Flats."[29] Hostility to the new proposal reached its zenith in January, 1938, when local leaders Felix Buchenroth, Peter Hansen, A. C. McCain, and Dr. Floyd C. Naegali organized an open meeting with Governor Leslie Miller. When a vote was taken following a one-sided discussion, 162 of 165 present voted against the Park Service proposal. The following month the group reconvened to endorse a set of resolutions condemning efforts at park extension.

Such determined opposition to an idea which had wide acceptance just a few years earlier demands analysis. Governor Miller, after receiving harsh treatment in the January, 1938, open meeting, reasoned that once again the Forest Service was the culprit. He was firmly convinced that resistance to park extension was "largely engendered by former and present representatives of the Forest Service" with a deep antagonism to the National Park Service.[30] The governor's impression was buttressed by certain facts. Robert Miller had passed from the scene, entrusting his leadership to Felix Buchenroth. Buchenroth had served as a Forest Service ranger, and was, as Harold Fabian put it, "a man Friday for Bobby Miller."[31] This close relationship extended to banking, and by 1938 Buchenroth was president of the Jackson State Bank, a position of considerable power and prestige in the community. A self-made man still possessing a German accent, Buchenroth was an unrelenting foe of the Snake River Land Company and the National Park Service. The logic of his opposition is not entirely clear, for his bank was thriving during a time of depression, partly as a result of tourism and the financial transactions of the Snake River Land Company. However, his loyalty to Miller and his Forest Service past, as well as his cattlemen customers, ran deep.

Supportive to Buchenroth was A. C. McCain, the retired supervisor of Teton National Forest. McCain had lived for some twenty-six years in Teton County and was widely known and respected. Forest Service hegemony in Teton County was a cause he had long espoused. Since the early 1920s he had played the game; by 1938 he was a master. Furthermore, because he was no longer restrained by the exigencies of his official position, he could forcefully speak his mind. Buchenroth found him a loyal and dependable ally.

In Washington, after a temporary truce, perhaps imposed

by Senator Nye, the Forest Service once again moved from a position of concurrence to one of opposition. Larger issues served to fracture any cordiality and unity of purpose between the two services. Harold Ickes's ambition was the primary cause. The secretary of the interior was convinced that the Forest Service belonged under his department rather than under Henry Wallace and the Department of Agriculture. Whenever possible Ickes publicly and privately proselytized for the change, much to the chagrin of Wallace, the Forest Service, and the Department of Agriculture.[32] An atmosphere in which one government department is attempting to swallow the agency of another breeds conspiracy, not cooperation. It is not surprising that Washington columnist Theodore Huntley, writing in 1939, was of the belief that each time the Teton project reared its head the Forest Service set "in motion a fresh flood of propaganda" to defeat it.[33]

With such united opposition it was a wonder that the Wyoming congressional delegation did not simply denounce the Park Service bill and be done with it. There was plenty of provocation to do so, particularly since the livestock interests, an historically powerful lobby in the state, vehemently condemned Park Service expansion. Yet, if the cattleman had political leverage, so did the Department of the Interior. Wyoming politicians, in spite of considerable rhetoric to the contrary, could not treat Interior in a cavalier fashion. Wyoming wanted revisions in the Taylor Grazing Act of 1934, completion of the Hart Mountain division of the Shoshone reclamation project, and an increased appropriation for the Casper-Alcova reclamation project. The town of Cody demanded the completion of the Yellowstone National Park approach road, and many individuals and companies throughout the state wished to obtain oil drilling permits and leases on federal lands. Most of these needs and desires involved large expenditures of federal funds, and all of the requests had to be channelled through the Department of the Interior. Wyoming was in many ways "a child of federal subsidy."[34] State politicians could and did condemn Interior, but they could not afford to ignore the department, and particularly its boss, Harold Ickes.

With pressure from both sides, the Wyoming congressional delegation looked to political expediency. The solution was to avoid the issue by asking for another special Senate committee to investigate. This did not please either side. The National Park Service and the Rockefeller interests wanted their bill introduced. They did not relish another hearing. Park opponents, now locally organized as the "Jackson Hole Committee," feared that the Park Service would somehow come out the victor as it had in the 1933 hearings. Perhaps journalist Theodore Huntley was correct in satirically implying that the only beneficiaries were the senators:

Whenever it begins to get warm in Washington, members of the Senate Committee on Public Lands and Surveys begin to wonder if it wouldn't be well to inspect the Grand Canyon, the Teton and Yellowstone National Parks, and perhaps go on out to Yosemite to see how things are going there. And frequently they do.[35]

Thus in August, 1938, the town of Jackson again hosted a Senate Subcommittee of the Committee on Public Lands and Surveys. In contrast to the 1933 hearings, it was the anti-park faction that had organized themselves to present their viewpoint by the most effective means. The "Jackson Hole Committee" made arrangements to wine and dine the senators so effectively that when Arno Cammerer proffered the aid of Park Service personnel and facilities, Senator O'Mahoney politely declined, informing the director that other arrangements had been made.[36] This time the visiting politicians would hear another point of view during those important unofficial conversations and tours.

The most important coup by the "Jackson Hole Committee" came in the committee hearings. Milward Simpson was allowed to conduct the hearings as a representative of the Jackson Hole Committee. Simpson was a capable local Wyoming attorney, who, as the son of William Simpson, was well versed in the arguments against park extension. He was a talented prosecutor who would go on to a political career as governor of Wyoming (1955–1959) as well as United States Senator (1963–1969). Simpson immediately took charge, presenting an overwhelming number of petitions, resolutions, and personal statements against the Park Service and the idea of park extension. Relentlessly he used his witnesses, his arguments, and his facts to sledgehammer the opposition. The best that the pro-park group could muster was the defensive reaction of Richard Winger that Simpson had "done a very good job of assembling more kinds of misinformation and . . . done the best job of spreading propaganda by innuendo that I have ever heard of . . ."[37] Of course Simpson's objectivity was never an issue, and by the conclusion of the hearings it was evident that the "Jackson Hole Committee" had won the day. "The local committee has certainly been the winners in the tiff," declared the Jackson Hole *Courier*.[38] Few could question the newspaper's analysis.

The Wyoming congressional delegation quickly dropped the National Park Service bill from further consideration and it was never introduced. Without their support there was little hope for legislative action, for as Senator Henry Ashurst of Arizona had stated in the 1933 hearings, "the other States are not going to put over on Wyoming something that her two Senators do not want."[39] What was most evident was that by 1939 the Jackson Hole project had met an impassable logjam. For some nine years Rockefeller had offered approximately 32,000 acres of land (he had purchased an additional 7,000 acres during the 1930s), and Congress had refused the gift. Now opposition on the local level was in the ascendency. About the only solace that park proponents could find was to believe in Dick Winger's almost cyclical theory of Jackson Hole attitudes, and that eventually the pendulum would swing to their position:

Jackson Hole is unique. Most of us here aren't happy unless we're miserable. We have our bitter feuds here, but we don't have any clan killings—we try to worry each other to death. Our idea of winning a battle is to put out as much propaganda as possible on one side and get the people with us, and then, when they lose interest, the other side puts out their propaganda and gets the people with them.[40]

But in 1939 all the trump cards were held by the anti-park side, and as Olaus Murie recalled: "There was no such thing as getting together and talking it over."[41] Albright's vision was dim indeed, and as Jackson Hole residents settled down into established routines, they felt they had once again defeated the National Park Service, perhaps for the last time.

In the meantime John D. Rockefeller, Jr., continued to hold his land through the Snake River Land Company. Retention of the property meant some expense, for his purpose was to return the land to a natural state. Thus, the buildings were removed and pasture land was used only by the wild animals of the region. This policy resulted in yearly losses to him of anywhere between $20,000 and $40,000, depending on certain variables. One inconstant figure was legal fees. For instance, Harold Fabian's fees in 1934, a year of considerable activity, were $9,200, whereas in 1936 they had diminished to $3,500.[42] During this decade there was a strong temptation to recover these losses by entering the tourist business, for inevitably when Rockefeller purchased land he also acquired working dude ranches. Why not operate the dude ranches until the government would accept the land? When Thomas Debevoise, one of Rockefeller's closest legal aides, inquired about the possibility, Vanderbilt Webb had to remind him of the limitations of the project. "Mr. Rockefeller did not wish," wrote Webb, "to undertake the operation of a hotel and tourist business through the Snake River Land Company." [43] This policy was upheld, although it was impossible to ignore responsibility for tourist facilities. Therefore, the Snake River Land Company would purchase a ranch, then lease it back to the seller with the understanding that the tourist operation would continue. This arrangement resolved the problem satisfactorily, although there were numerous charges of monopoly of tourist facilities and collusion with the National Park Service.

The evidence indicates these charges were baseless, but in one instance John D. Rockefeller, Jr., allowed family interests to influence his decision. The JY Ranch was perhaps the most scenic of all the dude ranches in Jackson Hole. Tucked at the base of the southern half of the Teton Range and hugging the shores of Phelps Lake, the ranch was without equal in the beauty of its surroundings. The site was homesteaded by Louis H. Joy in 1907, and for a time Struthers Burt joined him in partnership. However, Burt soon established the Bar BC Ranch, and Joy, in 1920, sold his place to Henry Stewart, a Pittsburgh, Pennsylvania, businessman. Under Stewart's ownership the JY prospered and the ranch was filled with well-heeled city folks almost all summer long.[44] The recreational value of Jackson Hole was obvious to Stewart and he was an active supporter of the national recreational area idea first presented at Maud Noble's cabin in 1923. In the following years he worked toward the establishment of the park and when this was finally achieved in 1929, the JY was included within the boundary.

But supporting an idea was one thing and selling his ranch was another. When the Snake River Land Company attempted to purchase the JY Ranch, Stewart demanded $250,000, a figure far in excess of the fair market valuation. However, according to Kenneth Chorley, by 1932 Stewart had managed his private life and loves so poorly that he was paying alimony to four wives! He needed money badly, and a purchase price of $90,000 was finally agreed upon.[45]

The JY Ranch became a great favorite of John D. Rockefeller, Jr., and his sons. Laurance Rockefeller spent his honeymoon at the ranch in 1934 as did David in 1941. The headquarters of the Snake River Land Company were moved from the Elbo Ranch to the JY. Within a very few years the Rockefeller family as well as their friends, associates and employees, formed a strong attachment to the scenic ranch on the shores of Phelps Lake.

Hence it came as no surprise when Rockefeller requested that the JY Ranch remain in the family possession. Since the JY had been in the original purchase schedule of the Snake River Land Company and was slated to be turned over to the National Park Service, Rockefeller, in August 1937, felt it necessary to write in confidence to Director Cammerer, explaining his decision:

The present Park line includes this ranch [JY] in its entirety, as I understand it. My children are greatly interested in this ranch and are anxious that I should retain it, for the present at least, for the general use of the family. This I shall presumably do. However, so long as the Park line remains as it is, it would be possible for me to give the whole or any part of this land to the Park at any time in the future without any government action. On the other hand, if our family should permanently retain it, no harm would be done.[46]

At the same time Kenneth Chorley gave the matter considerable thought, and then wrote a personal letter to Cammerer enumerating the advantages and disadvantages. Among the advantages of exclusion were that Rockefeller's guests might engage in hunting if they so desired and that Rockefeller would have absolute control of the land. The disadvantages, Chorley noted, would be that it would require an act of Congress should Rockefeller desire to donate the land to the park, and that the eastern millionaire could easily be "accused of trying to buy up the majority of the privately owned lands in the Jackson Hole country for inclusion in the national park and then reserving one of the best pieces of property for his own personal use . . ." [47]

Perhaps the most potent reason against being within the park was the possibility of condemnation. Chorley and the National Park Service officials were aware that a few prime pieces of property, such as that owned by Albert Gabbey, might have to be condemned, allowing the Park Service to acquire them by the power of eminent domain. If the Park Service was forced to move against Gabbey, questioned Chorley, would this not place Rockefeller "in a vulnerable position?" If the Park Service acquired land through the courts, would not the public be offended if no action was taken against the JY Ranch? [48]

To Chorley's carefully composed letter, Director Cammerer replied that he believed that the JY Ranch should remain within the proposed park. Park Service restrictions, such as a ban on hunting, would not apply, and should Rockefeller decide to deed over the ranch, this could be accomplished easily if the land was within park boundaries. On the sticky question of condemnation, Cammerer explained that such proceedings could only be carried out with an appropriation from Congress, a possibility he considered highly unlikely. [49]

As a result of this exchange the JY Ranch remained within the park. Although it was somewhat a violation of park principles, it was a wise decision. John D. and Laurance Rockefeller have been "ideal inholders," who have set a commendable example. Perhaps more important, the continued ownership of the ranch by the family has assured the Park Service that the Rockefellers' concern for Grand Teton National Park would not wane. Horace Albright continually favored retention of the ranch by the family. Certainly he was pleased that they enjoyed the JY Ranch, but beyond that he knew that visitations to the ranch would assure that John D. Rockefeller, Jr., would continue his interest in Jackson Hole. [50] Considering the nature and length of the controversy, Albright's reasoning was most sound.

Two years later Rockefeller purchased more land adjacent to the JY Ranch "to round out the . . . frontage on the lake." In an age when wealthy families were still aware of the Lindbergh kidnapping tragedy, it was felt necessary to have a

land buffer between them and the public. While he still acknowledged that the ranch might pass into government possession, for the present he would retain ownership, particularly
since it was "Laurance's desire not to have these lands pass into
other hands . . ."⁵¹

Of Rockefeller's five sons it was Laurance who would
share his father's interest in nature and conservation. And it
was Laurance Rockefeller who became the benefactor to Grand
Teton National Park. For Laurance the ranch became a favorite
retreat: a place where he could relax with his family and
friends, fish, and engage in such prosaic but healthy activities
as cutting and splitting wood for the ranch fireplace needs.⁵² So
associated with the JY Ranch did Laurance become that, without discussion, John D. Rockefeller, Jr., stipulated in his will
that the ranch would go to him. To this day the JY Ranch continues to be a summer retreat for this eastern-based family, and
it continues to insure that in the philanthropic concerns of the
family Jackson Hole and Grand Teton National Park will not
be forgotten.

Of course the continued ownership of one of the park's
prime areas of beauty has occasionally antagonized local residents. Furthermore, the irony of the most important philanthropic family in national park history contributing to one of
the national parks' greatest problems—private lands within the
parks—is bothersome. However, on balance the presence of the
family in Jackson Hole has been most beneficial to the park
and substantially aided the economy of Jackson Hole. Finally,
it should be added that Laurance Rockefeller has recently disposed of some 784 acres of the ranch, and it is the understanding of both National Park Service officials and Rockefeller executives that the JY Ranch will eventually revert to the National
Park Service.⁵³

Certainly the decision regarding the JY Ranch was not
uppermost in the thoughts of Rockefeller employees or National Park Service officials in the late 1930s. What was of
greater concern was that during the 1938 hearings the anti-park
faction had gained the upper hand and park expansion plans
had come to a virtual standstill. As the decade ended, the park
issue seemed settled, and Jackson Hole residents' thoughts
turned toward world events. The Wyoming congressional delegation acquiesced in this feeling of finality, for they feared the

political consequences of stirring up the old issue. And without the support of Senators Joseph O'Mahoney and Harry Schwartz and Representative Paul Greever, it was nearly impossible to create an enlarged Grand Teton National Park by act of Congress. Thus, in this atmosphere the National Park Service began to consider a politically undesirable, yet effective last resort: the creation of Jackson Hole National Monument.

V·I·I

THE HECTIC LIFE OF A
NATIONAL MONUMENT

"... a foul, sneaking Pearl Harbor blow."
Senator Edward V. Robertson, 1943

T HE difference between a national monument and a
national park has never been clearly defined. Some observers
have seen national monuments as "poor cousins to the national
parks," being essentially second-rate parks with second-rate
scenery and third-rate appropriations.[1] Horace Albright made
no such distinction between parks and monuments, declaring
that the two were "practically identical," except that monuments were usually smaller.[2] But there are many exceptions,
and perhaps the most appealing definition came many years
ago when author Frank Waugh, after pondering the problem,
argued that "the most clearly outstanding character of the National Monument is its complete inconsistency."[3]

When Congressman John Lacey of Ohio guided the Antiquities Act of 1906 to passage, he had a clear idea of what was
needed. Lacey wished to give protection to archeological, scientific and historical sites located on federal lands. Particularly in
the American Southwest, exploitation and outright vandalism
was rampant, with priceless relics being carried off without
consideration of their significance. The Antiquities Act of 1906
authorized the president of the United States to set aside by
proclamation areas of particular scientific or historic interest as
national monuments, therefore offering them a modicum of
protection.[4] From the establishment of Devil's Tower National

Monument (1906) in northeast Wyoming, the first national monument, to the present, confusion has reigned with regard to the meaning and function of national monuments. Certainly the choice of the word "monument" has perplexed national park officials and the public, for, in the words of one authority, "because of its funeral image, the name has been the source of much confusion and considerable hilarity . . ." [5]

For our purpose the major difference between parks and monuments is political. National parks must be created by an act of Congress, whereas national monuments may simply be proclaimed by presidential decree. This political reality has meant that some of our most scenic and vast parks, such as Grand Canyon, Bryce, and Zion, were monuments at their inception.[6] Thus the idea of bypassing Congress was not unique in national park history, but never would it be more controversial.

On November 27, 1942, John D. Rockefeller, Jr., informed Secretary of the Interior Harold Ickes that unless the government accepted his land gift, he would consider disposing of it by other means.[7] Historians who have investigated the controversy have assumed that the monument idea was conceived with the arrival of this ultimatum.[8] This was not the case, however, and the letter merely activated an already well-developed plan. The idea of asking the president to establish Jackson Hole National Monument by proclamation had its origins in informal discussions during the Albright administration (1929–1933), but the idea was never formalized in writing.[9] The only mention of it found in those early days was a letter from Richard Winger to Harold Fabian. After commenting on his frustration over the scandalous editorials of *The Grand Teton*, Winger mused reflectively that " it would be nice if President Hoover would decide to make the territory embraced in the Jackson Hole Plan into a National Monument." [10]

Winger's thought was premature, but by 1938 the idea was formally considered by National Park Service and Snake River Land Company officials. With the political climate against them, Kenneth Chorley and acting director of the National Park Service Arthur Demaray exchanged letters exploring the feasibility of accomplishing park extension through establishment of a national monument.[11] By late January, 1939, Director Cammerer had ordered his staff to prepare a draft of a proclamation. By February 10th the draft was complete and ready for review within the Park Service.[12] In June, 1939, Acting Director Demaray wrote directly to John D. Rockefeller, Jr., informing him that the political climate in both Congress and Wyoming had deteriorated so badly that the Park Service was considering a plan to establish "Grand Teton National Monument." Enclosed with this letter Rockefeller would find a tentative draft of the proclamation as well as the historic and scientific justifications, written with the Antiquities Act of 1906 in mind.[13]

The Park Service proposal was not well received. Kenneth Chorley advised his boss that "the proclamation is not in any condition for your consideration." Even if it had been, Chorley questioned whether Rockefeller ought to take any position on such a controversial matter.[14] Chorley's advice reflected his growing disillusionment with the National Park Service leadership. He placed the blame for the situation in Jackson Hole on poor guidance from Washington, lamenting that he could not "recall seeing any organization decline . . . as much as the Park Service has since Mr. Albright left it."[15] While Chorley's analysis was hardly just, it was true that Director Arno Cammerer was terribly overworked and would resign in August, 1940, as a result of heart trouble, to be replaced by Newton B. Drury.[16]

While denegrating the efficacy of the Park Service, Chorley hoped that he, personally, could pull the project together. On the same day that he advised Rockefeller on the monument material, he left New York for the JY Ranch. He intended to spend some two months in Jackson Hole with the idea of working out a compromise solution. He had hopes, but, as he wrote Arthur Demaray, few illusions: "I am quite prepared to believe I may be entirely unsuccessful, but it seemed to us that it was worthwhile to make this final effort."[17]

A noble effort, but, as Chorley predicted, futile. In Jackson Hole during the summer of 1938 there was little goodwill evident for a man bent on a mission for John D. Rockefeller, Jr. Even if Chorley had been successful, the old taxation problem remained. The National Park Service had made continued efforts to have the Bureau of the Budget modify its earlier decision. However, on August 1, 1940, Arthur Demaray regretfully informed Secretary Ickes that the bureau refused to reconsider, concluding that "the establishment of the area as a national monument at the appropriate time appears to be the only course available."[18]

Thus by late 1940 the monument idea had taken firm hold as the only solution. Horace Albright, Rockefeller, Webb, Chorley and Fabian were all anticipating a proclamation and were deciding how the Snake River Land Company ought to respond to it.[19] By late 1941 Chorley had reversed his position, and urged Harold Ickes that proclamation of the monument was "the only way." Ickes responded that Chorley's views "coincide with my own," and that the idea was under serious consideration.[20]

Discussion of the monument idea was not confined to New York and Washington, D. C. Rangers in the field discussed the possibility in an open fashion. In late 1939, Grand Teton National Park Superintendent Thomas Whitcraft wrote the Washington office that he was forwarding some ideas of Park Naturalist Bennett T. Gale to justify the national monument.[21] A year and a half later Superintendent Charles Smith mentioned the possibility of a monument proclamation in a report as if it were common knowledge.[22]

Although the monument idea was widely understood among Park Service personnel, the possibility was not discussed publicly by the opponents. The evidence extant indicates few, if any, of the anti-park leaders were aware of this contingency. Perhaps they reasoned that the National Park Service would not dare to advocate such a move after their spanking defeat in 1938. Whatever the case, they seemed to be smugly satisfied and supremely confident that the issue was closed. Like the rest of the nation, their efforts and thoughts were centered on the war being fought on a worldwide front. When Andrew Kendrew, an architect and planner closely associated with Rockefeller's Williamsburg project, spent the summer of 1942 in Jackson Hole, he came away with the feeling "that the battle of Park extension, that I had heard and read so much about, had died down."[23]

The catalyst setting in motion the monument plan was John D. Rockefeller, Jr.'s, letter of November 27, 1942. It indicated to Ickes that Rockefeller had "definitely reached the conclusion, although most reluctantly," to "make permanent disposition of the property before another year has passed." If the government was not interested in the acquisition, then "it will be my thought to make some other disposition of it or, failing in that, to sell it in the market to any satisfactory buyers."[24] Although the letter left loopholes, the implied threat was that John D. Rockefeller, Jr.'s, patience was exhausted and that if the government did not act decisively he would sell the land to private interests.

The origin of this letter is of particular interest. Who drafted it? Did the National Park Service or Harold Ickes recommend this ultimatum to force governmental action? Unfortunately, a perusal of the written record gives us no clues. Neither the National Park Service files nor the Rockefeller family files contain any memoranda or letters on the subject predating the mailing of the letter to Ickes.[25] Uncharacteristically, there are no opinions by Chorley, Albright, or Webb regarding the wisdom of this move and the possible action by Ickes or President Roosevelt. One is led to three conjectures: (1) the papers were removed from the files, (2) all communication was done by oral agreement, or (3) John D. Rockefeller, Jr., acted independently. In view of previous patterns, the third option seems unlikely and one is certainly disposed to believe that the letter was discussed and drafted with government officials prior to its receipt. The close cooperation between the National Park Service staff and the Rockefeller people for more than fifteen years suggests that the letter arrived by design rather than chance. Yet this cannot be proved conclusively. Many years later, when asked if his father had consulted with Ickes or other government officials before sending the letter, Laurance Rockefeller theorized that it was "quite possible" and "it would make a lot of sense," but he had no clear idea of what actually happened.[26]

Another question that cannot be answered with certainty is that of Rockefeller's intent: would he have sold the land and abandoned the project as he implied? His close associates assure us that Rockefeller did not bluff. When he decided on a course of action and formalized it by correspondence he was not flexible. Horace Albright's recollection was that he, Vanderbilt Webb, Kenneth Chorley, and others had to convince Rockefeller not to sell in 1942. Albright maintained that Rockefeller was tired of paying taxes and that his patience had finally worn thin.[27]

Albright's interpretation is open to question. Rockefeller was frustrated, but patient. From 1927 to 1942 he continually pronounced that time was on his side and he would not sacrifice the ideal project for a quick compromise settlement. His financial resources discourage the idea that the property tax of some $13,000 a year was an intolerable burden. In fact, Rockefeller had indicated that in the event of the establishment of a monument, the continued payment of taxes would be acceptable to him.[28] Finally it should be mentioned that planner Andrew Kendrew spent two months in Jackson Hole in 1942 studying locations on Rockefeller land which might be used for tourist accommodations. His recommendations involved future land use planning—an activity inconsistent with selling.[29]

Because we are dealing with conjecture, it might be well to give weight to the views of Laurance Rockefeller, who perhaps knew his father's proclivities and character as well as anyone. When asked if the Ickes letter indicated that his father's patience had run out, Laurance replied: "No . . . I would just like to feel that this was probably a good way of putting a little pressure on the people in Washington. . . ." Laurance believed his father had no thought of dumping the land on the open market, and the letter "was undoubtedly more of a bit of maneuver and pressure kind of thing than [an] indication of a change of purpose or policy."[30]

Although the evidence is not conclusive, one can say that John D. Rockefeller, Jr., was not prepared to abandon the Jackson Hole project and that his November 27th letter to Ickes was a cooperative effort written to support Ickes and the National Park Service in an action they wanted to take. Certainly the letter signalled a flurry of activity. After assuring Rockefeller that he fully understood his position, Ickes pledged that he would "do everything within [his] power to bring about the acceptance of your gift as an addition to the national park system."[31] Ickes was true to his word, for he moved with the kind of purpose and vigor that made him a great, albeit controversial, secretary of the interior. First, he called on Director Newton Drury to see if he agreed that the time was propitious to move on the monument idea. Ickes must have been disappointed, for the director neither favored nor rejected the idea, preferring to remain on the fence.[32] Almost on the eve of Christmas, Ickes met with Rockefeller. The two agreed that Ickes should press for monument action, and though there would surely be criticism, it would die down and be "followed shortly . . . by general approval." The two leaders immediately established a close friendship, Rockefeller having particular admiration for Ickes's courage, while Ickes respected the New York millionaire's patience and public service.[33]

The next step was for Ickes to see President Roosevelt, and although Ickes was on good terms with the president, to gain an interview was not always easy. In January, 1943, Roosevelt was in North Africa, occupied with the conduct and strategy of the Allied forces. However, by mid-February Ickes had lunched with the president and explained the monument plan to him. After the meeting, the Interior Secretary was confident, writing to Rockefeller that Roosevelt "seemed well disposed" to the idea and that the president would make a decision shortly.[34] When Ickes received no immediate word from the president, he dashed off a note to White House aide Major General Edwin M. Watson to the effect that he was very anxious to move on the Jackson Hole matter and that he would like another conference with Roosevelt.[35] Ickes's request was honored on March 12th, when the Interior Secretary again took lunch with the president. At that meeting Ickes candidly warned Roosevelt that if he signed a monument proclamation he could expect considerable criticism from Congress and that there might be an effort to strip from the president the power to establish national monuments. Having been apprised of the consequences, President Roosevelt "still seemed ready to go ahead."[36]

Ickes's warning was, in part, occasioned by conversations with Senator Joseph O'Mahoney. On the request of the Bureau of the Budget, Ickes met with the Wyoming senator in mid-February. At this meeting Ickes informed O'Mahoney of the forthcoming executive decree, suggesting that it would be handled "in such a way that he would be absolved from blame by any of his constituents." O'Mahoney voiced his concerns, asking for time so that something other than the monument plan could be worked out.[37] A week later Ickes received a letter from the Wyoming senator questioning the constitutionality of using the Antiquities Act of 1906 to accept a donation of land from private interests for the purpose of extending the boundaries of a national park. O'Mahoney concluded his objections by arguing that in his opinion "it would be contrary to sound public policy" for the president to act on an issue which the Congress had rejected.[38] Whatever effect O'Mahoney's objections had, they did little to dissuade Ickes from his purpose.

Thus on March 15, 1943, President Roosevelt put his signature to Executive Order 2578, a proclamation establishing Jackson Hole National Monument. Transferred into National Park Service control were 221,610 acres to the east of and adjacent to Grand Teton National Park. Some 99,345 acres were taken from Teton National Forest. Jackson Lake, combined with the lesser lakes, comprised 31,640 acres of water surface. The new monument also included 39,323 acres of withdrawn public lands, 1,406 acres of state lands, and 49,896 acres of private land, of which 32,117 were owned by Rockefeller's Jackson Hole Preserve.[39] Essentially, a bill which Congress would not consider in 1938 had become law five years later.

For those who had labored long and hard, this was an ecstatic moment. John D. Rockefeller, Jr., was jubilant. He dictated a note to Ickes apologizing because they could not get together to celebrate the news properly, but he wanted him to know that "except for your vision, your courage, your determination, there was every prospect that this uniquely beautiful area . . . would have been permanently lost. I take off my hat to you. Please know what a pleasure it has been to me to have a part in this matter which has lain close to my heart for so many years." [40]

Perhaps Rockefeller's enthusiasm and feeling that the matter was at last settled were premature. The majority of Jackson Hole residents had a different assessment of President Roosevelt's action. A verbal barrage erupted from the Jackson Hole *Courier,* and editor Charles Kratzer issued an extra on March 22nd entirely devoted to vilifying the proclamation. Wyoming Governor Lester Hunt, Senators Joseph O'Mahoney and Edward Robertson, and Representative Frank Barrett all expressed shock and indignation over the action, each proclaiming that he would vigorously oppose this federal action and that he could cut through the Gordian knot of federal fiat. The most common condemnation was provided by the accessible and understandable World War II analogy. Senator Robertson characterized the action as "a foul, sneaking Pearl Harbor blow." The Teton County Commissioners asked how the federal government could "reconcile taking away the homes of

men who are now fighting to preserve their homeland." [41]
Across the state, the Cheyenne *Tribune,* after quoting a portion
of Roosevelt's "Day of Infamy" speech, stated that "the effectiveness of the yellow barbarian's strategy and tactics was not
lost in Washington ... witness Jackson Hole national monument." [42]

The local press erroneously implied that the monument
proclamation had automatically displaced many Jackson Hole
residents. On April 8, 1943, the *Courier* proclaimed in bold
headlines: "150 Homes Are Involved in Nat'l Monument Area,"
but the article failed to mention that many of these residences
were owned by Rockefeller's Jackson Hole Preserve. Furthermore, the story neglected to state that home owners within the
monument would be allowed to continue to live in their homes
and use their land in any way they saw fit. The local press
chose to associate the creation of the monument with immediate condemnation proceedings against all private holdings, the
loss of economic livelihood, and the displacement of numerous
families. Many thought of the monument as a death knell for
Jackson Hole, as witnessed by this piece of doggerel published
in the *Courier*:

> We love you and we want to stay,
> But higher powers we must obey.
> We know we have to go,
> Because they have the dough.
> We buy our bonds, we work, we strive,
> We also put over our Red Cross drive.
> Our best beloveds have we sent,
> And now we are but a monument.
> Good bye, Jackson Hole. We must leave
> you now.[43]

Governor Lester Hunt vigorously condemned the monument in a nationwide radio address and a strongly worded letter
to President Roosevelt.[44] Hunt argued that the monument proclamation was a flagrant violation of states' rights. By casting the
issue in terms of states' rights versus the federal government
Hunt was assured of striking a sympathetic chord among fellow
westerners. No section of the country accepted the "New
Dealers" with more reluctance than the Far West. For many who
talked, thought, and dressed western, the struggle for Jackson
Hole represented the last of the rugged individualists doing bat-

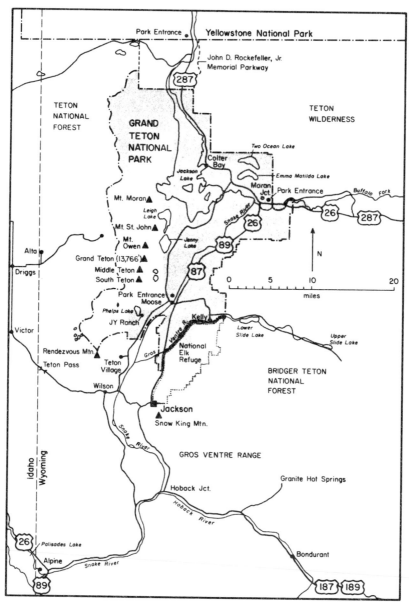

Jackson Hole National Monument, 1943

tle with the planned society of slick Washington bureaucrats. The fact that the American West had often fed at the trough of federal subsidy did not bother Hunt. Like many western politicians, he had mastered the art of insisting on large federal favors while stoutly resisting any inference of dependence on the federal largesse.

Governor Hunt found sympathetic ears when he spoke to the Western Governors' Conference, meeting in early April, 1943, at Salt Lake City. The governors, most of whom were at odds with Washington on land matters, listened attentively as Lester Hunt lambasted Ickes and the Washington bureaucracy. However, even those politicians attuned to anti-Washington rhetoric were forced to take notice when the Wyoming governor declared: "I shall utilize all police authority at my disposal to exit from the proposed Jackson Hole National Monument any federal official who attempts to assume authority." It was one of the most flagrant nullification threats since the Civil War. The *Courier* was so delighted with Hunt's bold declaration that for four months its editor emblazoned the newspaper's masthead with the quote. The western governors responded predictably by passing a resolution condemning the "autocratic act of a meddling bureaucracy," but failed to follow the suggestion of California governor Earl Warren that they act in concert to frame a bill repealing the Antiquities Act of 1906.[45]

In Congress the Wyoming congressional delegation was able to capitalize on the growing friction between Congress and President Roosevelt. By the 1940s many congressmen had grown to resent the usurpation of power by the executive branch. From the time of the "100 Days," through the "court packing" scheme, and on the questions of neutrality in the late 1930s, it seemed that President Roosevelt continued to acquire power at the expense of Congress. His election to an unprecedented third term in 1940 confirmed their worst suspicions. Yet critical congressmen held their collective tongues, for the United States was at war, and clearly the man needed at the helm during this time of national crisis was President Franklin Delano Roosevelt.

Yet when Roosevelt signed Executive Order 2578 establishing Jackson Hole National Monument, it had nothing to do with the war effort. The executive branch could not rightly claim that in this case the use of executive power was necessary for the conduct of the war. Thus, when Senator Joseph

O'Mahoney rose on the Senate floor to attack the monument order, he knew how to gain the attention of his colleagues. And his speaking against Roosevelt was not altogether a novelty, for back in 1937 the unknown senator had boldly denounced the ill-fated "court packing" scheme. Now his audience listened attentively as he rose "to make a record here this afternoon of what I regard to be a rather extraordinary instance of the direct use of Executive power to accomplish an objective which could not be accomplished by legislative action." O'Mahoney reviewed the legislative attempts to expand the park, noting that these attempts had been rejected by both the people of Wyoming and the Congress of the United States. In closing his address, he again appealed to many of his fellow senators, who knew nothing of Jackson Hole, by castigating Ickes and Roosevelt for engaging in "the very bad practice" of circumventing the Congress to obtain concessions which Congress would not grant.[46]

While speeches in Congress and volatile rhetoric in Wyoming might interest a few, the Jackson Hole situation was hardly material for the national press. This changed on the morning of May 2, 1943, when a group of heavily armed ranchers met near the border of the Jackson Hole National Monument. In the vanguard was the flamboyant movie star and erstwhile cowboy Wallace Beery. During the day the group defiantly trailed some 550 yearlings across the monument to their summer range without a permit. The scene might have been a Hollywood set for any one of the many cowboy-genre films of the decade. One could almost expect Indians to sweep down from the surrounding mountains at any moment. However, this was not make-believe, and the enemy was not Amerinds but the rangers of the National Park Service. Wisely the monument superintendent, Charles Smith, ignored this trespass, and direct confrontation was avoided.[47]

For the ranchers, defiance of the newly established monument, although an act of civil disobedience, was primarily a publicity stunt designed to draw attention to their plight. According to some, the ride, which Ickes cynically described as "mock heroics" by a bunch of "ghost-hunting cowboys" wearing their "best mail-order regalia," was the invention of the imagination of Stanley Resor. Resor was the president of J. Walter Thompson Company, an advertising firm with offices in the principal cities of the United States and throughout the world. In the late 1920s the advertising executive became infatuated with the Jackson Hole country, bought a small place north of Wilson, and decided to become a summertime, gentleman rancher. During the 1930s he increased his ranch holdings to well over 5,000 acres. While Resor took no public stance regarding Rockefeller's land purchases, behind the scene he was an ardent opponent and a persuasive force among local ranchers.[48] The reason for his antipathy is not evident, but more than likely he aspired to be the dominant economic force in the valley, and certainly Rockefeller's presence stifled that ambition. If a publicity stunt might help to abolish the monument, then Resor was the man to organize it.

No less important was Wallace Beery, a nationally known film actor whose name was synonymous with the cowboy ethos of individualism and rugged masculinity. Though an aging figure in 1943, who, it was said, had to be assisted by a ladder in mounting his horse, Beery was still a colorful character whose antics were newsworthy. To give Berry legitimacy he was reported to be a Jackson Hole rancher. This was surely stretching the truth, for Beery held a Forest Service permit for a cabin and ½ acre of land bordering Jackson Lake, and his one milk cow had recently died.[49] But this was a quibbling concern, for the actor desired publicity and the ranchers were anxious for any means available to raise their hue and cry to the country.

Like any effective advertising stunt, the ride accomplished its goal. *Time* magazine picked up the story. Although remaining neutral on the issue, the widely circulated weekly featured a photograph of Beery on horseback and a provocative statement by Felix Buchenroth that: "It may be a monument to Ickes, but it's a tombstone to me."[50] Other national media picked up the story and condemned Roosevelt's action. Journalist Westbrook Pegler, whose column appeared in the Scripps-Howard newspapers and the United Features syndicate, had such a field day equating the monument proclamation with the dictatorial methods of the Axis powers that few Americans could read his column dispassionately. The actions of Roosevelt and Ickes followed "the general lines of Adolf Hitler's seizure of Austria. They anschlussed a tract of 221,610 acres for Ickes's domain ...," a man who might be likened "to that of the Nazi governor of Poland." [51] Strong words in those days, and Horace Albright wrote Pegler to tell him so; but the damage was done.[52]

Particularly disturbing to conservationists was the position of the *Saturday Evening Post*. Although long a friend of conservation causes, the popular weekly surprisingly took the position that the hard working ranchers of Jackson Hole had not reckoned with "the ease with which Franklin D. Roosevelt can pluck just the right rabbit out of the Federal statutes." The *Post* would not predict the outcome of the controversy, but was confident that the episode would "serve to warn millions of Americans of the power available to the determined bureaucracy." [53] Again, preservationists protested. Harlean James, executive secretary of the American Planning and Civic Association, chastised Frederic Nelson, associate editor of the *Post*, for taking a simplistic view of the question. The issue, James contended, had more than two sides. "Indeed, it is polygonal, and it is with some difficulty that any of us trots around an entire polygon." [54]

Whatever the complexity, the editorial staff of the *Post* felt certain they had clearly identified the political principle at stake. In response to criticism from Albright and George Lorimer, *Post* editor Ben Hibbs argued that conservationists missed the point of the editorial. Certainly conservation was important, but "the conservation of our democratic processes is even more important. The trouble with so many conservationists," continued Hibbs, "is that they are zealous, and most zealots so completely lose their sense of proportion that they finally come to believe the noble end justifies any means at all." [55]

It soon became evident that whatever the beneficial result of the monument, it was being submerged in a flood of condemnation of the method by which it had been established. The Jackson Hole monument question was becoming a *cause célèbre* for those who knew nothing of the land use issues involved, but simply wished to use the issue to denigrate President Roosevelt, Rockefeller, the Department of the Interior, the National Park Service, or all four. Yet, Editor Hibbs's faultfinding was telling. Park proponents were guilty of a certain righteousness that allowed them to assume a "higher law," or at least to circumvent Congress. On the other hand, it could be maintained that the national interest had been blocked for many years by a "tyranny of a minority" of local interests and livestock lobbyists. If conservation matters had been left strictly in the hands of Congress there would be few forests or grazing lands in the West free from private exploitation.

As opposition to Jackson Hole National Monument coalesced, Wyoming Representative Frank Barrett emerged as its leader. A Republican known for folksiness and attention to the needs of his constituents, Barrett had long sympathized with the livestock interests and opposed conservation goals and federal land control.[56] His avid defense of "sacred cows" later prompted the historian-conservationist Bernard DeVoto to describe Barrett as "gaudy, gorgeous, and inflammatory."[57] Barrett's immediate response to Executive Order 2578 was to introduce H.R. 2241, a bill "To Abolish the Jackson Hole National Monument."[58]

The Barrett bill was a negative approach, but, considering the sentiment of the day, its chances of congressional approval were good. In late May and early June, 1943, the House Committee on the Public Lands held hearings on the bill. Barret had organized well. Residents from Jackson Hole testified and Stanley Resor came down from New York to add his opposition. The hearings turned into a polemical circus with ringmaster Barrett directing the show. Monument apologists such as National Park Director Newton Drury and Horace Albright were treated roughly, and Secretary of the Interior Ickes concluded his appearance with the observation that next time he "would like to have questions, but . . . not . . . protracted argument."[59]

In the Senate, Pat McCarran of Nevada and Joseph O'Mahoney co-sponsored a bill (S. 1046) to repeal the Antiquities Act of 1906.[60] With related bills in both branches of Congress, a joint congressional committee was appointed to investigate and take testimony. Once again the town of Jackson would host its periodic August visit by congressmen junketing in the Rocky Mountain West. In the official party were Senators Robertson and O'Mahoney from Wyoming, Senator Gerald Nye from North Dakota and Senator Chan Guerney from South Dakota. The House was represented by Frank Barrett, James O'Conner from Montana, J. E. Chenoweth of Colorado, Hugh Peterson of Georgia, J. W. Robinson of Utah, and J. Hardin Peterson of Florida, chairman of the House Committee on Public Lands. Assisting this joint committee were high Interior officials such as

Michael Straus, first assistant secretary of the interior, Newton Drury, director of the National Park Service, and R. H. Rutledge, director of the Grazing Service, and a number of lesser officials.[61] Harold Ickes did not accompany this diverse group, but the military terminology of his instructions to Michael Straus indicated his concern: "You are the commanding officer of this brigade.... I hope that our forces are being carefully mobilized and that they will be vigorously led."[62]

Considering how volatile the issue had become, perhaps Ickes's instructions were appropriate. Some years later, Conrad Wirth, then assistant director of the National Park Service charged with organizing the committee's visit, recalled that when he telephoned Congressman Barrett to discuss arrangements, Barrett warned him twice that if Wirth entered Jackson Hole he was "just as apt to get shot as not." No shootings occurred, but at Old Faithful in Yellowstone Barrett became so incensed at Wirth regarding the car assignments of the party, that the two men had to be pulled apart to avoid physical blows.[63] Tempers were strained, especially since the "Jackson Hole Anti-monument Committee," comprised of Felix Buchenroth, Milward Simpson, Cliff Hansen, Charles Kratzer and others, joined the congressmen and officials. After spending the night at Signal Mountain Lodge, the party continued into Jackson Hole, stopping for viewing and discussion at Hedricks Point, the very place where Albright and Rockefeller had envisioned the park some sixteen years earlier. It was another spectacular day, clear and beautiful. Conrad Wirth recalled that as the visitors looked across the Snake River they were enthralled with the majesty of the scene, for "the mountains were up there just ready to fall over on top of you . . ."[64]

The next day, August 17th, the committee sat in Jackson to take testimony. In the morning Director Drury was allowed to present arguments for the monument, but the afternoon was devoted totally to anti-monument testimony, featured by Milward Simpson's eloquent denunciation. At the conclusion of the day a standing vote was taken in which some 650 persons present voted for abolition of the monument while half a dozen or so remained seated. No one had the courage to stand in favor of the monument.[65]

Notwithstanding the domination of the anti-monument forces, many of the visiting congressmen were impressed with the potential of Jackson Hole as an extraordinary national park. They could not give up the idea easily. Also, the anti-monument committee realized that even if Barrett's bill cleared Congress it would surely face a presidential veto. It seemed a compromise might be in the offing. On September 4, 1943, Governor Lester Hunt convened a meeting in Cheyenne attended by National Park Service and Department of the Interior representatives, the Wyoming congressional delegation, and members of the Jackson Hole Anti-monument Committee. The meeting was cordial, and, although nothing definite was agreed to, there was a feeling of optimism. Grazing Director R. H. Rutledge expressed the feeling of those in attendance when he wrote Ickes that "we made a break in the opposition ranks and . . . the matter was almost at a point of settlement." [66] However, the following week Clifford Hansen sent letters to Barrett and Governor Hunt informing them that the people of Jackson Hole would not compromise.[67] They wanted total victory, or, in the parlance of the day, "unconditional surrender" by the National Park Service. By the middle of September it was understood that the Wyoming congressional delegation would push hard for passage of H. R. 2241, the bill to abolish the monument.

The following year the House Committee on Public Lands voted out the Barrett bill (12 to 7) and the House passed H. R. 2241 (178 yea, 107 nay, 142 not voting). In the Senate there was no objection and no roll call; thus the bill passed by unanimous consent.[68] As anticipated, President Roosevelt vetoed the bill, although conceding in his veto message that he would support legislation to guarantee grazing privileges for ranchers and provide for tax concessions to Teton County. By the end of 1944 the monument had withstood its first sustained attack, yet, as the *Washington Post* remarked, the issue was not settled: "President Roosevelt's pocket veto of the bill to abolish the Jackson Hole Monument at least has the virtue of giving Congress a new start toward solution of the problem at which the bill was aimed." [69]

Meanwhile the state of Wyoming determined to seek redress through the courts. The question Wyoming wished to test was whether the president had the statutory authority to proclaim the monument under the Antiquities Act of 1906. State Deputy Attorney General John J. McIntyre was convinced he did not. "We don't think the pretended monument is legally constituted," McIntyre explained to Jackson Hole residents, "... we believe that the entire proceeding is illegal." [70] Many agreed with him, for, although the definition of a national monument was unclear, the language of the Antiquities Act was quite specific in stipulating that monuments must have significant historic or scientific interest.

In *State of Wyoming v. Franke* the state sought to prove that the area within Jackson Hole National Monument contained no objects of particular scientific or historic interest. Evidence was heard from August 21–24, 1944, before the Twelfth District Court in Sheridan, Wyoming. Both the state of Wyoming and the United States Attorney General's Office paraded expert witnesses who testified to the scientific and historic uniqueness or mediocrity of the monument area. McIntyre relied primarily on state agency officials and professors from the University of Wyoming to argue his side. The case presented by Chief Counsel Jackson Price of the Attorney General's Office was well planned and executed. Price established the historic connection between Jackson Hole and the fur trade through the testimony of western historians Leroy R. Hafen and Merrill J. Mattes. In was Mattes, in particular, who did extensive research to verify that Jackson Hole was indeed a crossroad of the fur trade in the Rocky Mountain West. His exhaustive testimony would shortly take the form of a pamphlet and scholarly articles.[71] The scientific importance of Jackson Hole was established primarily by biologist Olaus Murie and geologist Fritiof M. Fryxell. Fryxell, who had written his doctoral dissertation on Jackson Hole, was particularly important in establishing that the area was of geological significance.[72]

However, when Judge T. Blake Kennedy ruled in February, 1945, it was not on the merits of the arguments presented. After noting the evidence, Kennedy dismissed the case, declaring that it was "a controversy between the legislative and executive branches of the Government in which ... the Court cannot interfere." It was the burden of Congress to pass "remedial legislation" as "the disposition of government lands inherently rests in its Legislative branch." [73] Thus the court found "generally for the defendant" and it was clear that redress for the state of Wyoming lay only in congressional action.[74] Wyoming was willing to pursue this legislative course, for immediately following the judge's adverse ruling, the state legislature appropriated up to $50,000 to continue the struggle to abolish the monument.[75]

While Congress and the courts debated, the National Park Service took control of its newest possession. In early April, 1943, Regional Director Lawrence C. Merriam arrived in Jackson Hole to make contact with local leaders and generally survey the attitude of the populace. His primary mission, however, was to arrange a "changing of the guard" with F. C. Koziol, supervisor of Teton National Forest.[76] This would not necessarily be routine, for, although Merriam found Koziol "cordial," beneath this decorum was considerable bitterness. From the beginning the Forest Service had openly or covertly opposed National Park Service objectives in Jackson Hole. Now it was difficult to admit defeat and graciously turn over some 130,000 acres of land and lakes.

And Koziol didn't, as the following example will illustrate. Koziol and Merriam had agreed on the transfer of ranger stations within the monument. However, when the Forest Service evacuated in June, 1943, it was not done with what one might call a spirit of camaraderie. Not only were the furniture and equipment taken from the Jackson Lake Ranger Station, but *all* the plumbing in the basement, kitchen, and bathroom was removed. Even doors, cupboards, drawers, and cabinets, plus the accompanying hardware, were considered "movable equipment." Well tubing was removed, and an underground tank unearthed and packed away. To complete the task a four-foot square hole was cut in the living room floor, severing not only the flooring but the floor joists as well. In short, the station was uninhabitable.[77]

The incident led to some heated correspondence between Merriam and C. N. Woods, regional superintendent for the Forest Service. Woods, in turn, demanded accountability from Koziol, asking for a full report "of just what you did." He then defined "fixture" in case Koziol "may not have clearly in mind the difference between furniture and equipment on the one hand and fixtures on the other." Koziol replied rather weakly, claiming that he needed the fixtures for other forest stations since they were unavailable in the wartime market. Having determined that Koziol acted rashly and independently, the Forest Service disavowed his actions, transferred him to another national forest, and agreed to make such repairs and replacements as were needed to make the Jackson Lake quarters livable.[78]

Although Regional Forester Woods was infuriated at his subordinate's indelicate action, he was no less miffed at the Washington office's willingness to cooperate with the National Park Service. Specifically, the Forest Service agreed to man certain fire lookout stations protecting monument land until such time as the Park Service might find funds to assume the task. In a forthright, perhaps insolent, letter to Chief Forester Lyle F. Watts, Woods charged that this policy "may cause trouble with the public and with Congress. So far this Region has managed to ward off what might have been bad effects of your policy." Woods accused the Washington office of being directed by the National Park Service, then concluded his missive with the request that "in the interest of good administration and as a considerable safety factor, I hope you will henceforth consult this Region before you enter into any important agreement with the Park Service." [79]

Woods's apparent anger was surely the result of his desire to see the Forest Service speak out—to fight for what it had lost. Surrounded as he was by westerners enraged by the president's proclamation, he could smell the scent of victory on this issue if only his superiors would seize the opportunity.

It fell to Assistant Chief Forester L. F. Kneipp to answer his regional superintendent's bombastic letter. With admirable tact, Kneipp reminded Woods that there were bigger questions at stake than the jurisdiction of some 130,000 acres in Jackson Hole. Kneipp sketched a picture of a much-beleaguered and much-maligned Forest Service, which had taken second best for many years in the struggle for congressional appropriations. Now a perceptible change was evident and certainly accelerated by the Jackson Hole National Monument incident. The Forest Service had the advantage, and Kneipp was not about to risk it by such incidents as "the stripping of the ranger station" or an "inopportune fire." As to Woods's suggestion that the Washington office check with the regional office before decision making, Kneipp gave his superintendent a political primer in the realities of power, concluding that for the "Chief to wholly divest himself of powers of decision, or to exercise them only after the concurrence of his Regional Foresters would be a poor way for him to discharge the responsibilities of his position." [80]

Aside from a gentle rebuke of Woods's views, Kneipp's

letter outlined official Forest Service policy. In spite of personal feelings, the Forest Service attitude toward the monument would be one of cooperation and non-involvement. It would remain on the sidelines, content to let others do battle. Adherence to this policy is evident in Forest Service testimony before congressional committees and its reluctance to become involved in the *State of Wyoming v. Franke* case.[81]

The Forest Service found no shortage of others willing to cudgel the monument into oblivion. Senator Joseph O'Mahoney devitalized the new Park Service possession through the "power of the purse." In 1943 he attached an amendment to the Interior Department Appropriation Act prohibiting the use of any monies for any new administration, maintenance, or protection which might be occasioned by the establishment of a new national monument. This amendment remained in effect for three years, restricting the Park Service to maintenance alone, a limiting but not crippling situation.[82]

The primary objective of the Wyoming congressional delegation was to kill the new monument by congressional action. From 1944 through 1947 they continuously kept the issue before Congress. Their harangues fell on many sympathetic ears. Barrett's first bill, H. R. 2241, had been defeated, but through no fault of Congress. Thus Roosevelt's veto simply signalled the introduction of similar legislation. Wyoming politicians reasoned that if they could push legislation through Congress, then President Harry Truman, who came to power in April, 1945, on the death of Roosevelt, would be more sympathetic to their cause. They hoped that the issue might provide Truman with the opportunity to declare his independence from Secretary of the Interior Ickes, whose favoritism to the National Park Service was well known.[83] Thus, in February, 1945, H. R. 2109 was introduced, reiterating the abolishment theme, while H. R. 2691, presented in March, 1945, would turn over administration of Jackson Hole National Monument to the Forest Service. In January, 1947, Senator Edward Robertson of Wyoming introduced S. 91, a bill to remove the president's power to create national monuments, retroactive to December 7, 1941. Truman was never tested, for all of these bills died in committee.[84]

Congressman Frank Barrett's final attempt to abrogate the monument came in January, 1947, with the introduction of H. R. 1330. Like earlier versions, this bill aimed to abolish the monument and return the lands therein to their previous status. When hearings were held in Washington, however, it was evident that the moral outrage of 1943 was gone. Whereas in 1943 the anti-monument forces dominated the hearings, in 1947 over half of the statements favored retention. Representative Barrett had taken three days to present his case in 1943, but his testimony in favor of H. R. 1330 was completed in an hour and a half. Some of the old arguments had lost their meaning. The issue of executive usurpation of power died with Roosevelt. So also did the charge of Hitlerian tactics lose its impact with the successful conclusion of World War II. Some opponents sought to replace Hitler and fascism with Stalin and communism, but the nation was not quite ready for McCarthyism.[85]

On the other hand, with the close of the war, it had become evident to conservation groups that the public lands must be preserved and, if possible, expanded. Millions of Americans who had endured the depression years and the personal sacrifices demanded by World War II were now eager to relax and enjoy an extended vacation, often in the West. By 1947 such groups as the National Audubon Society, the Izaak Walton League, the American Planning and Civic Association, the Sierra Club, the Wilderness Society, and other local organizations were determined that Jackson Hole would not be sacrificed to commercial development. Their political campaign was influential, and, in the end, successful. Evidence of their impact came from Representative Preston Peden of Oklahoma. Peden, who knew virtually nothing of Jackson Hole, expressed his incredulity that he had received "more correspondence and telegrams on this particular issue than in any one heretofore . . ."[86] Peden had no explanation for this, but in truth the American public was stirring itself and conservation forces were rapidly gaining strength. Jackson Hole had become a challenge in their determination to curb needless exploitation and the attempted "land grab" by certain western cattlemen.

In a sense the Jackson Hole issue was a forerunner of the Echo Park fight in the 1950s. At Echo Park, a valley formed by the confluence of the Yampa and Green Rivers within Dinosaur National Monument, preservationists made a determined stand against the dam builders. This time they were victorous, and the Bureau of Reclamation left the confrontation with new respect for the political clout of the aesthetic conservationists.

Jackson Hole was different in its particulars, yet the basic issue of whether areas of exceptional beauty would be preserved for all time or immediately exploited was present in each case.

Times were changing, and H. R. 1330 was a victim of that change. Although Barrett was able to see the bill voted out of committee, twice it was objected to on the floor of the House, and finally on January 19, 1948, it was stricken from the calendar.[87] The legislative attempt to slay the National Park Service colossus was over.

V·I·I·I

CREATING A NEW
GRAND TETON NATIONAL PARK

"The project . . . has taken much longer to
work out than either of us dreamed."
John D. Rockefeller, Jr., to Horace Albright, 1950

LIKE many great national parks, the establishment of Grand Teton National Park transpired in steps. The small park encompassing the mountains, established in 1929, was the first phase. The proclamation of Jackson Hole National Monument fourteen years later represented the second phase. The final step would be the amalgamation of the monument and the park, thus establishing Grand Teton National Park as it is today.

This final step did not take place easily. The National Park Service, Rockefeller, and the various conservation organizations all felt relief that the monument had survived, yet they knew that it offered no assurance of permanence. It was a necessary transitional phase. When in early 1945 Harold Ickes suggested that the Jackson Hole Preserve, Inc., transfer its land to the government, Rockefeller responded that he would not do so until "the Government's position assured the successful completion of the project."[1] Thus the monument was understood as a holding action that stretched the meaning of the Antiquities Act of 1906 to its very limits. It represented a standoff, a *status quo*, until such time as the conservation forces could muster the strength to consummate the final phase.

In 1945 that final phase seemed remote, for while the National Park Service had successfully fended off the enemy from without, factionalism from within played havoc with any effort to incorporate the monument lands into Grand Teton National Park. As in the 1930s, many leading members of the National Parks Association continued to question the wisdom of the inclusion in the park of Jackson Reservoir and the sagebrush flats. They feared that the dam builders, who continually cast covetous eyes upon the national parks, would seize on Jackson Reservoir as an example of how the national parks and reservoirs might exist in harmony. By 1943 the association was hopelessly divided on the issue. Eventually the National Parks Association Board of Trustees drafted a resolution opposing the inclusion of Jackson Lake, but they agreed "to have no action taken against the monument in any way."[2] By taking no *public* stand, the board negated the effect of its resolution.

While the board remained silent, some prominent conservationists spoke out. Robert Sterling Yard, a respected veteran, attacked the monument and the Jackson Reservoir in the October, 1943, issue of the *Living Wilderness*.[3] Many supporters were incredulous. Struthers Burt, still fighting for the park, was astonished and regretted that one of his most intimate and admired friends "must be becoming senile."[4]

Many conservationists continued to question inclusion in the park of the commonplace sagebrush country to the east of the Snake River. Viewed alone, it was not of national caliber. However, as Olaus Murie once commented, the beauty of these sagebrush lands "all depends on which direction one points the camera."[5] From the beginning, Horace Albright and John D. Rockefeller, Jr., had in mind the preservation not of the land but of the view. And the mountains and the flat valley each enhanced the other. They were both necessary. "We cannot have a beautiful valley," testifed Murie, "without the mountains. We cannot have the mountains without the flat country adjacent."[6] It was the incomparable vista from the valley that Murie and so many others wished to keep inviolate. Therefore, the character of the land was of no real signifcance. Some conservationists, however, continued to disagree.

Another "inhouse" issue that muddied the waters was the question whether historic values or pristine nature should take precedence in the proposed park. Rockefeller, Albright and ranchers, such as Struthers Burt, had always maintained that the northern Jackson Hole area ought to be scenic, but also historic. Since the early 1920s they had in mind continuance of a number of guest ranches, thus retaining the flavor of "the old West." This flavor meant continuation of cattle grazing, often at the expense of competing wildlife. On the other side of the environmental fence was Newton Drury, the new Director of the National Park Service. Drury believed that wilderness and pristine nature must come first in importance over the preservation and restoration of the cattleman's frontier in Jackson Hole. The two positions came into conflict at a December, 1944, meeting, when Chorley reminded Newton Drury of Rockefeller's interest in history. "Mr. Rockefeller," Chorley instructed Drury, "had in mind perpetuating the picturesque features of Jackson Hole as a cattle country." [7] In this exchange the issue of concern was a particularly delightful spread called the Elk Ranch. Drury suggested eliminating the ranch and allowing the land to return to a natural state. At issue was the priority of elk, for use of the Elk Ranch for cattle would be at the expense of the elk herd, and vice versa. In this instance cattle and history won, for Drury backed off, quickly stating that he was sure their differences could be resolved.[8]

Of a more serious nature was the continual discord that centered about the activities and policies of the Jackson Hole Preserve, Inc. Throughout the 1930s, Struthers Burt had chastised the executives of the Snake River Land Company for disregarding local interests and creating needless tensions. In the 1940s, after the Snake River Land Company had reincorporated into the Jackson Hole Preserve, Inc., the critic was Olaus Murie. Since 1927, Murie had been employed in Jackson Hole as a Fish and Wildlife Service biologist studying the elk herd. Over the years the utilitarian conservation tendencies of the Fish and Wildlife Service often clashed with Murie's personal environmental convictions. Late in 1945 he retired from government service to become national director of the Wilderness Society and an activist in the Izaak Walton League, both of which allowed him to fight for his beliefs. He was a man who combined scientific knowledge and love of the wilderness with honesty and openness.[9]

When Vanderbilt Webb appointed Murie to the Jackson Hole Preserve, Inc., Board of Directors, he was pleased to have local representation. However, Murie soon took offense at what he perceived as neglect of local residents' opinions. Furthermore, with the exception of Harold Fabian and himself, the directors all resided in New York, and usually conducted their meetings in the rather cloistered confines of the Rockefeller Center. Murie's opinions were seldom heard.

Murie's discontent with the board surfaced over an incident with Coulter Huyler, owner of the Bear Paw Ranch, a dude ranch just south of Rockefeller's JY Ranch. The incident is worth exploring, for it is illustrative of how the penchant for corporate orderliness of the Jackson Hole Preserve, Inc., directors occasionally was destructive of good public relations. Coulter Huyler had first offered to sell "Bear Paw" in 1932, but Arthur Woods indicated that the property was outside the area of purchase. Nine years later Kenneth Chorley approached Huyler, but the two men could not agree on a price. At that time Harold Fabian discovered that the legal right-of-way for two roads to Huyler's ranch, which both crossed Rockefeller land, was unclear. Determined to settle the matter, Chorley offered the legal right-of-way on one road but not the other. Since Huyler had used both roads for many years, he refused this compromise. The Jackson Hole Preserve, Inc., directors hastily decided to settle the matter in court.[10] Shortly before the trial date, Huyler wrote to Laurance Rockefeller in an attempt to avoid the expense and inconvenience of a trial, stating that he could not "quite believe that either you or your father wish to deprive Bear Paw of the use of either of these roads." But even if they did, Huyler suggested that until the war was over and the land issue in Jackson Hole settled, Huyler and Rockefeller might "exchange documents in which we would agree that the use of the roads in question from this date on would not constitute a waiver by either side of any rights which we both might have." Huyler felt sure that when they could go over the matter on the ground, a mutually satisfactory arrangement could be found. "If not," proposed Huyler, "the case could go on and the matter be adjudicated in the regular way."[11] This was an eminently practical solution, although Huyler did not mention the most obvious advantage to Rockefeller: the avoidance of adverse publicity that would surely accompany a trial involving a small dude rancher and one of the wealthiest families in America. Huyler received a rather curt letter from young Laurance stating that the positions that "Father's associates have taken ... are imminently [sic] fair and just. ... I am afraid there is nothing I can do in the matter." [12]

One associate who was not consulted was Murie. When he received word of the pending suit, he demanded an explanation. In a lengthy letter Chorley reviewed the history of the disagreement, stating that Huyler had made rather unreasonable demands and it was finally decided that the whole matter ought to be submitted to the courts "in a friendly way ...." Chorley's explanation was unsatisfactory to Murie, who responded that "bringing on this suit at this time is a mistake. I can visualize serious repercussions." [13]

Murie's analysis was sound. The case was adjudicated and the Rockefeller interests lost. By January, 1949, Rockefeller had purchased the Bear Paw Ranch, so it mattered very little. In fact, the issue never was of importance, and it was remarkable that Rockefeller's advisors, particularly Chorley, would risk adverse publicity when it could so easily have been avoided. But good public relations, as Chorley later admitted, were not the forte of the Jackson Hole Preserve, Inc., and ineptness in this area was, perhaps, the company's most serious shortcoming.[14]

As evidenced in the Huyler case, in the 1940s, many of the responsibilities and problems associated with Jackson Hole fell to Laurance Rockefeller. During that decade John D. Rockefeller, Jr., wisely delegated more and more responsibility for his multi-faceted projects to his five sons. It was Laurance who inherited his father's love of nature and interest in conservation; therefore it was natural that the completion of the Jackson Hole plan should fall to him. Before making this decision, John D. Rockefeller, Jr., in his typically organized fashion, asked Kenneth Chorley's opinion. Chorley favored the transfer of responsibility to Laurance, for it would relieve his father of the "cost and annoyance of the project," and allow "one of your sons to carry out a project which you originated." The most persuasive argument was that the transfer would give Laurance Rockefeller a project on which "he might center his interest" and "further explore his interest in the West and in conservation, and at the same time demonstrate ways and means of caring for visitors to national parks and monuments on a non-profit basis, which might be of great value to the future of the Park Service." [15]

Thus it was that on October 1, 1945, the senior Rockefeller turned over to Laurance some 29,937 acres of Jackson Hole land, retaining the 3,288 acres comprising the JY Ranch in his name. It was agreed that Laurance would "assume the cost of maintaining all properties held by Jackson Hole Preserve, Inc., and all that involves . . . ." [16]

Soon after the transfer Laurance Rockefeller began to wield considerable influence. In much the same fashion as Stephen Mather or Horace Albright, who often acted in an advisory capacity, the younger Rockefeller commenced to develop tourist attractions designed to appeal to those with limited time and a reluctance to stray far from their automobile. Under his leadership the Jackson Hole Preserve, Inc., undertook to conserve and restore some of the buildings and places of historic interest. One of the most successful was carried out by Harold Fabian and his wife, Josephine, who planned and completed the restoration of the Menor's Ferry spanning the Snake River at Moose.[17] Plans were discussed to allow the Elk Ranch, one of the most profitable operations within the monument, to be a model working cattle ranch, thus carrying on the historic livelihood of the area. Director Newton Drury was hardly enthusiastic, but he was in no position to oppose or obstruct these projects.

Perhaps the most serious rift between the conservation factions occurred over the Jackson Hole Wildlife Park. The wildlife park was the idea of Laurance Rockefeller and his good friend, Fairfield Osborn, executive director of the New York Zoological Society. To be located downstream from the Jackson Lake dam along the Snake River at Oxbow Bend, the wildlife park would be carved from land destined to become part of Grand Teton National Park. Within the confines of this fenced wildlife park would reside big game animals of the West, such as buffalo, deer, antelope, and elk, to be studied by scientists and viewed by tourists.

Surely Laurance Rockefeller had every right to pursue this interest, but it was unfortunate that the views of the National Park Service were not given greater consideration. Ever since the 1920s when Superintendent Albright displayed wildlife at Mammoth Hot Springs in Yellowstone, the National Park Service had been moving away from such garish activities. By the 1940s the idea of confinement and exhibition of wild animals could find few if any Park Service supporters. Yet it was the height of impolitic behavior for the Park Service to bite the hand that feeds; thus Director Drury confined his opposition to off the record remarks. In one conversation, Drury resigned himself to the inevitable, reasoning that the wildlife park would "turn out to be a good experiment to justify the policy of the Park Service."[18] In other words, it would fail.

While Drury found it advantageous to remain impartial, Olaus Murie could not restrain his feelings. As a wildlife biologist who had spent the better part of his life studying the habits of free-roving animals in Alaska and Jackson Hole, he knew that confinement was the antithesis of a healthy habitat for big game. He had always accepted the National Elk Refuge in Jackson Hole as a necessary compromise rather than an ideal situation. In truth, Murie opposed anything that was artificial in altering the habitat of wildlife. He found incredulous the argument that the wildlife park could offer scientists an opportunity to study big game animals. "Imagine naturalists, particularly ecologists, thrilling at the opportunities presented by a group of animals under fence . . . ," wrote Murie with more than a hint of irony and ridicule.[19]

Of course, Rockefeller and Osborn advocated that the wildlife park would act as an educational instrument to sensitize the public to the special problems of wildlife, and "to inform visitors of the great need of forest protection and of maintaining the inviolability of primitive and wilderness areas."[20] While these were admirable objectives, the means to achieve them were in question. Murie could see little real possibility of changing attitudes or increasing sensitivity by allowing the busy tourist to view wild animals with a minimum of effort. The naturalist, who had spent many arduous years in tracking and observing wildlife in Alaska, Canada, and Labrador, believed that a person's appreciation of nature was proportionate to the effort expended. Sighting a moose in the wild after a strenuous hike was an altogether different experience than emerging from one's automobile to peer through a fence at the identical animal. It was difficult to define, but clearly the elements of wonder, surprise, danger, and appreciation were missing. "The experiences that stay in the memory," wrote Murie, "are those enjoyed through one's own effort."[21]

For Murie, the proposed wildlife park was one more step in a direction that he did not think the United States should go.

He feared the mechanized, push-button world that dictated that Americans be spectators, rather than participants. He feared a "national laziness" sweeping the nation, which demanded "extra service, easy entertainment, and pleasure with the least possible exertion." He realized that he could do little to reverse the trend, but at least the National Park Service could combat these tendencies by opposing "well-meant attempts to draw the essence out of a landscape for presentation to the tourist by the roadside, which thereby cheapens it and places it in the category of the souvenirs that can be purchased over the counter." [22] The wildlife park, which he profaned with the epithet "zoo," was one more vulgar show to be resisted.

To Murie's charges supporters of the idea could only reply that his views were idealistic, but impractical. Fairfield Osborn branded Murie an elitist; one of a tiny minority of admirable but out-of-touch Americans. Only a "pitifully small minority have the time or ability to pack off into the wilderness." The wildlife park would be for the general public; "for the many and not the few." [23]

To conservationists, the differences between Murie and Osborn have a certain classic ring, and, of course, there is no easy compromise. Thus when the Jackson Hole Preserve, Inc., Board of Directors made public the wildlife park plans, Murie felt obliged to resign from the board.[24] Sincere efforts by Harold Fabian, Vanderbilt Webb, and Fairfield Osborn could not persuade him to reconsider.[25] Murie seemed to understand that his divergent views would only cause him needless frustration if he remained on the Jackson Hole Preserve, Inc., Board of Directors. Furthermore, he was about to accept a position in an organization where his convictions would be more compatible: the executive directorship of the Wilderness Society. From this post he would continue to fight for the establishment of Grand Teton National Park.

Although Murie often disagreed with the policies of the Jackson Hole Preserve, Inc., seldom did he publicly voice his differences. He understood that dissension over detail would endanger the ultimate objective of an enlarged Grand Teton National Park. He was able to place principles above personalities, and he realized that his differences with other conservationists were but cracks rather than chasms. By 1947 these cracks had been sealed. This was most evident in April of that year, when such conservationists as Murie, Osborn, Kenneth Reid, Executive Director of the Izaak Walton League, Fred Packard, Field Executive of the National Parks Association, and Howard Zahniser, editor of *The Living Wilderness* and executive secretary of the Wilderness Society, all testified against H. R. 1330, Barrett's final legislative attempt to abolish the monument.[26] It was evident that the Izaak Walton League, supported by such organizations as the American Planning and Civic Association, the National Parks Association, the Wilderness Society, the Sierra Club, and the National Audubon Society should now take the offensive.

On the local level, the conclusion of World War II brought a change to Jackson Hole. Americans were on the move. With money saved during the war and gasoline no longer rationed, hordes of vacation-hungry Americans descended on the valley. While the cattle business remained steady, the tourist business boomed. Clearly such prophets of doom as Felix Buchenroth were wrong. Grass was not growing in the streets of Jackson: in fact the most evident green was that of the dollar. An Izaak Walton League leaflet entitled, "Dollars and Sense About the Jackson Hole National Monument" gave revealing facts.[27] Deposits in the Jackson State Bank had risen from approximately $1,000,000 in 1943 to over $2,300,000 in 1946. Retail sales tax doubled between the same years. Real estate values were skyrocketing. Two vacant lots that sold in 1942 for $3,000 were priced at $10,000 in 1946. Within the monument a three-acre plot with some old log structures which had sold in 1943 for $8,000 was resold in 1946 for $20,000. Up and down the economic charts, from telephone installations to liquor sales, the indicators were that Jackson Hole was experiencing economic prosperity. Certainly this prosperity could not be credited wholly to Jackson Hole National Monument. On the other hand it was increasingly evident that Horace Albright was right —the future prosperity of Jackson Hole was in tourism, not the cattle industry. In this light, many saw the monument as an asset rather than a liability. A local opinion poll conducted in February, 1947, indicated that while 182 persons opposed the monument, 142 favored it and 234 expressed no strong opinion.[28] While this represented no tidal wave, it was evident that the ebb and flow of public opinion was moving toward acceptance.

Increased tourism had effects other than economic. Many residents viewed the throngs of tourists with apprehension. Up until the post-war period they had seen no real threat to the pristine nature of the valley. Now they perceived that a new era had begun, one which could seriously effect the quaint and unsullied lifestyle of Jackson Hole. In truth, almost all the residents were aesthetic conservationists at heart. They wished to preserve the beauty which they so treasured, but they felt that they needed no outside help. They thought preservation ought to be a local affair. Particularly, they did not want the restrictions that had come to be synonymous with Park Service control. In the 1938 hearings Holly Leek, the son of pioneer Stephen Leek, expressed the individualism that they did not want to lose: "You can't holler in Yellowstone. You can't build a fire where you want to. They can get up and holler at 4 o'clock in the morning here and nobody cares. They build a fire where they please, and they are free here; they are enjoying themselves." [29] In that same year, Albert Schwabacher, a wealthy San Francisco investor, voiced his opposition to inclusion of his Jackson Hole property in the park along similar lines. Schwabacher feared that rules and regulations would be imposed upon his family and guests to the point that they might "kill off our enthusiasm for the complete freedom which we have always enjoyed in the past." [30]

The issue of freedom versus regulations struck a responsive chord with many. Residents did not want a twentieth century bureaucracy to maintain a nineteenth century environment. However, after the war it became most evident that to have the latter you must accept the former. Continuation of the helter-skelter individualism expressed by Holly Leek would only result in the worst type of chaos and profiteering. The valley needed sound planning, but local government was not equal to the task. It would take an organization such as the National Park Service, with all its bureaucratic trappings, to do the job, or, as Struthers Burt put it, "*to zone properly* one of the most famous counties in the world, to prevent its selfish, or careless despoliation, and to keep a proper balance between the various interests in the valley." [31]

In that balance, a continuing problem was summer home leases on Jackson Lake. Many locals would not give up their private dream of an idyllic mountain retreat. And, of course, without Park Service control this would be possible. Olaus Murie was convinced that "establishing summer homes is the avowed purpose, possibly the main purpose, of a group of anti-monument people."[32] They argued that Teton County's tax problem could be alleviated by summer homes on the lake, and that summer homes were less offensive than hordes of tourists and campers. Murie did not agree, for the people would still come, and to preempt much of the shoreline for private cabins would be elitist and undemocratic.[33]

This disagreement could not be easily resolved, but the changing position of the Forest Service gave the summer home hopefuls less confidence in their position. As noted, the Forest Service determined to remain publicly neutral on the monument issue. However, after the war they had to reassess their "friends" and "enemies." What was most evident was that the Forest Service-cattleman alliance was under severe strain. From 1930 on the Forest Service and the cattlemen had sought the same objective: restraining the National Park Service and keeping the land open to livestock grazing. However, in 1946 the livestock interests, championed by Senator Edward Robertson and Representative Frank Barrett, both of Wyoming, turned against the Forest Service. The cattle interests lobbied for legislation that would transfer unappropriated and unreserved federal lands to the individual states. It was generally assumed that the states would then sell the land to ranchers at bargain prices, possibly retaining the mineral rights to augment the state treasury. This attempt, as introduced by Senator Robertson in Senate bill 1945, was vigorously opposed by conservationists. Bernard DeVoto claimed that "the ultimate objectives of the biggest land grab in our history are to extinguish the public interest in all lands now held by the government that can be used by cattle, sheep, mining, lumber, or power companies."[34]

In pursuing this objective Representative Barrett found it necessary to vilify the Forest Service, attempting to expose the agency's ineptness in land management. Public hearings in the West, which DeVoto labelled "Barrett's Wild West Show," were stacked against the Forest Service, with the general objective of intimidating "the Forest Service if you can; if you can't, then bleed it to death by cutting down its appropriation."[35]

Although the livestock interests were not successful in their "land grab," it was not surprising that the Forest Service would reassess its role in the monument fight. Obviously it was not in their interest to support Barrett's attempt to return about 100,000 acres of Jackson Hole land to their control while simultaneously the Wyoming representative was determined to strip millions of acres from Forest Service jurisdiction. It was evident that while the rivalry between the Forest Service and the National Park Service would continue, at times it was necessary to present a common front against a determined enemy.

Thus, while the Forest Service gave testimony favorable to their control of Jackson Hole lands in the 1933, 1938, and 1943 hearings, in 1947 Barrett received no supportive testimony from the Forest Service. On the local level Teton National Forest Supervisor Art Buckingham found that he had much in common with John McLaughlin, his counterpart in Grand Teton National Park. When state senator Felix Buchenroth sponsored a memorial backing the proposed transfer of public lands to the states, which passed almost unanimously, Buckingham expressed his desire to join the Izaak Walton League, which not only opposed the land transfer but also supported the monument. After some private discussion, it was agreed that if Supervisor Buckingham joined the league it might place him in an embarrassing position and "cause a local demand for his transfer." [36] It was evident that local opponents of the National Park Service could no longer count on their traditional ally.

By late 1948 only a small but influential group of local businessmen and ranchers continued to actively oppose National Park Service jurisdiction in Jackson Hole. And even these enemies had to admit that this jurisdiction could no longer be disputed. They had made numerous forays by many circuitous routes, yet the Park Service prevailed. Defeated at every turn and with public opinion changing, the Wyoming congressional delegation was prepared to accept the permanent presence of the Park Service by resolving the matter. Throughout 1948 the talk on both sides was that it was time to get together, settle differences and fashion the compromises into legislation. In April, 1948, former governor Leslie Miller attempted to organize a conference, but his efforts were undermined by Felix Buchenroth.[37] In January, 1949, Harry Miner, President of the Wyoming Izaak Walton League, sent out letters to all important parties proposing a conference in Washington. Miner's efforts were well received, and in April, 1949, a three-day conference was held in Washington, D.C., with the intent of drawing up a bill to end the controversy. The meeting was attended by twenty-two persons, representing all of the various interest groups. Among those present were Senator O'Mahoney and Senator-elect Lester Hunt, Representative Barrett, Under Secretary of the Interior Oscar Chapman, Acting Director of the National Park Service Arthur Demaray, Leslie Miller and Harold Fabian representing the Jackson Hole Preserve, Inc., Lester Bagley of the Wyoming Game and Fish Commission, and Felix Buchenroth and Clifford Hansen, both of Jackson.[38]

During the initial meeting Teton County Commissioner Clifford Hansen sounded a note of conciliation. There were, according to Hansen, only three problems that Wyoming people wanted resolved. These three stumbling blocks were the control of the elk herd, grazing rights across the monument, and the property tax problem.[39] For the next two days a working committee of six hammered out acceptable compromises. Grazing privileges were quickly conceded by the National Park Service and it was reluctantly agreed that Teton County ought to be reimbursed for the property tax loss that it would suffer with the establishment of the enlarged park. The equity of this request from a county with only 4½ percent of its total acreage on the tax tolls was never in dispute, but just how to accomplish this reimbursement had escaped the collective wisdom of both conservation and commercial interests for close to twenty years. The Bureau of the Budget agreed that removal from the tax rolls of 33,562 of only 114,491 taxable acres posed a serious problem, yet they still feared creation of an unwanted precedent.[40] Thus, while the end was agreed upon, the means were still elusive.

The knottiest problem was the management of the elk herd. Wyoming Game and Fish Commissioner Lester Bagley was particularly fearful that the state was gradually losing control of its property. The National Park Service was most reluctant to allow hunting within a national park. After protracted and heated debate, the committee determined that a "Jackson Hole Elk Herd Advisory Committee" ought to be established to advise both the National Park Service and the Wyoming Game and Fish Commission on the yearly management of the herd. At the conclusion of the conference almost all of the participants indicated that the solutions proposed were not what they wanted, but they were solutions that might work. The recommendations were incorporated in an unsigned report, dated April 15, 1949, which they all agreed, some reluctantly, that they would try to sell to all interested parties.[41]

An important step had been taken. All concerned groups had met together and found that their differences were not insolvable. So confident was John D. Rockefeller, Jr., that he and Laurance determined that it was finally time to deed over to the government the 33,562 acres of land that had been held for some twenty years. A ceremony of acceptance was held on December 16, 1949. A modicum of caution prevailed, however, for the deed stipulated that should the lands be used for other than public park purposes, they would automatically revert to the Jackson Hole Preserve, Inc.[42] In the spirit of the occasion, Senator O'Mahoney suggested by letter to Harry Truman that Jackson Hole now be considered as a summer home site "for the President of the United States."[43] Evidently Truman was not interested in locating west of Missouri.

In early 1950 all barriers seemed to fall. A few dissidents condemned the compromise as "spurious appeasement" to a "bureaucratic dream," but most were ready to call a halt to discord.[44] Senator Joseph O'Mahoney found it possible to draft a bill and introduce it in the Senate on April 12th. Senate bill 3409 provided that Jackson Hole National Monument be abolished and the lands incorporated into a greater Grand Teton National Park. As might be expected, some amendments altered earlier decisions. The Bureau of the Budget, in a predictable action, objected to tax concessions in perpetuity to Teton County. It was finally agreed that Teton County would be compensated at a rate very similar to that which the Bureau had rejected in 1934: for four years the county would receive the full amount of the annual taxes last assessed, then for the next twenty years payment would decrease by 5 percent each year.[45]

The bill provided that the management of the elk herd within the new park would be the joint responsibility of the federal government and the state of Wyoming. The secretary of the interior and the governor of Wyoming would approve an annual conservation plan drafted by the Wyoming Game and Fish Commission and the National Park Service. When the agencies agreed that hunting in the park was necessary, hunters would be licensed by the Wyoming Game and Fish Commission and deputized as temporary rangers by the National Park Service.[46]

One interesting provision within the bill allowed that "no further extension or establishment of national parks or monuments in Wyoming may be undertaken except by express authorization of the Congress." [47] In this fashion the Wyoming congressional delegation finally succeeded in stripping from the president the power to decree monuments under the Antiquities Act of 1906, albeit only in the state of Wyoming.

The question of grazing privileges, so long debated and so often misunderstood, was resolved by guaranteeing each rancher continuance of his lease for twenty-five years and "thereafter during the lifetime of his heirs, successors, or assigns, but only if they were members of the immediate family on such date, as determined by the Secretary of the Interior." [48] Thus, the bill protected rancher's grazing rights within the proposed park for the lifetime of the rancher or that of his immediate family living in 1950.

With these compromises and hard work by such men as Senator O'Mahoney and Carl D. Shoemaker, lobbyist for the National Wildlife Federation, the bill moved easily through Congress and was signed by President Harry Truman on September 14, 1950.[49] Jackson Hole National Monument died, but a new park emerged. The American people would be assured that this crucible of beauty set in the Rocky Mountains would remain in its natural state for generations to come.

The establishment of Grand Teton National Park in 1950 was a notable victory for the preservationist cause at a time when the wilderness movement was struggling.[50] Not only was it the culmination of years of strife, but in a sense, it was a prelude to the spirited offense the wilderness movement would take in the 1960s and 1970s. Over and above the question of conservation and park-making, the issue may be seen as a victory for the democratic process. Throughout the years there was plenty of anger, vituperation, and bitterness. There were deals, there was deceit, but amidst it all the democratic process continued. There were threats, but there was no violence. No one picked up a gun or a bomb, although at times they were sorely tempted. Order remained, and, without question, the national will of the majority prevailed.

Seven years earlier John D. Rockefeller, Jr., had written Ickes with unconcealed pleasure when the monument was established. Now, once again, the elderly gentleman, in his seventy-sixth year, wrote his friend, Horace Albright. In a reminiscent mood, Rockefeller noted that "the project which you then initiated, and the significance of which I was quick to appreciate, has taken much longer to work out than either of us dreamed." [51] That it did, but in 1950 Rockefeller, Albright, and many other conservationists could take immense pleasure in the fruition of a project that may have been the most difficult in conservation history.

I·X

POSTSCRIPT FOR A PARK

"They don't know this land was
once a battleground."

JACKSON HOLE NEWS, *September, 1975*

EARLIER in the struggle the editor of the Jackson
Hole *Courier* remarked with a certain pernicious wisdom: "Personal motives are always selfish, which explains why a wise
man will sometimes change his mind."[1] In the 1950s there
were a great number of wise men in Jackson Hole, or, at least,
persons who changed their minds. Of course, the bitter feelings
of many did not simply vanish, but generally they were harbored within rather than channeled outward into the community. They accepted the 1950 settlement as final; it was something they must learn to live with. Others, perhaps a majority,
bowed to the presence of the new park much more graciously.
They agreed with Lewis Bates, a Wyoming journalist, who admitted that he was one who took exception to the park, but
found it "not difficult to say that we were wrong."[2]

The reason for this change of mind, this willingness not
only to tolerate but to encourage the new park, was based on
the reality of economic prosperity. The economic boom, which
commenced with the close of the war, accelerated in the 1950s.
In Jackson Hole this new affluence was associated with the park
and tourism. It came as no surprise when in 1959 a team of
economists from the University of Wyoming concluded that
over 72 percent of the basic income of Teton County was derived from tourism. In looking to the future they remarked that
"Teton County is so intimately connected with the growth in

the American vacation trade, that it seems hardly worth while
to consider anything else."[3] Similar studies in 1967 and 1979
only reinforced the fact that the local economy was and is based
on the tourist trade.[4]

As could be expected, the thriving economy was directly
related to increased visitation to the park. The popularity of
Grand Teton National Park has been little short of phenome-
nal. The number of visitors has risen steadily, until by the mid-
1970s the total passed over the 3½ million mark. Though Teton
Park has not enjoyed the fame of Yellowstone National Park,
statistics seem to indicate that motorists drawn to Yellowstone
often stay to praise the beauty of the young park to the south.
In 1965 more than 2½ million vacationers enjoyed Grand
Teton while only slightly more than 2 million visited Yellowstone.[5] And Teton Park continues to hold the numerical advantage.

Prosperity heals wounds. In the 1950s and 1960s the summertime presence in Jackson Hole of John D. Rockefeller, Jr.,
Laurance Rockefeller, and their friends and associates was
viewed positively. Horace Albright soon corresponded in a
friendly fashion with such men as Frank Barrett, Clifford Hansen, and Milward Simpson.[6] Perhaps the changing attitude of
Clifford Hansen, who continued his political career as governor
of Wyoming (1963–1967) and senator from Wyoming (1967–
1979), is symbolic. Throughout the 1940s Hansen was a stead-
fast opponent of park extension. He never engaged in inflammatory rhetoric, yet he worked diligently and effectively for
the cattle interests and against the National Park Service. By
the 1960s Hansen had not undergone any metamorphosis regarding conservation matters, but he did accept the necessity
of the enlarged park. He freely admitted that Grand Teton National Park was an asset to the community and the state. Furthermore, Hansen realized that the small park he had favored
in the 1940s, which would have been confined to the west side
of the Snake River, would not have been feasible. To funnel
millions of visitors through the "westside" park would have
created havoc. With changing conditions Hansen could now
appreciate why the Rockefeller interests and the National Park
Service "felt that as much land as was taken in should be taken
in."[7]

It is to their credit that many of the National Park Service's enemies acquiesced to the necessity of the park. They preferred to think of the old days when Jackson Hole consisted of a small, rather isolated community of individualists who enjoyed a high degree of personal liberty in an idyllic setting. But those days are gone forever. As the twentieth century closes in on Jackson Hole with increasing crowds, crime and commotion, the park has become a sanctuary, at least in the sense that it is largely free from the threats of subdivision and mammonism. Residents realize this and appreciate it.

And, of course, park or no park, throngs of people would have descended on Jackson Hole, for it does not take the National Park Service to inform visitors that this is a place of exceptional natural beauty. They would have come, but had not Rockefeller, Albright, Struthers Burt, Olaus Murie and so many others fought with infinite patience and determination, they would have found a different valley. Perhaps it is not proper in a work of this nature to indulge in futuristic scenarios, but one can not help but speculate on what might have been. The southern end of Jackson Lake would have been festooned with some four hundred summer homes, possibly attractive, yet preventing access for the general public. We can also assume that Jackson Lake would have faced pollution problems from seeping sewage, not unlike Lake Tahoe, California. Inevitably the land would have been scarred by construction and the valley bisected with power lines. Jackson Lake might have been desecrated further by a small logging operation, utilizing logs on the west side of the lake, transporting them across the lake to a small lumber mill. The mill might have been located at Moran. As is so often the case with a logging operation, air quality would have been diminished. We might also expect the lake would have been drained, particularly during drought years, to the point of being an eyesore.

Inevitably, the road from Jackson to Jenny Lake would have become an extension of the town of Jackson. Motels would have been built further north, each claiming the best view of the Cathedral Group, and yet collectively diminishing the pleasure of that scene by their very existence. Along with the motels we could expect fast and cheap food service, facilities for automobiles, and crowded campgrounds featuring electricity and sewer hookups in lieu of trees.

The bypass road on the east side of the Snake River might have been spared such intense development. However, since this is the route of the tourist-in-a-hurry, we might expect the most audacious commercialism to slow him down. Perhaps a model might be Highway 16 from Rapid City to Mount Rushmore. "Gravity spots," reptile gardens, aquatic displays, a "wild" animal park, and the ubiquitous Indian souvenir shop, *ad infinitum,* could be expected, replete with billboards out of all proportion in size and number to the attractions advertised.

Perhaps this scenario is unduly pessimistic. Let us presume that this development would have been done tastefully, eliminating the worst excesses. The result would still have detracted from the pristine beauty of Jackson Hole. It would have focused the tourist's attention on man-made objects and on individual transient needs, rather than allowing his spirit to soar briefly to the heights of this awe-inspiring mountain range as he hurriedly traveled the highway east of the river.

Of course, none but the most crass, opportunistic resident would have sanctioned this scenario at any time during the long struggle over land use, but inevitably it would have happened. It would have happened because those who opposed the National Park Service favored individualism, property rights and local control. Given the conservatism of local residents and their attachment to "laissez-faire" economic principles, it is difficult to see any other outcome. Certainly the group that met at Maud Noble's cabin in 1923 recognized this scenario for the valley and were determined to remove somehow the land use decision-making power from local control. They knew that although there might be professions to the contrary, money would be the measure in Jackson Hole and unrestrained development would be the result. And why shouldn't that be the pattern? Why should Jackson Hole be spared? That is a question which perhaps will never be answered.

Although the 1950 park law assured the preservation of northern Jackson Hole, not all problems or issues terminated in that year. First, the Rockefellers' association with the park continued. Inevitably, the Jackson Hole Preserve, Inc., entered the tourist business to the extent that by the late 1940s Harold Fabian's time was spent less in purchasing land and more in managing and leasing tourist facilities. The influence of the

Rockefeller family continues to this day, for the Jackson Hole Preserve, Inc., owns the Grand Teton Lodge Company, the prime concessionaire for Grand Teton National Park.

The family's presence has been positive in Jackson Hole, as it has been for many other national parks. Laurance Rockefeller has followed in his father's tradition to funnel large amounts of money through the Jackson Hole Preserve, Inc., to upgrade and expand the tourist facilities within the park, a task which the National Park Service undertook in other parks through its "MISSION 66" program. This expansion, primarily the construction of the Colter Bay facilities and Jackson Lake Lodge, was accompanied by the expected charge that the Rockefeller interests would profit, and that tourist facilities ought to remain outside the park and in the hands of local interests. Whatever the merits of this argument, in the 1950s the facilities were needed, and Laurance and his father were willing to provide the capital. The job was done.[8]

Perhaps the most ambitious undertaking has been the construction of Jackson Lake Lodge, a project which, according to Kenneth Chorley, brought John D. Rockefeller, Jr., "great satisfaction" in his declining years.[9] Shortly after the establishment of the enlarged park it became evident that the lack of overnight facilities was causing much inconvenience as well as sanitary problems. In a decade when the idea of visitor quotas was unthinkable, the only alternative was to provide the needed facilities. On one of his yearly sojourns to the JY Ranch, John D. Rockefeller, Jr., faced the problem. According to Kenneth Chorley, Rockefeller reasoned that he was somewhat responsible for bringing tourists to the park, therefore the facilities problem was his. When Chorley asked what he could do about it, the elderly Rockefeller replied: "I suppose I ought to build a hotel." [10]

The Jackson Lake Lodge took some three years to build at a cost of over $5 million. John D. Rockefeller, Jr., was intimately involved in the project from beginning to end. He approved the site, a place adjacent to Lunch Tree Hill where he had first viewed the Teton Range in 1926, and then worked diligently on the architectural plans for this "gift to the American public."

Once completed, the lodge received much acclaim. Few persons remain unaffected as they enter into the spacious lounge and view Jackson Lake and the whole Teton Range spread out before them. This unparalleled view, framed by magnificent windows, was a tribute to the elder Rockefeller's dedication and planning, and has been, indeed, a "gift" to the American public. Unfortunately, while all acclaim the view, few approve of the architecture of the lodge. Constructed of poured concrete, the structure, in the opinion of many, fails to blend with its surroundings. Criticisms range from Homer Richards's gentle rebuke that it "could have been built a little more rustic-like," to author Frank Calkins's evaluation that the lodge "is by far the ugliest building in Western Wyoming, rising out of its ugly compound like a great steel and cement excrescence predetermined to be the ugliest of all its surveys." [11] While Calkins's estimate is extreme, it is unfortunate that the lodge did not incorporate some of the more natural qualities of Old Faithful Inn, Timberline Lodge at Mt. Hood, Oregon, or the Ahwahnee Hotel in Yosemite. Regrettably, the lodge was planned at a time when architects of national park structures had abandoned the idea that a structure ought to be indigenous to the area, in favor of modernism and efficiency. [12]

Mistakes are inevitable, but fortunately some of them are easily corrected. Such was the case with the Jackson Hole Wildlife Park dedicated in 1948. The project came from the imagination of Laurance Rockefeller and Fairfield Osborn, and the two provided the capital and enthusiasm to push the project to completion. As noted, the National Park Service was lukewarm at best in its support. After a few rather difficult and not altogether successful years, Laurance Rockefeller was ready to phase out his involvement in the venture. By 1953 the National Park Service had allowed the objectionable display to die a natural death. The buildings were turned over to the University of Wyoming, to be operated in conjunction with the New York Zoological Society as the Jackson Hole Biological Station. [13] The station operated at this site until the summer of 1978 when its agreement with the New York Zoological Society terminated and its headquarters were moved to the AMK Ranch on the shores of Jackson Lake. [14] The wild animals were eventually released and presumably flourished. Thus ended a well-intended but ill-founded attempt to bring the park to the people.

Certainly the actions of families of wealth will continue

to be controversial; however, by 1970 few residents of Jackson Hole failed to acknowledge the Rockefellers' contribution to preservation of the valley and the greater Yellowstone region. Hence, when in 1972, Congress authorized the transfer of some 24,000 acres of Forest Service land as the John D. Rockefeller, Jr., Memorial Parkway, there was little opposition. The parkway now serves as a corridor and link between Yellowstone and Grand Teton National Park. Officially, the purpose of the land transfer was twofold: to commemorate the many significant contributions to the cause of conservation in the United States by Rockefeller, and "to provide both a symbolic and desirable physical connection between the world's first national park, Yellowstone, and the Grand Teton National Park." [15] The symbolic importance is rooted in history. Not only did the parkway addition fall on the centennial year of the establishment of Yellowstone, but some ninety years had passed since General Philip Sheridan had first proposed a "Greater Yellowstone" concept. The parkway signified another step in the effort to provide unified management for the northwest corner of Wyoming.

Of course General Sheridan and other early advocates of the "Greater Yellowstone" idea fought to preserve wildlife. They watched the lower elevation and level lands taken up by pioneer settlers, with the resultant loss of winter habitat. This problem still remains and is becoming more crucial each year. As population pressure builds, much less desirable land is being subdivided for home construction. This land often does not have the picture-window view of the Grand Teton, but it is of crucial importance if the wildlife continuity of the lands around the parks is to be preserved.[16] Controversy in Jackson Hole and on the Forest Service lands often centers on the needs of wildlife versus the needs of an expanding human population.

An ongoing wildlife problem of complexity is the fate of the Jackson Hole elk herd. From the beginning to the end of the park battle, the destiny of this noble animal has been an influential factor. Since 1950 perhaps it is the proliferation rather than the survival of the elk herd that concerns many federal and state personnel, wildlife experts and interested sportsmen and conservationists. The elk have thrived to the point that each year it is necessary to thin the herd by hunting. Since the majority of the migrating elk cross the park en route to their winter grounds, killing elk within the Grand Teton National

Park has become an annual event. For park personnel it is a painful violation of park principles, especially since many of the hunters congregate along Antelope Flats and do most of their stalking, waiting and watching from the confines of their automobiles. "The Firing Line" has been deplored for years, yet no satisfactory alternative has been found.

The present elk hunting arrangement was one of the most heated matters discussed in 1950. The final compromise hammered out by the Wyoming Game and Fish Commission and the National Park Service essentially stated that the two agencies would determine the yearly kill, then the state of Wyoming would license hunters, and the National Park Service would deputize the hunters as rangers. No one was enthusiastic over this compromise, and later Director Newton Drury admitted that he was a party to it "with great reluctance." [17] Lester Bagley, head of the Wyoming Game and Fish Commission in 1950, commented at the time that the idea of appointing hunters as rangers "is very clumsy, but if that is the system the Park Service wishes to employ it is their problem." [18] Historian John Ise, in his study of the national parks, termed the compromise an "unfortunate concession to the selfish demands of Wyoming sportsmen," and "an insult to the Park Service and common decency." [19] Ise may have momentarily lost his objectivity, for the whole elk matter is too complex for quick condemnation. The fundamental problem is that the elk is an intelligent, resourceful wild animal that is artificially fed in the winter and protected ten months out of the year. Thus winter no longer takes its toll and natural predators, aside from man, such as the wolf and mountain lion, were systematically hunted to near extinction early in the century. Having eliminated the natural controlling factors of the elk herd, it has now fallen to man to manage the Jackson Hole elk herd. This has not been, is not, and will not be easy. [20]

As the elk population has posed problems, so has the burgeoning human population of Teton County. The development of a major Jackson Hole ski area in 1965 has expanded the brief summer tourist season. The flight from the nation's cities has brought a wave of urban expatriates. These newcomers find Jackson Hole a refreshing place to live, combining clean air, unparalleled scenery, and a certain cosmopolitan, arty atmosphere tempered by the conservatism of an established ranching community. Generally these new residents are environmentally aware, yet by their very presence they demand services and housing, which translates into pressure to subdivide the ranches still remaining in private hands. South of Jackson open space is disappearing rapidly. In a sense it is unfortunate that Rockefeller did not undertake to purchase lands south as well as north of Jackson. However, in the 1920s the population was miniscule and the acquisition of southern Jackson Hole would have compounded an already complex and difficult preservation task. Even in 1950 the population of Teton County numbered only 2,593, most of whom were concentrated in the town of Jackson. However, times change, and it appears to some that in the future the park could share Jackson Hole with a small city of up to 40,000 residents. As one author lamented: "The nation loves Jackson Hole. And it is in danger of smothering the very object of its affection." [21] To forestall such a fate local citizens organized and drafted legislation in 1977 to create a Jackson Hole Scenic Area. The bill would provide the monies necessary to purchase development rights on private ranch lands. Although it passed the House, the bill was shelved in the Senate. In the meantime in spite of a local land use plan the subdivision continues and open space diminishes.[22]

As in the past, the conflicting claims of commercialism and conservation are often joined, resulting in spirited and often heated debate. Should the National Park Service consent to the expansion of Jackson airport to accommodate larger, commercial jet aircraft? Should the residents of Teton County accept and support a county land use plan that will limit development? Should residents support the efforts of the National Park Service to limit severely the building rights of landowners within the park? Should local land owners support federal efforts to create a national scenic area to protect ranches adjacent to the park from subdivision? [23] These questions indicate that conflicting values do exist and will continue to exist in Jackson Hole.

Meanwhile, within the park, the National Park Service staff wrestles with such problems as hunting within the park, snowmobile use, elimination of residential and concessioner facilities within the park, possible introduction of mass transportation, and the determination of a numerical limit on summer visitors. These problems are not unique to Grand Teton

National Park, but are representative of the problems many parks face throughout the nation. In recent years the parks have realized a popularity that Stephen Mather could not have envisioned in his wildest fantasies. Such popularity has created unprecedented problems. The most obvious solution would be a quota system, limiting the numbers of visitors allowed to enter the park, to float the river, and to hike in the wilderness. But this solution is difficult to square with the tradition of individualism and freedom dear to many westerners. In 1938 Holly Leek complained that visitors wouldn't be able to "holler" in Grand Teton National Park. In the future they may be prevented from even entering the park at their own leisure. However, the problem may resolve itself. National parks far removed from centers of population may experience less visitation. Gasoline price increases, shortages, or rationing could be significant. In 1979, a year of gasoline shortages, visitation to Wyoming's six National Park Service areas dropped 22.1 percent. Grand Teton National Park dropped from a 1978 figure of 4,159,490 visitors to 3,466,350 in 1979, a 17 percent loss.[24] No one can foretell the future, but it is possible that isolated parks such as Grand Teton may have to adjust to a population far less mobile than in the past.

Whatever the problems faced by park administrators, local elected officials, and the public, it can be assumed that they will be addressed in a more cooperative attitude than in the first half of the century. Most residents embrace the objective of resolving land use disputes equitably, yet ecologically. That is not to say that there is not debate, anger and hurt, but the majority of residents no longer can identify with the burning issues of earlier generations. Today many residents realize they live in a special place; a place that often demands that individual freedom be subservient to nature's limitations. They recognize they are but stewards for the preservation of nature in the national interest.

This national interest has dictated from 1915 to the present that Jackson Hole remain pristine, an unspoiled valley from which to view the Teton mountains. No end of bickering, argument and downright ruthlessness accompanied the carrying out of the national interest. But today few remember. When Grand Teton National Park celebrated its twenty-fifth anniversary in September, 1975, the Jackson Hole *News* nostalgically commemorated the past, and yet recognized that our collective memory is short, and generations pass, one then another:

They are old now, or dead, the actors in the park drama. Rockefeller, dead, Roosevelt, dead. Horace Albright, in his eighties. Harold Fabian, no longer active, his memory almost gone. Josephine Fabian, wispy and frail, her voice faded to a hushed whisper, but still fighting the good fight. For her, even a quarter, even a half a century later, the people, the memories are still alive. But for the three and a half million who view this land each year, there is nothing. No memories. They don't know this land was once a battleground.[25]

Perhaps they need not know. Perhaps it should be enough to know that so many Americans find spiritual and physical renewal in visiting such a place of natural beauty. Yet, it seems important that future generations know that the park commemorates not only the grandeur of nature but the spirit of man acting for a noble cause. It is a park not of chance, but of man's design.

NOTES

Abbreviations Used

GT	Grand Teton
NA	National Archives
NPS	National Park Service
RG	Record Group
SRLCo	Snake River Land Company
USFS	United States Forest Service
WHRC, UW	Western History Research Center, University of Wyoming
YNP	Yellowstone National Park

1 A Country for Controversy

1. Alexander Ross, *The Fur Hunters of the Far West*, ed. Kenneth A. Spaulding (Norman: University of Oklahoma Press, 1956, 1st Ed., 1855), p. 136.
2. See Gary A. Wright, "The Shoshoneans' Migration Problem," *Plains Anthropologist* 23 (May, 1978): 117–20.
3. Perhaps the best discussion of Colter's route regarding Jackson Hole is by David J. Saylor, *Jackson Hole, Wyoming* (Norman: University of Oklahoma Press, 1970), pp. 26–34, 216–17. For a geographically argued position that Colter never entered Jackson Hole, see Frank Calkins, *Jackson Hole* (New York: Alfred A. Knopf, 1973), pp. 39–53.
4. Fred Gowans, *Rocky Mountain Rendezvous: A History of the Fur Trade Rendezvous, 1825–1840* (Provo, Utah: Brigham Young University Press, 1976), pp. 97–258, *passim*: Merrill J. Mattes, "Jackson Hole, Crossroads of the Western Fur Trade, 1807–1829," *Pacific Northwest Quarterly* 37 (April, 1946): 87–108.
5. Saylor, *Jackson Hole*, pp. 54, 63.
6. Aubrey L. Haines, *The Yellowstone Story*, 2 vols (Boulder: Colorado Associated University Press, 1977), I: 64.

7. See William H. Goetzmann, *Exploration and Empire* (New York: Alfred A. Knopf, 1966).
8. Ibid., pp. 489–529.
9. Saylor, *Jackson Hole*, p. 107.
10. For a cynical account of Arthur's visit see Calkins, *Jackson Hole*, pp. 150–55.
11. Saylor, *Jackson Hole*, p. 118.
12. Margaret and Olaus Murie, *Wapiti Wilderness* (New York: Alfred A. Knopf, 1966), p. 113.
13. Olaus Murie, *The Elk of North America* (Harrisburg, Penn.: Wildlife Management Institute, 1951), pp. 19–20.
14. Calkins, *Jackson Hole*, p. 133.
15. Saylor, *Jackson Hole*, pp. 161–62.
16. William E. Smythe, *The Conquest of the Arid West* (Seattle: University of Washington Press, 1969 ed. first ed., 1899), p. 221.
17. T. A. Larson, *History of Wyoming* (Lincoln, Nebraska: University of Nebraska Press, 1965), pp. 355–57.
18. Later there was much criticism, but at the time there was little or no protest.
19. Benjamin Hibbard, *History of the Public Land Policies* (Madison, Wisconsin: University of Wisconsin Press, 1965 ed., first published in 1924), pp. 438–39.
20. Struthers Burt, *The Diary of a Dude-Wrangler* (New York: Charles Scribner's Sons, 1938), p. 118.
21. Saylor, *Jackson Hole*, p. 156.
22. Burt, *Diary of a Dude-Wrangler*, pp. 49, 57.
23. Ibid., pp. 49–51.

II Genesis of an Idea

1. Alfred Runte, *National Parks: The American Experience* (Lincoln, Nebraska: University of Nebraska Press, 1979), pp. 2–3.
2. George Catlin, *North American Indians: Being Letters and Notes on their Manners, Customs, and Conditions, Written during Eight Years' Travel amongst the Wildest Tribes in North America, 1832–1839*, 2 vols. (London, 1880). Selection in Roderick Nash, ed., *The American Environment: Readings in the History of Conservation* (Reading, Mass.: Addison-Wesley Publishing Co., 1968), p. 9.
3. Henry David Thoreau, "Chesuncook," *Atlantic Monthly* 2 (1859): 317.
4. Frederick Law Olmsted, "The Yosemite Valley and the Mariposa Big Trees," *Landscape Architect* 43 (1952). Selection in Nash, *The American Environment*, p. 23.
5. Marion Clawson, Burnell Held, *The Federal Lands: Their Use and Management* (Baltimore: The Johns Hopkins University Press, 1957), pp. 22–7.
6. Runte, *National Parks*, pp. 5–9.
7. Still the classic work on the arid West is Walter Prescott Webb's, *The Great Plains* (Boston: Ginn and Company, 1931).
8. Roderick Nash, "The American Invention of National Parks," *American Quarterly* 22 (1970): 726.

9. Runte, *National Parks*, pp. 11–47.
10. U.S., Congress, House, *Letter from the Secretary of the Interior*, House Doc. 500, 57th Cong., 1st sess.
11. Quoted from Richard A. Bartlett, *Nature's Yellowstone* (Albuquerque, New Mexico: University of New Mexico Press, 1974), pp. 195–6.
12. Carl P. Russell, *100 Years in Yosemite* (Berkeley: University of California Press, 1947), p. 148.
13. See Alfred Runte, "The National Park Idea: Origins and Paradox of the American Experience," *Journal of Forest History* 21 (April, 1977): 71–2.
14. Alfred Runte, "Worthless Lands–Our National Parks," *The American West* 10 (May, 1973): 4–11. See also Runte, *National Parks*, pp. 48–64.
15. John Ise, *Our National Park Policy: A Critical History* (Baltimore: Johns Hopkins University Press, 1961), pp. 20–29.
16. Linnie Marsh Wolfe, *Son of the Wilderness: The Life of John Muir* (New York: Alfred A. Knopf, Inc., 1945), p. 157.
17. See Stewart Udall, *The Quiet Crisis* (New York: Avon Books, 1963).
18. See Samuel P. Hays, *Conservation As Efficiency* (Cambridge, Massachusetts: Harvard University Press, 1959).
19. See J. Leonard Bates, "Fulfilling American Democracy: The Conservation Movement, 1907–1921," *Mississippi Valley Historical Review* 44 (June, 1957): 29–57.
20. Marion Clawson, Burnell Held, *The Federal Lands*, pp. 16–17.
21. See particularly Turner's essays, "The Significance of the Frontier in American History," and "Contributions of the West to American Democracy," in George Rogers Taylor, ed., *The Turner Thesis Concerning the Role of the Frontier in American History* (Lexington, Mass.: D. C. Heath and Co., 1972, 3rd. Ed.)
22. For a full discussion of this idea see Roderick Nash, *Wilderness and the American Mind* (New Haven, Connecticut: Yale University Press, 1967), pp. 141–60.
23. Gifford Pinchot, *The Fight for Conservation* (New York: Harcourt, Brace, 1910), pp. 42–3.
24. See Holway R. Jones, *John Muir and the Sierra Club: The Battle for Yosemite* (San Francisco: Sierra Club, 1965). Also Nash, *Wilderness*, pp. 161–81.
25. Struthers Burt, *The Delectable Mountains* (New York: Charles Scribner's Sons, 1927), pp. 198–9.
26. Harold Steen, *The U.S. Forest Service: A History* (Seattle: University of Washington Press, 1976), pp. 26–7.
27. Leo H. Dieterich, et al., *Jackson Hole National Monument, Wyoming: A Compendium of Important Papers Covering Negotiation in the Establishment and Administration of the National Monument* (4 Vols., Washington: Department of the Interior, ca. 1945, 1950) I: 1. Copy in WHRC, UW.
28. See Harold Pinkett, *Gifford Pinchot: Forester* (Urbana, Illinois: University of Illinois Press, 1974).
29. Dieterich, et al., *Compendium*, I: 1.

III   Another Way—Enter the National Park Service

1. Aubrey L. Haines, *The Yellowstone Story*, 2 vols. (Boulder, Colorado: Colorado Associated University Press, 1977) I: 267–8.

2. David J. Saylor, *Jackson Hole, Wyoming* (Norman: University of Oklahoma Press, 1970), p. 159.

3. U.S., Congress, Senate, *Letter from the Secretary of the Interior*, Sen. Doc. 39, 55th Cong., 3rd sess., pp. 5–6.

4. Ibid.

5. U.S., Congress, House, *Letter from the Secretary of the Interior*, House Doc. 500, 57th Cong., 1st sess.

6. See John Ise, *Our National Park Policy: A Critical History* (Baltimore: Johns Hopkins University Press, 1961); Robert Shankland, *Steve Mather of the National Parks* (New York: Alfred A. Knopf, 1954); Donald Swain, *Wilderness Defender: Horace M. Albright and Conservation* (Chicago: University of Chicago Press, 1970); and William C. Everhart, *The National Park Service* (New York: Praeger Publishers, 1972).

7. Swain, *Wilderness Defender*, p. 38.

8. See Duane Hampton, *How the Calvary Saved Our National Parks* (Bloomington: University of Indiana Press, 1971).

9. Everhart, *The National Park Service*, pp. 15, 21.

10. Swain, *Wilderness Defender*, pp. 34–7.

11. Ibid., pp. 48–53; Shankland, *Steve Mather*, pp. 68–74.

12. "Interview with Mr. Horace Albright by Assistant Superintendent of Grand Teton National Park Haraden and Chief Naturalist Dilley at Jackson Lake Lodge, September 12, 1967," p. 7. Typescript in the Horace Albright Collection, WHRC, UW.

13. Horace M. Albright to Wilford Neilson, April 5, 1933, in *Mr. John D. Rockefeller, Jr.'s Proposed Gift of Land for the National Park System in Wyoming* (n.p., n.d.), p. 4. This booklet was published in 1933 to present the Snake River Land Company position regarding their land purchases.

14. "Interview with Mr. Horace Albright . . . ," p. 9.

15. Horace Albright to J. A. Breckons, Sec. to Senator Warren, October 6, 1917 in File 602, pt. 2, Box 460, YNP, NPS, RG 79, NA.

16. Leo H. Dieterich, et al., *Jackson Hole National Monument, Wyoming: A Compendium of Important Papers Covering Negotiation in the Establishment and Administration of the National Monument* (4 Vols., Washington: Department of the Interior, ca. 1945, 1950), II: 1, Exhibit 1.

17. H. S. Graves to Stephen Mather, October 26, 1918, File 602, pt. 3, Box 460, YNP, NPS, RG 79, NA.

18. Dieterich, *Compendium*, II: 1, Exhibit 5.

19. George Goodwin, NPS, to Horace Albright, October 26, 1918, File 602, pt. 4, Box 460, YNP, NPS, RG 79, NA.

20. H. S. Graves to Frank Mondell, May 13, 1919, File 602, pt. 5, Box 460, YNP, NPS, RG 79, NA.

21. See Horace Albright to Stephen Mather, October 21, 1919, ibid.

22. F. J. Hagenharth to Stephen Mather, May 13, 1919, File 602, pt. 4, Box 460, YNP, NPS, RG 79, NA.

23. *Jackson Hole Courier*, September 22, 1919.

24. Horace M. Albright to Wilford Neilson, April 5, 1933, in *Mr. John D. Rockefeller, Jr.'s Proposed Gift*, p. 9.

25. "Interview with Mr. Horace Albright . . . ," pp. 17–18.

26. Swain, *Wilderness Defender*, pp. 110–77.

27. Horace M. Albright to Wilford Neilson, April 5, 1933, in *Mr. John D. Rockefeller, Jr.'s Proposed Gift*, pp. 10–11.

28. Horace Albright to author, July 16, 1979.

29. H. Cantwell Wallace, Secretary of Agriculture to Secretary of the Interior, March 9, 1923 in "Forest Service Comments," Box 290, GT, NPS, RG 79, NA.

30. L. F. Kneipp, Acting Forester, to Stephen Mather, August 17, 1922; Horace Albright to Arno Cammerer, September 2, 1922; Arno Cammerer to William Greeley, Chief Forester, September 30, 1922, File 602, pt. 7, Box 461, YNP, NPS, RG 79, NA.

31. "Report on Wyoming Segregation List No. 97 under the Carey Act: Jackson Hole Irrigation Company," submitted by C. D. Avery, Carey Act Inspector, General Land Office, undated, but written in late 1919, in File 112.1, Box 465, YNP, NPS, RG 79, NA.

32. For detailed correspondence on the subject see File 112.1, ibid.

33. Frank Emerson to Horace Albright, October 17, 1921; Albright to Emerson, October 20, 1921, ibid.

34. R. H. Rutledge, District Forester, to Horace Albright, October 21, 1921, ibid.

35. Struthers Burt to Frank Mondell, September 25, 1922, File 602.1, Box 461, YNP, NPS, RG 79, NA.

36. Struthers Burt, "The Jackson Hole Plan," *Outdoor America* (November–December, 1944). Reprint in Dieterich, *Compendium*, II: 2, Exhibit 31.

37. "Interview with Mr. Horace Albright . . . ," pp. 2–5, 31–2; Horace Albright to Wilford Neilson, April 5, 1933, in *Mr. John D. Rockefeller, Jr.'s Proposed Gift*, pp. 15–17.

38. Horace Albright to Dr. W. T. Hornaday, Director of the New York Zoological Park, November 28, 1923, in "Albright—Jackson Hole Correspondence, 1923–1927," National Park Service section, Yellowstone Archives, YNP.

39. Horace Albright to Struthers Burt, November 21, 1923, in ibid.

40. Horace Albright to Wilford Neilson, April 5, 1933 in *Mr. John D. Rockefeller, Jr.'s Proposed Gift*, p. 17.

41. Dieterich, *Compendium*, I: 6.

42. Horace Albright to Wilford Neilson, April 5, 1933, in *Mr. John D. Rockefeller, Jr's Proposed Gift*, pp. 18–19.

43. "Plan for Administering Those Portions of Teton and Targhee National Forests Included in Executive Order of January 28, 1921, in the Event the Temporary Withdrawal is Released," 45-page typescript in "History of Teton Forest" folder, Box II, Teton National Forest Collection, WHRC, UW. Also see "Memorandum on Lands for Timber Surveys," in "Timber Surveys, 1908–1950" folder, Box 32165, USFS, RG 95, Federal Record Center and Archives, Denver.

44. William B. Greeley to Stephen Mather, December 11, 1924, and "Memorandum to Members of the Coordinating Commission on National Parks

and Forests," by L. F. Kneipp, Acting Forester, 1925, both in "Forest Service Comments" folder, Box 290, GT, NPS, RG 79, NA.

45. Michael Frome, *Battle for the Wilderness* (New York: Praeger Publishers, 1974), pp. 117–19; Harold K. Steen, *The U.S. Forest Service: A History* (Seattle: University of Washington Press, 1976), pp. 153–9.

46. Robert Marshall, *Alaska Wilderness*, edited and with an introduction by George Marshall (Berkeley; University of California Press, 1970 ed.), pp. 24–5.

47. Stephen Mather to William Greeley, January 19, 1925, "Forest Service Comments" folder, Box 290, GT, NPS, RG 79, NA.

48. "Report of the Coordinating Committee on National Parks and Forests," October 25, 1925, in U.S., Congress, Senate, *Hearings before the Committee on Public Lands and Surveys on S. 2570, S. 2571, and S. 3071,* 70th Cong., 1st sess., pp. 6–8.

49. Quoted in T. A. Larson, *History of Wyoming* (Lincoln: University of Nebraska Press, 1965), p. 449.

50. U.S., Congress, Senate, *Hearings before the Committee on Public Lands and Surveys on S. 3176, S. 3427, S. 3428, S. 3433, S. 4073, S. 4209, S. 4258, and H. R. 9387,* 69th Cong., 1st sess., pp. 26–9.

51. Senator Peter Norbeck to the National Park Service, April 25, 1927, in Dieterich, *Compendium*, I: 8.

52. U.S., Congress, Senate, *Hearings before the Committee on Public Lands and Surveys on S. 2570, S. 2571, and S. 3071,* 70th Cong., 1st sess., p. 13.

53. Ibid., p. 16.

54. U.S., Congress, Senate, *Hearings before the Committee on Public Lands and Surveys pursuant to S. 237,* 70th Cong., 2nd sess, Part 2, p. 21.

55. Ibid., pp. 22–3.

56. See U.S., Congress, Senate, *Hearings before a Subcommittee of the Committee on Public Lands and Surveys ... pursuant to S. Res. 250,* 75th Cong., 3rd sess., p. 242; also Horace Albright to Wilford Neilson, April 5, 1933, in *Mr. John D. Rockefeller, Jr.'s Proposed Gift,* p. 32.

57. Dieterich, *Compendium,* I: 9.

58. Ise, *Our National Park Policy,* p. 329.

IV Philanthrophy and Property

1. Aldo Leopold, *A Sand County Almanac* (New York: Sierra Club/Ballantine Book, 1970 ed.), p. 239. For an argument that natural objects have legal "standing," see Christopher Stone, *Should Trees Have Standing?* (New York: Discus Books, 1974).

2. Joe Frantz, *Aspects of the American West* (College Station, Texas: Texas A & M University Press, 1976), p. 69.

3. Horace Albright to Wilford Neilson, April 5, 1933, in *Mr. John D. Rockefeller, Jr.'s Proposed Gift of Land for the National Park System in Wyoming* (n. p., n.d.), p. 2.

4. Horace Albright to Rose Phelps, undated, File 602.1, Box 461, YNP, NPS, RG 79, NA.

5. Donald Swain, *Wilderness Defender: Horace M. Albright and Conservation* (Chicago: University of Chicago Press, 1970), p. 154.

6. Raymond B. Fosdick, *John D. Rockefeller, Jr.: A Portrait* (New York: Harper & Brothers, 1956), pp. 36–7.

7. John D. Rockefeller, Jr., to Horace Albright, August 15, 1924, in "Yellowstone National Park Contributions," Box 98, Cultural Interests, RG 2, Private Archives of Messrs. Rockefeller, New York.

8. Fosdick, *Rockefeller*, p. 309.

9. Horace Albright to Wilford Neilson, April 5, 1933, in *Mr. John D. Rockefeller, Jr.'s Proposed Gift*, p. 24.

10. Struthers Burt, "The Battle of Jackson's Hole," *The Nation* 122 (March 3, 1926): 225–7.

11. Nathaniel Burt, "Jackson Hole Journal," pp. 163–4, quoted in John Daugherty, "Struthers Burt: Dude Rancher, Author, and Conservationist, Jackson Hole, Wyoming." (Denver: Regional Historic Preservation Team, National Park Service, 1979), p. 24.

12. Kenneth Chorley to Struthers Burt, March 17, 1926, copy in "Albright–Jackson Hole Correspondence, 1923–1927," National Park Service section, Yellowstone Archives, YNP.

13. Horace M. Albright to Struthers Burt, October 19, 1926, in ibid.

14. Horace M. Albright to Wilford Neilson, April 5, 1933, in *Mr. John D. Rockefeller, Jr.'s Proposed Gift*, p. 25.

15. "Interview with Mr. Horace Albright," by Assistant Superintendent of Grand Teton National Park Haraden and Chief Naturalist Dilley at Jackson Lake Lodge, September 12, 1967," p. 41.

16. William A. Welsh to Horace M. Albright, February 23, 1927, in "Albright—Jackson Hole Correspondence, 1923–1927," National Park Service section, Yellowstone Archives, YNP.

17. "Interview with Mr. Horace Albright," p. 42.

18. John D. Rockefeller, Jr., to Arthur Woods, February 28, 1927, in "Jackson Hole Property," Box 98, Cultural Interests, RG 2, Private Archives of Messrs. Rockefeller, New York.

19. Fosdick, *Rockefeller*, p. 309.

20. See ibid., pp. 272–301.

21. Horace M. Albright to John D. Rockefeller, Jr., February 16, 1927, in U.S., Congress, House, *Hearings Before the Committee on the Public Lands . . . on H.R. 2241*, 78th Cong., 1st. sess., p. 163: Struthers Burt to Horace M. Albright, February 10, 1927, in "Albright—Jackson Hole Correspondence, 1923–1927," National Park Service section, Yellowstone Archives, YNP.

22. Arthur Woods to John D. Rockefeller, Jr., March 29, 1927, in "Jackson Hole Property," Box 98, Cultural Interests, RG 2, Private Archives of Messrs. Rockefeller, New York.

23. "Interview with Kenneth Chorley," by Ed Edwin, April 13, 1966, pp. 10–11, Oral History Collection of Columbia University, New York. Copy furnished the author by the Jackson Hole Preserve, Incorporated, is deposited in the WHRC, UW.

24. For a brief biographical sketch of Harold Fabian, see the pamphlet en-

titled, "Harold Pegram Fabian" deposited in the library, Grand Teton National Park, Moose, Wyoming.

25. Arthur Woods to John D. Rockefeller, Jr., March 29, 1927, in "Jackson Hole Property," Box 98, Cultural Interests, RG 2, Private Archives of Messrs. Rockefeller, New York.

26. U.S., Congress, Senate, *Hearings Before a Subcommittee of the Committee on Public Lands and Surveys . . . Pursuant to S. Res. 226*, 72nd Cong., 2nd sess., p. 36.

27. "Jackson Hole Agreement," dated June 15, 1927, in "Jackson Hole Property," Box 98, Cultural Interests, RG 2, Private Archives of Messrs. Rockefeller, New York.

28. Ibid.

29. Harold P. Fabian to Wilford Neilson, April 6, 1933, in *Mr. John D. Rockefeller, Jr.'s Proposed Gift*, pp. 46–7.

30. Ibid., pp. 47–51.

31. Ibid., p. 48.

32. Robert Miller to Harold Fabian, October 26, 1927, in ibid., p. 50.

33. "Snake River Land Company Chronology of Events, March 10, 1927 to December 30, 1932," p. 9, typescript in Box 293, GT, NPS, RG 79, NA. This manuscript was prepared by Harold Fabian's office in preparation for the 1933 Senate Subcommittee hearings in Jackson. From this chronology Fabian wrote his letter to Wilford Neilson, published in *Mr. John D. Rockefeller, Jr.'s Proposed Gift*. . . . The manuscript, hereafter referred to as "SRLCo, Chronology of Events," is important for its detail and frank assessment of people and events.

34. *Jackson Hole Courier*, August 25, 1927. The September 15, 1927 *Courier* also mentioned "Mr. Chorley" in an editorial.

35. Ibid.

36. "SRLCo. Chronology of Events," p. 23.

37. Harold P. Fabian to Wilford Neilson, April 6, 1933, in *Mr. John D. Rockefeller, Jr.'s Proposed Gift*, pp. 51–2.

38. "Jackson Hole Agreement," amended December 5, 1927, in Box 98, Cultural Interests, RG 2, Private Archives of Messrs. Rockefeller, New York.

39. "Interview with W. C. Lawrence," by Ed Edwin, July 12, 1966, p. 6, in Oral History Collection of Columbia University, New York.

40. T. A. Larson, *History of Wyoming* (Lincoln, Nebraska: University of Nebraska Press, 1965), pp. 412–18, *passim*.

41. "1945 Transfer to Jackson Hole Preserve, Inc.," in Box 101, Cultural Interests, RG 2, Private Archives of Messrs. Rockefeller, New York. This 1945 document gave a detailed description of such purchases as Ben Sheffield's land and structures at Moran.

42. J. H. Rayburn to Wilford W. Neilson, April 21, 1933, in *Mr. John D. Rockefeller, Jr.'s Proposed Gift*, pp. 82–4.

43. Ibid., p. 85.

44. Verne E. Chatelain, "A Memorandum Dealing with the Question of the Jackson Hole Region in Wyoming in its Relationship to the National Park Service," typescript prepared by the National Park Service, 1933, pp. 39–40. Copy in WHRC, UW.

45. J. H. Rayburn to Wilford W. Neilson, April 21, 1933, in *Mr. John D. Rockefeller, Jr.'s Proposed Gift*, p. 87.
46. Ibid., p. 88.
47. Vanderbilt Webb to Robert Miller, February 21, 1928, in U.S., Congress, Senate, *Hearings Before a Subcommittee of the Committee on Public Lands and Surveys . . . Pursuant to S. Res. 226*, 72nd Cong., 2nd sess., pp. 39–40.
48. "SRLCo. Chronology of Events," p. 30.
49. Ibid., p. 35.
50. Ibid., p. 40.
51. Struthers Burt to Kenneth Chorley, April 12, 1928, in "SRLCo. Corres., 1928," Box 293, GT, NPS, RG 79, NA.
52. Kenneth Chorley to Struthers Burt, April 26, 1928, in ibid.
53. Horace Albright to Struthers Burt, March 7, 1928, in ibid.
54. Horace Albright to Kenneth Chorley, June 22, 1929, in "SRLCo. Corres., 1929," Box 293, GT, NPS, RG 79, NA.
55. Harold Fabian to Horace Albright, July 2, 1929; Kenneth Chorley to Horace Albright, July 2, 1929, in ibid.
56. Ibid.
57. Harold Fabian to Vanderbilt Webb, August 6, 1929, in ibid.
58. Ibid.
59. Arno Cammerer to Kenneth Chorley, January 16, 1929, in ibid.
60. "Interview with Conrad L. Wirth," by Ed Edwin, June 21, 1966, pp. 5–7, in Oral History Collection of Columbia University, New York.
61. Harold Fabian to Kenneth Chorley, August 10, 1929, in "SRLCo. Corres., 1929," Box 293, GT, NPS, RG 79, NA.
62. "Interview with Homer C. Richards," by Ed Edwin, July 19, 1966, pp. 1–10, in Oral History Collection of Columbia University, New York.
63. Kenneth Chorley to Arno Cammerer, December 8, 1928; Arno Cammerer to Kenneth Chorley, December 11, 1928, in "SRLCo. Corres., 1928," Box 293, GT, NPS, RG 79, NA.
64. For a strongly-worded argument on this issue see *The Grand Teton*, January 5, 1932.
65. Harold Fabian to Wilford Neilson, April 6, 1933, in *Mr. John D. Rockefeller, Jr.'s Proposed Gift*, pp. 57–8.
66. Frank Emerson to Vanderbilt Webb, September 29, 1930, in "SRLCo. Chronology of Events," p. 63.
67. Horace Albright to Kenneth Chorley, June 18, 1929, in "SRLCo. Corres., 1929," Box 293, GT, NPS, RG 79, NA.
68. Harold Fabian to Vanderbilt Webb, January 21, 1930, in "SRLCo. Corres., 1930," Box 294, GT, NPS, RG 79, NA.
69. W. H. Gray to Ray Lyman Wilbur, January 27, 1930, in ibid.
70. "SRLCo. Chronology of Events," p. 50.

V *The Brew Boils*

1. The term "expectant capitalist" is meant to define that person who is intent on acquiring material wealth. In *The American Political Tradition* (New York: Vintage Books, 1948), p. 57, Richard Hofstadter characterizes

this American as "a hardworking, ambitious person for whom enterprise was a kind of religion."

2. *Jackson Hole Courier*, June 5, 1930.

3. Struthers Burt, "The Battle of Jackson Hole," *The Nation* 122 (March 3, 1926): 225–7. Frederick Law Olmsted's defense of a primitive Yosemite Valley may be found in a report to the state of California (1865), excerpts of which have been reprinted in Roderick Nash, ed., *The American Environment: Readings in the History of Conservation* (Reading, Mass.: Addison Wesley Pub. Co., 1968), pp. 18–24.

4. U.S., Congress, Senate, *Hearings Before a Subcommittee of the Committee on Public Lands and Surveys . . . Pursuant to S. Res. 226*, 73rd Cong., 2nd sess., pp. 412–3.

5. *The Grand Teton*, June 28, 1932.

6. In *Mr. John D. Rockefeller, Jr.'s Proposed Gift of Land for the National Park System in Wyoming*, (n. p., n. d.), pp. 36–7, 61–3.

7. Ibid., p. 37.

8. *Hearings . . . Pursuant to S. Res. 226*, pp. 206–7.

9. *Jackson Hole Courier*, April 30, 1931.

10. Ibid., May 7, 1931.

11. See *Hearings . . . Pursuant to S. Res. 226*, pp. 470–2.

12. See Jeanne Robertson Vap, "The Grand Teton: Frontier Newspaper in the Twentieth Century," *Annals of Wyoming* 42 (October, 1970): 149–82. This article should be read with discretion, for it contains many errors of fact and interpretation.

13. *The Grand Teton*, May 24, 1932.

14. Ibid., June 21, 1932.

15. Ibid., February 2, 1932.

16. Ibid., December 13, 1932.

17. Sam T. Woodring to Horace Albright, February 7, 1933, File 601-01, pt. 24, Box 1056, GT, NPS, RG 79, NA.

18. Horace Albright to Sam Woodring, February 16, 1933, in ibid.

19. Dick Winger to Harold Fabian, December 27, 1931, "Grand Teton" file, Box 289, GT, NPS, RG 79, NA.

20. See Lewis Gould, *Wyoming: A Political History, 1868–1896* (New Haven, Conn.: Yale University Press, 1970), pp. 251–2.

21. Harold Fabian to Vanderbilt Webb, September 29, 1930, in "SRLCo. Chron. of Events," p. 63.

22. Harold Fabian's notes, in ibid., p. 70.

23. Ibid., p. 99.

24. Ibid., p. 100.

25. Ibid., pp. 101–9; also Harold Fabian to Wilford Neilson, April 6, 1933, in *Mr. John D. Rockefeller, Jr.'s Gift*, p. 77, and the *Rocky Mountain News*, September 11, 1931.

26. Harold Fabian to Vanderbilt Webb, January 27, 1930, Harold Fabian to Vanderbilt Webb, April 16, 1930, in "SRLCo. Chron. of Events," pp. 47, 52.

27. Harold Fabian to Horace Albright, January 3, 1932, in ibid., p. 117.

28. John D. Rockefeller, Jr., to Horace Albright, October 24, 1931, in ibid., p. 113.

29. *Jackson Hole Courier*, December 29, 1932.
30. Robert Carey to Horace Albright, September 5, 1932, in "SRLCo. Chron. of Events," pp. 121–2.
31. Harold Fabian to Vanderbilt Webb, January 27, 1933, File 601–01, pt. 24, Box 1056, GT, NPS, RG 79, NA.
32. John Kendrick, Robert Carey, Vincent Carter to Hon. Ray Lyman Wilbur, December 12, 1932, in "SRLCo. Correspondence, 1932," Box 296, GT, NPS, RG 79, NA: Arthur Woods to Ray Lyman Wilbur, December 23, 1932, in "Hearings, 1933, 1938," Box 98, Cultural Interests, RG 2, Private Archives of Messrs. Rockefeller.
33. Arthur Woods to Robert Carey, December 23, 1932; Robert Carey to Arthur Woods, December 27, 1932; Arthur Woods to Robert Carey, December 29, 1932; Robert Carey to Arthur Woods, December 31, 1932, in File 610-01, pt. 24, Box 1056, GT, NPS, RG 79, NA: Copies also in "Hearings 1933, 1938," Box 98, Cultural Interests, RG 2, Private Archives of Messrs. Rockefeller.
34. "Interview with Kenneth Chorley," by Ed Edwin, April 13, 1966, p. 39, Oral History Collection of Columbia University.
35. Confidential memo from Horace Albright to Harold Fabian, Kenneth Chorley, and Vanderbilt Webb, February 4, 1933, File 601-01, pt. 24, Box 1056, GT, NPS, RG 79, NA.
36. Struthers Burt to Horace Albright, February 7, 1933, ibid.
37. "Interview with Leslie Miller," by Ed Edwin, April 26, 1966, p. 8, Oral History Collection of Columbia University.
38. Harold Fabian to Vanderbilt Webb, February 23, 1933, File 601-01, pt. 24, 1056, GT, NPS, RG 79, NA.
39. Horace Albright to Harold Fabian, January 17, 1933, ibid.
40. "SRLCo., Chron. of Events," March 10, 1927, to December 30, 1932, 135-page typescript in Box 293, GT, NPS, RG 79, NA.
41. Memo from John D. Rockefeller, Jr., undated, "Jackson Hole Property," Box 98, Cultural Interests, RG 2, Private Archives of Messrs. Rockefeller.
42. Verne Chatelain, "A Memorandum Dealing with the Question of the Jackson Hole Region in Wyoming in its Relationship to the National Park Service," 101-page typescript. Copy in the WHRC, UW.
43. Kenneth Chorley to Harold Fabian, Horace Albright and Vanderbilt Webb, July 27, 1933, File 610-01, pt. 24, Box 1056, GT, NPS, RG 79, NA.
44. Charles C. Moore to Horace Albright, September 24, 1931, "Miscellaneous" folder, Box 285, GT, NPS, RG 79, NA.
45. Horace Albright to Kenneth Chorley, February 25, 1933; Horace Albright to L. H. Larom, March 13, 1933, File 610-01, pt. 24, GT, NPS, RG 79, NA.
46. Marie H. Erwin, ed., *Wyoming Historical Blue Book* (Denver: Bradford-Robinson Printing Company, 1946), p. 1313.
47. *The Grand Teton*, June 27, 1933.
48. See Donald Swain, *Wilderness Defender: Horace M. Albright and Conservation* (Chicago: University of Chicago Press, 1970), pp. 71–2, 103–4.
49. Interview with Horace Albright by author, September 9, 1976.
50. Swain, *Wilderness Defender*, p. 214.
51. Horace Albright to Arthur Woods, January 13, 1933, in "Hearings, 1933,

1938," Box 98, Cultural Interests, RG 2, Private Archives of Messrs. Rockefeller.
52. Swain, *Wilderness Defender*, p. 214.
53. Hofstadter, *The American Political Tradition*, p. 99.
54. Horace Albright to F. S. Burrage, July 26, 1933, File 610-01, pt. 28, Box 1057, GT, NPS, RG 79, NA.
55. *Denver Post*, July 14, 1933.
56. *New York Herald Tribune*, July 17, 1933.
57. Peter Norbeck to Horace Albright, undated, File 610-01, pt. 28, Box 1057, GT, NPS, RG 79, NA.
58. "Interview with Harold Fabian," by Ed Edwin, July 11, 1966, p. 49, Oral History Collection of Columbia University.
59. Ibid., pp. 49–50.
60. *The Rocky Mountain News,* August 7, 1933.
61. *Hearings . . . Pursuant to S. Res. 226*, pp. 2–3.
62. Ibid., pp. 4–7.
63. Ibid., p. 304, also pp. 308–9, 4–5.
64. Ibid., pp. 221–231.
65. Ibid., pp. 300–330.
66. Ibid., pp. 151–182, 343–360.
67. As quoted in "Interview with Harold Fabian," by Ed Edwin, July 11, 1966, pp. 51–2, Oral History Collection of Columbia University.
68. *The Rocky Mountain News,* August 12, 1933.
69. Gerald Nye to Horace Albright, August 19, 1933, "Hearings, 1933, 1938," Box 98, Cultural Interests, RG 2, Private Archives of Messrs. Rockefeller.

VI   A Decade Without a Solution

1. Memo by Kenneth Chorley for the files, October 5, 1933, "Jackson Hole Property," Box 98, Cultural Interests, RG 2, Private Archives of Messrs. Rockefeller.
2. *Jackson Hole Courier*, May 24, 1934.
3. Arno Cammerer to Gerald Nye, April 12, 1934; J. N. Darling to Arno Cammerer, May 14, 1934; Ferdinand Silcox to Arno Cammerer, April 25, 1934, File 610-01, pt. 30, Box 1056, GT, NPS, RG 79, NA.
4. Harold Steen, *The U.S. Forest Service: A History* (Seattle: University of Washington Press, 1976), pp. 198–9.
5. Hillory Tolson to Horace Albright, June 2, 1934, File 610-01, pt. 30, Box 1057, GT, NPS, RG 79, NA.
6. Leo H. Dieterich, et. al., *Jackson Hole National Monument, Wyoming: A Compendium of Important Papers Covering Negotiations in the Establishment and Administration of the National Monument* (4 Vols., Washington: Department of the Interior, ca. 1945, 1950), II: 1, Exhibit 8.
7. *Jackson Hole Courier*, May 31, 1934.
8. Dieterich, *Compendium*, I: 11.
9. Lewis W. Douglas, Esq., Director, Bureau of the Budget, to Vanderbilt Webb, June 26, 1934, Series 21.1, Box P-4, Bureau of the Budget, RG 51, NA.
10. Ibid.

11. Memo to Senator Robert Carey from Vanderbilt Webb, May 23, 1935, File 601-01, pt. 33, Box 1058, GT, NPS, RG 79, NA.
12. Henry A. Wallace to D. W. Bell, Director, Bureau of the Budget, Series 21.1, Box P-4, Bureau of the Budget, RG 51, NA.
13. John Ise, *Our National Park Policy: A Critical History* (Baltimore: Johns Hopkins Press, 1961), pp. 296–7.
14. *National Parks Bulletin*, 68 (July, 1940): 5.
15. William P. Wharton, President of the NPA, to Arno Cammerer, June 15, 1935, File 602.1, Box 1055, GT, NPS, RG 79, NA.
16. "Memorandum for the Press on the Clean-up of Jackson Lake," dated October 24, 1934, File 501-23, Box 1052, GT, NPS, RG 79, NA.
17. Ibid.
18. Henry B. Ward to Arno Cammerer, May 22, 1935, File 602-1, Box 1055, GT, NPS, RG 79, NA.
19. Arno Cammerer to Henry B. Ward, June 4, 1935, ibid.
20. Ibid.
21. Arno Cammerer to William Wharton, June 22, 1935, ibid.
22. Arno Cammerer to Henry B. Ward, June 4, 1935, ibid.
23. Henry Ward to Harold Ickes, June 12, 1935; Henry Ward to Arno Cammerer, June 12, 1935; William Wharton to Harold Ickes, June 24, 1935, File 610-01, pt. 33, Box 1058, GT, NPS, RG 79, NA.
24. Ise, *Our National Park Policy*, pp. 352–3, 437–9.
25. Kenneth Chorley to Leslie Miller, November 10, 1937; Leslie Miller to Kenneth Chorley, November 13, 1937, File 610-01, pt. 34, Box 1058, GT, NPS, RG 79, NA.
26. Memorandum from Harold Ickes to Arno Cammerer, July 26, 1937, ibid.
27. Dieterich, *Compendium*, II: 1, Exhibit 11.
28. *Jackson Hole Courier*, December 2, 1937.
29. See *Jackson Hole Courier* issues of December 2, 9, 16, 23, and 30, 1937, January 8, 30, February 3, 10, 1938.
30. Leslie Miller to Senator Joseph O'Mahoney, Senator Harry Schwartz, Representative Paul Greever, January 12, 1938, "Teton Park Correspondence," Box 36, Joseph O'Mahoney Collection, WHRC, UW.
31. "Interview with Harold Fabian," by Ed Edwin, July 11, 1966, p. 45, Oral History Collection of Columbia University.
32. Steen, *The U.S. Forest Service*, pp. 239–40; Ise, *Our National Park Policy*, pp. 439–40.
33. Theodore Huntley, "Mr. Rockefeller Strikes a Snag," *The Senator* 1 (May 6, 1939): 12–14.
34. See Joe Frantz, "The American West: Child of Federal Subsidy," in *Aspects of the American West: Three Essays*, by Joe Frantz (College Station, Texas: Texas A & M Press, 1976), pp. 70–82.
35. Huntley, "Mr. Rockefeller Strikes a Snag," pp. 12–14.
36. Arno Cammerer to Joseph O'Mahoney, June 14, 1938; Joseph O'Mahoney to Arno Cammerer, July 11, 1938, "Teton Park Correspondence," Box 36, Joseph O'Mahoney Collection, WHRC, UW.
37. U.S., Congress, Senate, *Hearings Before a Subcommittee of the Committee on Public Lands and Surveys . . . Pursuant to S. Res. 250*, 75th Congress, 3rd sess., p. 221.

38. *Jackson Hole Courier*, August 11, 1938.

39. U.S., Congress, Senate, *Hearings Before a Subcommittee of the Committee on Public Lands and Surveys . . . Pursuant to S. Res. 226*, 73rd Cong., 2nd sess.

40. *Hearings . . . Pursuant to S. Res. 250*, pp. 215–6.

41. Margaret and Olaus Murie, *Wapiti Wilderness* (New York: Alfred A. Knopf, 1966), p. 121.

42. "Jackson Hole Property," Box 98, Cultural Interests, RG 2, Private Archives of Messrs. Rockefeller.

43. Memo from Vanderbilt Webb to Thomas V. Debevoise, June 4, 1936, "Jackson Hole Property," Box 98, Cultural Interests, RG 2, Private Archives of Messrs. Rockefeller.

44. Josephine C. Fabian, "Preliminary Draft of a Story About the History of the J.Y. Ranch," dated August 15, 1975, pp. 1–4. Typescript loaned to the author.

45. "Interview with Kenneth Chorley."

46. John D. Rockefeller, Jr., to Arno Cammerer, August 31, 1937, File 610-01, pt. 34, Box 1058, GT, NPS, RG 79, NA.

47. Kenneth Chorley to Arno Cammerer, October 28, 1937, ibid.

48. Ibid.

49. Arno Cammerer to Kenneth Chorley, November 18, 1937, ibid.

50. Horace M. Albright to author, July 16, 1979.

51. John D. Rockefeller, Jr., to Kenneth Chorley, October 24, 1939, "Jackson Hole Property," Box 98, Cultural Interests, RG 2, Private Archives of Messrs. Rockefeller.

52. "Interview with Kenneth Chorley," pp. 109–11.

53. Sherman Swenson, National Park Service to author, July 13, 1978; Horace M. Albright to author, July 16, 1979; telephone interview by author with George Lamb, Jackson Hole Preserve, Inc., July 16, 1979.

VII   The Hectic Life of a National Monument

1. Harold Wood, "Protecting Nature's Monuments," *Sierra Club Bulletin*, 59 (March, 1974): 4–7.

2. John Ise, *Our National Park Policy: A Critical History* (Baltimore: Johns Hopkins University Press, 1961), p. 154.

3. Ibid., p. 155.

4. For a thorough discussion of the Antiquities Act of 1906, see ibid., pp. 143–62.

5. William C. Everhart, *The National Park Service* (New York: Praeger Publishers, 1972), p. 13.

6. Ise, *Our National Park Policy*, pp. 233, 241–2, 289.

7. John D. Rockefeller, Jr., to Harold Ickes, November 27, 1942, in Leo H. Dieterich, et al., *Jackson Hole National Monument, Wyoming: A Compendium of Important Papers Covering Negotiations in the Establishment and Administration of the National Monument* (4 Vols., Washington: Department of the Interior, ca. 1945, 1950), II: 2, Exhibit 13.

8. Ise, *Our National Park Policy*, p. 298; Donald Swain, *Wilderness Defender: Horace M. Albright and Conservation* (Chicago: University of

Chicago Press, 1970), p. 262; David J. Saylor, *Jackson Hole, Wyoming* (Norman: University of Oklahoma Press, 1970), p. 200; William C. Everhart, *The National Park Service* (New York: Praeger Publishers, 1972), pp. 136–7.

9. Interview with Horace M. Albright by author, September 7, 1975.

10. Richard Winger to Harold Fabian, January 7, 1932, "Grand Teton" folder, Box 289, GT, NPS, RG 79, NA.

11. Kenneth Chorley to Arthur Demaray, April 12, 1938; Arthur Demaray to Kenneth Chorley, April 14, 1938, File 610-01, pt. 34, Box 1058, GT, NPS, RG 79, NA.

12. A number of memos on the monument subject may be found in ibid., Box 1059, pt. 35.

13. Arthur Demaray to John D. Rockefeller, Jr., June 8, 1939, in ibid., pt. 36.

14. Memorandum to Mr. John D. Rockefeller, Jr., from Kenneth Chorley, June 24, 1939, "Jackson Hole Property," Box 98, Cultural Interests, RG 2, Private Archives of Messrs. Rockefeller.

15. Kenneth Chorley to John D. Rockefeller, Jr., July 31, 1939, in ibid.

16. Ise, *Our National Park Policy*, pp. 442–3.

17. Kenneth Chorley to Arthur Demaray, June 24, 1939, File 610-01, pt. 35, Box 1059, GT, NPS, RG 79, NA.

18. Memorandum from Arthur E. Demaray to Harold Ickes, August 1, 1940, in File 610-01, pt. 36, Box 1059, GT, NPS, RG 79, NA.

19. Kenneth Chorley to Harold Fabian, October 7, 1941, "Jackson Hole Property," Box 98, Cultural Interests, RG 2, Private Archives of Messrs. Rockefeller.

20. Kenneth Chorley to Harold Ickes, November 12, 1940; Harold Ickes to Kenneth Chorley, November 28, 1940, NPS, National Monuments, Jackson Hole, pt. 1, File 12-46, Department of the Interior, RG 48, NA.

21. Thomas Whitcraft to Director, December 12, 1939, File 610-01, pt. 36, Box 1059, GT, NPS, RG 79, NA.

22. "A Preliminary Plan for Grand Teton National Park . . . ," by Charles Smith, Superintendent, July 28, 1941, Box 1054, GT, NPS, RG 79, NA.

23. "Comments on Plans and Reports For the Development of Teton National Park," by A. E. Kendrew, August, 1942, ibid.

24. John D. Rockefeller, Jr., to Harold Ickes. November 27, 1942, in Dieterich, *Compendium*, II: 2, Exhibit 13.

25. For the National Park Service files see File 610-01, pt. 36, Box 1059, GT, NPS, RG 79, NA. For the Rockefeller files see "Jackson Hole Property— Offer and Controversy," Box 107, Cultural Interests, RG 2, Private Archives of Messrs. Rockefeller.

26. "Interview with Laurance Rockefeller," by Ed Edwin, January 10, 1967, pp. 34–5, Oral History Collection of Columbia University.

27. Interview with Horace Albright by author, September 7, 1975.

28. Kenneth Chorley to Harold Fabian, October 7, 1941, "Jackson Hole Property," Box 98, Cultural Interests, RG 2, Private Archives of Messrs. Rockefeller.

29. "Comments on Plans and Reports For the Development of Teton National Park," by A. E. Kendrew, August, 1942, Box 1054, GT, NPS, RG 79, NA.

30. "Interview with Laurance Rockefeller," by Ed Edwin, January 10, 1967, pp. 33–4, Oral History Collection of Columbia University.
31. Harold Ickes to John D. Rockefeller, Jr., December 4, 1942, in Dieterich, *Compendium*, II: 2, Exhibit 13.
32. Memorandum for Secretary Ickes from Director Drury, December 18, 1942, File 610-01, pt. 36, Box 1059, GT, NPS, RG 79, NA.
33. John D. Rockefeller, Jr., to Harold Ickes, January 5, 1943, NPS—National Monuments, Jackson Hole, pt. 1, File 12-46, Department of the Interior, RG 48, NA; Harold Ickes to John D. Rockefeller, Jr., January 7, 1943, "Jackson Hole Project—Offer and Controversy," Box 107, Cultural Interests, RG 2, Private Archives of Messrs. Rockefeller.
34. Harold Ickes to John D. Rockefeller, Jr., February 19, 1943, NPS—National Monuments, Jackson Hole, pt. 1, File 12-46, Department of the Interior, RG 48, NA.
35. Harold Ickes to Major General Edwin M. Watson, February 27, 1943, in ibid.
36. Harold Ickes to John D. Rockefeller, Jr., March 12, 1943, in ibid.
37. Harold Ickes to John D. Rockefeller, Jr., February 19, 1943, in ibid.
38. Joseph O'Mahoney to Harold Ickes, February 23, 1943, in ibid.
39. Dieterich, *Compendium*, II: 2, Exhibits 14, 15.
40. John D. Rockefeller, Jr., to Harold Ickes, March 17, 1943, NPS—National Monuments, Jackson Hole, pt. 1, File 12-46, Department of the Interior, RG 48, NA.
41. *Jackson Hole Courier*, March 22, 1943.
42. Quoted in the *Jackson Hole Courier*, March 25, 1943.
43. *Jackson Hole Courier*, March 22, 1943.
44. Ibid.
45. Ibid., April 15, 1943. The quote was on the *Courier* masthead from April 15, 1943 through August 16, 1943.
46. *Congressional Record*, March 19, 1943, pp. 2233–5.
47. *Jackson Hole Courier*, May 6, 1943.
48. For a statement by Resor of his involvement in the Jackson Hole country, U.S., Congress, Senate, *Hearings Before a Subcommittee of the Committee on Public Lands and Surveys . . . Pursuant to S. Res. 250*, 75 Cong., 3rd sess., pp. 111–2.
49. See Dieterich, *Compendium*, II: 2, Exhibit 32.
50. *Time Magazine*, 41 (May 17, 1943): 21.
51. See Dieterich, *Compendium*, II: 2, Exhibit 32.
52. Horace Albright to Westbrook Pegler, September 17, 1943, copy "Correspondence—Jackson Hole," Box I, Struthers Burt Collection, WHRC, UW.
53. Editorial in *The Saturday Evening Post*, (August 28, 1943), copy in Dieterich, *Compendium*, II: 2, Exhibit 32.
54. Harlean James to Frederic Nelson, September 3, 1943, in NPS—National Monuments, Jackson Hole, pt. 2, File 12-46, Department of the Interior, RG 48, NA.
55. Memo from Ben Hibbs to George Lorimer, undated, copy in "Correspondence—Jackson Hole," Box I, Struthers Burt Collection, WHRC, UW.

56. T. A. Larson, *History of Wyoming* (Lincoln: University of Nebraska Press, 1965), p. 498.
57. Bernard DeVoto, "Sacred Cows and Public Lands," *Harper's Magazine* 197 (July, 1948): 52.
58. Dieterich, *Compendium*, II: 2, Exhibit 16.
59. U.S., Congress, House of Representatives, *Hearings Before the Committee on Public Lands . . . Pursuant to H. R. 2241*, 78th Cong., 1st sess., p. 274.
60. *Jackson Hole Courier*, June 17, 1943.
61. Ibid., August 19, 1943.
62. Note for Mr. Straus from the secretary of the interior, August 3, 1943, NPS—National Monuments, Jackson Hole, pt. 2, File 12-46, Department of the Interior, RG 48, NA.
63. "Interview with Conrad Wirth," by Ed Edwin, June 21, 1966, pp. 10–12, Oral History Collection of Columbia University.
64. Ibid., p. 15.
65. *Jackson Hole Courier*, August 19, 1943. Also see Dieterich, *Compendium*, II: 2, Exhibits 24 and 25, for the testimony of the August 17th hearing and a report by Conrad Wirth on the committee's visit to Jackson Hole.
66. Memorandum for the secretary of the interior from R. H. Rutledge, September 16, 1943, in Dieterich, *Compendium*, II: 2, Exhibit 28.
67. *Jackson Hole Courier*, September 14, 1943.
68. Dieterich, *Compendium*, I, 16–18.
69. *Washington Post*, December 31, 1944.
70. *Jackson Hole Courier*, April 29, 1943.
71. The planning and thought that went into the government case are witnessed by the voluminous correspondence in Files 775, 776, 778, Merrill J. Mattes Papers, WHRC, UW.
72. Fryxell's testimony may be found in File 776, Merrill J. Mattes Papers, WHRC, UW.
73. Later, in his memoirs, Judge Kennedy commented that the government had given effective evidence of scientific and historic interest, indicating that he would have ruled for the National Park Service. See T. Blake Kennedy, "Memoirs," pp. 736–9, typescript in the WHRC, UW.
74. *State of Wyoming v. Franke, Federal Supplement*, LVIII, 96. Also see Dieterich, *Compendium*, II: 3, Exhibit 42.
75. *Scottsbluff Star-Herald* (Nebraska), February 13, 1945.
76. Confidential Memorandum for the director from Lawrence C. Merriam, April 10, 1943, "Conferences, 1943," Box 76453, NPS, RG 79, Federal Record Center and Archives, Denver.
77. Lawrence C. Merriam to C. N. Woods, July 1, 1943, "Organization—Teton National Monument, 1943–1945," Box 32186, United States Forest Service, RG 95, Federal Record Center and Archives, Denver.
78. For correspondence see ibid.
79. C. N. Woods to Lyle F. Watts, July 21, 1943, ibid.
80. L. F. Kneipp to C. N. Woods, August 24, 1943, ibid.
81. A number of Forest Service letters indicating a policy of not testifying in *State of Wyoming v. Franke* may be found in ibid.
82. Dieterich, *Compendium*, II: 2, Exhibit 30.

83. See Elmo R. Richardson, *Dams, Parks and Politics* (Lexington, Kentucky: University of Kentucky Press, 1973), pp. 7–10.

84. Dieterich, *Compendium*, II: 3, Exhibits 43, 44, 46.

85. U.S., Congress, House of Representatives, *Hearings Before a Subcommittee on Public Lands of the Committee on Public Lands . . . Pursuant to H. R. 1330*, 80th Cong., 1st sess., p. 196.

86. Ibid., p. 25.

87. Dieterich, *Compendium*, I, pp. 22–3, II: 3, Exhibit 47.

VIII Creating a New Grand Teton National Park

1. John D. Rockefeller, Jr., to Harold Ickes, January 16, 1945, in Leo H. Dieterich, et al. *Jackson Hole National Monument, Wyoming: A Compendium of Important Papers Covering Negotiations in the Establishment and Administration of the National Monument* (4 Vols., Washington: Department of the Interior, ca. 1945, 1950), II, Pt. 3, Exhibit 41.

2. Devereux Butcher to Olaus Murie, June 3, 1943, "Correspondence, 1943," Box I, Olaus and Margaret Murie Collection, WHRC, UW.

3. Robert S. Yard, "Jackson Hole National Monument Borrows Its Grandeur From Surrounding Mountains," *The Living Wilderness* 8 (October, 1943): 3–5.

4. Struthers Burt to Olaus Murie, November 7, 1943, "Correspondence, 1943," Box I, Olaus and Margaret Murie Collection, WHRC, UW.

5. Olaus Murie to Kenneth Reid, June 5, 1943, ibid.

6. U.S., Congress, House of Representatives, *Hearings Before a Subcommittee on Public Lands of the Committee on Public Lands . . . Pursuant to H. R. 1330*, 80th Cong., 1st sess., p. 191. Perhaps the best article seeking to explain the physical and spiritual tie between the mountains and the valley was Olaus Murie's, "The Spirit of Jackson Hole," *National Parks Magazine* (October–December, 1943): 3–7.

7. Handwritten notes of a meeting between Kenneth Chorley, Vanderbilt Webb, Horace Albright, and Newton Drury, December 18, 1944, copy in "Misc. Notes" folder, Box I, Newton Drury Collection, WHRC, UW.

8. Ibid.

9. See Gregory Kendrick, "An Environmental Spokesman: Olaus J. Murie and a Democratic Defense of Wilderness" (unpublished M.A. thesis, Department of History, University of Wyoming, 1977).

10. Correspondence and notes may be found in the "Colter D. Huyler" folder, Box 98, Cultural Interests, RG 2, Private Archives of Messrs. Rockefeller.

11. Coulter Huyler to Laurance Rockefeller, September 12, 1944, ibid.

12. Laurance Rockefeller to Coulter Huyler, September 20, 1944, ibid.

13. Olaus Murie to Kenneth Chorley, September 1, 1944, "Correspondence, 1943," Box I, Olaus and Margaret Murie Collection, WHRC, UW.

14. "Interview with Kenneth Chorley," by Ed Edwin, April 13, 1966, p. 42, Oral History Collection of Columbia University.

15. Kenneth Chorley to John D. Rockefeller, Jr., May 29, 1945, "1945 Transfer to Jackson Hole Preserve" folder, Box 101, Cultural Interests, RG 2, Private Archives of Messrs. Rockefeller.

16. Memorandum from John D. Rockefeller, Jr., to Laurance S. Rockefeller, September 20, 1945, in ibid.
17. The ferry is still operational today.
18. Andrew Kendrew to Kenneth Chorley, February 7, 1946, "Jackson Hole Preserve," Box 101, Cultural Interests, RG 2, Private Archives of Messrs. Rockefeller. In this letter Kendrew related his off-the-record talk with Drury.
19. Olaus Murie, "Improving Jackson Hole," *National Parks Magazine* 46 (January–March, 1946).
20. "Project Memorandum: Jackson Hole Preserve, Inc., Jackson Hole Wildlife Park, Inc., and Grand Teton Lodge and Transportation Company," dated July 30, 1947, in "Jackson Hole Preserve, Inc.," folder, Box 101, Cultural Interests, RG 2, Private Archives of Messrs. Rockefeller.
21. Murie, "Improving Jackson Hole."
22. Ibid.
23. Fairfield Osborn to Emmet T. Hooper, undated, in "Grand Teton Park" folder, Box 17, Horace Albright Papers, UCLA.
24. Olaus Murie to Vanderbilt Webb, November 4, 1945, "Correspondence, 1945," Box I, Olaus and Margaret Murie Collection, WHRC, UW.
25. See Harold Fabian to Laurance Rockefeller, November 30, 1945, "Jackson Hole Preserve," Box 101, Cultural Interests, RG 2, Private Archives of Messrs. Rockefeller; also see Vanderbilt Webb to Olaus Murie, November 20, 1945, and Olaus Murie to Vanderbilt Webb, November 26, 1945, "Correspondence, 1945," Box I, Olaus and Margaret Murie Collection, WHRC, UW.
26. *Hearings . . . Pursuant to H. R. 1330.*
27. "Dollars and Sense About the Jackson Hole National Monument," a four-page brochure by the Izaak Walton League of America, in "Miscellaneous" folder, Box 2, Izaak Walton League Collection, WHRC, UW.
28. Confidential memorandum for the director from John S. McLaughlin, February 26, 1947, "Proposed Legislation, 1944–1947," Box 76453, NPS, RG 79, Federal Archives and Record Center, Denver.
29. U.S., Congress, Senate, *Hearings Before a Subcommittee of the Committee on Public Lands and Surveys . . . Pursuant to S. Res. 250,* 75th Cong., 3rd sess., p. 156.
30. Albert E. Schwabacher to Senator Joseph O'Mahoney, September 24, 1938, "Teton Park Correspondence," Box 36, Joseph C. O'Mahoney Collection, WHRC, UW.
31. Struthers Burt, "The Jackson Hole Plan," *Outdoor America* 9 (November–December, 1944).
32. Olaus Murie to Earnest Linford, February 26, 1948, "Correspondence, 1948," Box I, Olaus and Margaret Murie Collection, WHRC, UW.
33. Olaus Murie to Arthur Carhart, October 23, 1947; Olaus Murie to Frank Barrett, May 24, 1947, "Correspondence, 1947," ibid.
34. Bernard DeVoto, "Easy Chair," *Harper's Magazine* 194 (June, 1947): 546.
35. Bernard DeVoto, "Easy Chair," *Harper's Magazine* 196 (January, 1948): 31. For other articles by DeVoto on the subject of conservation and cattlemen in the West, see: Bernard DeVoto, "The West Against Itself," *Harper's Magazine* 194 (January, 1947); Bernard DeVoto, "Sacred Cows and Public

Lands," *Harper's Magazine* 197 (July, 1948); Bernard DeVoto, "Easy Chair," *Harper's Magazine* 197 (July, 1948). Also see Arthur Carhart, "Flank Attack in Jackson Hole," *Sports Afield* (February, 1948).

36. Confidential Memorandum for the regional director from John S. Mc-Laughlin, March 11, 1947, "Proposed Legislation, 1944–1947," Box 76453, NPS, RG 79, Federal Archives and Record Center, Denver.

37. Leslie Miller to Wilford Neilson, May 17, 1948, copy in "Jackson Hole" folder, Box 131, Joseph C. O'Mahoney Collection, WHRC, UW.

38. The account of this meeting is based primarily on a Memorandum for the Director from Conrad Wirth, April 21, 1949, in Dieterich, *Compendium*, II: 4, Exhibit 56.

39. Ibid.

40. The figures used are from a letter from Clifford Hansen to Lester Bagley, January 5, 1950, in Lester Bagley file on Jackson Hole National Monument, in the possession of Rex Corsi, Wyoming Game and Fish Commission, Cheyenne.

41. Memorandum for the director from Conrad Wirth, April 21, 1949, in Dieterich, *Compendium*, II: 4, Exhibit 56.

42. Ibid., Exhibit 56A.

43. Joseph O'Mahoney to President Harry Truman, December 12, 1949, "Jackson Hole" folder, Box 131, Joseph O'Mahoney Papers, WHRC, UW.

44. Clifford Wilson to Senator Lester Hunt, February 4, 1950, in Lester Bagley file on Jackson Hole National Monument, in the possession of Rex Corsi, Wyoming Game and Fish Commission, Cheyenne.

45. The bill may be found in Dieterich, *Compendium*, II: 4, Exhibit 60.

46. Ibid.

47. Ibid.

48. Ibid.

49. Ibid.

50. The wilderness movement was on the defensive, according to Michael McCloskey, "Wilderness Movement at the Crossroads, 1945–1970," *Pacific Historical Review* 41 (August, 1972): 346–61.

51. John D. Rockefeller to Horace Albright, January 10, 1950, "Rockefeller Correspondence" folder, Box I, Horace Albright Papers, UCLA.

IX   Postscript for a Park

1. *Jackson Hole Courier*, February 16, 1928.

2. *Wyoming State Tribune*, October 11, 1959.

3. Floyd K. Harmston, Richard E. Lund, J. Richard Williams, *A Study of the Resources, People, and Economy of Teton County, Wyoming* (Laramie, Wyoming: University of Wyoming, 1959), pp. 32, 75.

4. Dwight M. Blood, Floyd K. Harmston, G.R. Rajender, *A Study of the Resources, People, and Economy of Teton County, Wyoming* (Laramie, Wyoming: University of Wyoming, 1967), p. 65: Garnet E. Premer, et al., *Recreation and Tourism in the Teton County Economy* (Laramie: University of Wyoming, 1979), p. 23.

5. David J. Saylor, *Jackson Hole, Wyoming* (Norman: University of Oklahoma Press, 1970), p. 205.

6. Horace Albright to Frank Barrett, February 1, 1951, B Correspondence file, Box I; Horace Albright to Milward Simpson, July 26, 1954, S Correspondence File; Milward Simpson to Horace Albright, December 21, 1962; Clifford Hansen to Horace Albright, November 26, 1962, "Grand Teton" file, Box 4, all in Horace Albright Papers, UCLA.
7. "Interview with Governor Clifford Hansen," by Ed Edwin, July 15, 1966, pp. 47–53, Oral History Collection of Columbia University.
8. See John Ise, *Our National Park Policy: A Critical History* (Baltimore: Johns Hopkins University Press, 1961) *passim*, for numerous problems associated with the various concessioners. For criticism of the Grand Teton Lodge Company see Frank Calkins, *Jackson Hole* (New York: Alfred Knopf, 1973), pp. 171–8.
9. "Interview with Kenneth Chorley," by Ed Edwin, April 13, 1966, p. 81, Oral History Collection of Columbia University.
10. Ibid., pp. 81–2.
11. "Interview with Homer C. Richards," by Ed Edwin, July 18, 1966, p. 34, Oral History Collection of Columbia University: Calkins, *Jackson Hole*, pp. 172–3.
12. Devereux Butcher, "Resorts or Wilderness," *Atlantic Monthly* 207 (February, 1961): 49.
13. See James R. Simon, "When Winter Comes to Jackson Hole Wildlife Park," *Animal Kingdom* (January–February, 1949), pp. 10–14. In this article James Simon, the park director, reported on the winter difficulties of the animals. For considerable correspondence on the dissolving of the wildlife park, see "Jackson Hole Wildlife Park," folder, Box 104, Cultural Interests, RG 2, Private Archives of Messrs. Rockefeller.
14. *Jackson Hole News*, September 8, 1977.
15. Quoted in "Draft Statement For Management: John D. Rockefeller, Jr., Memorial Parkway," (Grand Teton National Park: Office of the Superintendent, *circa* 1972), p. 11.
16. Philip M. Hocker, "Yellowstone: The Region Is Greater Than the Sum of Its Parks," *Sierra* 64 (July/August, 1979): 8–12.
17. "Comments on Conservation, 1900 to 1960," an interview with Horace M. Albright and Newton B. Drury conducted by Amelia R. Fry, March 21, 1961, pp. 37–8, Regional Cultural History Project, Bancroft Library, U.C., Berkeley.
18. Lester Bagley to Henry Burgess, May 15, 1950, in Lester Bagley file on Jackson Hole National Monument, in the possession of Rex Corsi, Wyoming Game and Fish Commission, Cheyenne.
19. Ise, *Our National Park Policy*, p. 507.
20. The continuing interest in this problem is evident from the holding of an "Elk Ecology and Management Symposium," April 3–5, 1978, at the University of Wyoming campus, in which over forty papers were presented on various aspects of the care and management of elk.
21. Jean Hocker, "Jackson Hole: Are We Loving It to Death," *Sierra* 64 (July/August, 1979): 15.
22. Ibid., 16. For more discussion of population pressures in Jackson Hole see: *Los Angeles Times*, May 27, 1978; *The Wall Street Journal*, Decem-

ber 10, 1979; and Jean Hocker, "The League Defends Jackson Hole," *Izaak Walton News* 4 (April/May, 1980): 1–3.
23. For more detail on these contemporary problems see the *Jackson Hole News*, October 23, November 6, and November 20, 1975; January 8, January 22, February 5, February 19, March 3, March 31, September 29, 1976; May 4, August 24, and September 21, 1977.
24. *Jackson Hole Guide*, March 27, 1980.
25. *Jackson Hole News*, September 11, 1975, Grand Teton National Park Supplement.

BIBLIOGRAPHY

1 Primary Sources

A. MANUSCRIPT COLLECTION

Because the heart of this study is based on primary sources it might be well to comment briefly on them. The voluminous records of the National Park Service provided a storehouse of material. The National Archives in Washington divides the documents by parks. The Yellowstone National Park file was useful for the early years; after 1929 the Grand Teton National Park file provided much unused material. These records include communications among department officials and correspondence between staff and field officials with private persons and organizations, state officials, state and federal administrators and legislators. Furthermore, they include many in-house reports not found elsewhere. These reports are too numerous to list, but may be found in the notes. The records of the Bureau of Reclamation provided supplementary information, as did those of the Bureau of the Budget and the Department of the Interior.

Materials were also available in the Federal Archives and Record Center, Denver. Sometimes these documents duplicate Washington, but much local park correspondence, memorandums, and reports that never reached headquarters may be found from this source. The records of Grand Teton National Park and the United States Forest Service were particularly significant.

Of course the accomplishment of the park involved a combined effort of government and private enterprise. For a complete story the Snake River Land Company records would have to be consulted. These records, as well as those of John D. Rockefeller, Jr.'s and Laurance Rockefeller's varied conservation interests and projects, may be found in the Private Archives of Messrs. Rockefeller, Rockefeller Center, New York.

Finally, the University of Wyoming Western History Research Center assisted by providing materials on Teton National Forest, various conservation figures, and state and federal officials.

Collections that were most helpful are as follows :

National Archives, Washington.
     National Park Service (Record Group 79).
     Yellowstone National Park.
     Grand Teton National Park.
     United States Forest Service (Record Group 95).
     Bureau of the Budget (Record Group 51).
     Department of the Interior (Record Group 48).
Federal Archives and Record Center, Denver.
     Grand Teton National Park (Record Group 79).
     United States Forest Service (Record Group 95).
Private Archives of Messrs. Rockefeller, Rockefeller Center, New York.
     Cultural Interests (Record Group 2).
Western History Research Center, University of Wyoming, Laramie.
     Horace Albright Collection.
     Struthers Burt Collection.
     Izaak Walton League Collection.
     John B. Kendrick Collection.
     T. Blake Kennedy Collection.
     Richard Leigh Collection.
     Merrill J. Mattes Collection.
     Olaus and Margaret Murie Collection.
     Joseph C. O'Mahoney Collection.
     William L. Simpson Collection.
     Teton National Forest Collection.
Yellowstone Archives, Yellowstone National Park.
     Albright Correspondence—Grand Teton National Park, 1923–1927.
University of California at Los Angeles Archives.
     Horace M. Albright Papers.

B. PERSONAL INTERVIEWS.

Albright, Horace M.
Fabian, Josephine
Lamb, George
Mattes, Merrill
Murie, Margaret

C. ORAL HISTORY TRANSCRIPTS.

Oral History Collection of Columbia University. Jackson Hole Preserve, Incorporated. This collection consists of thirteen interviews by Edward Edwin in 1966 of prominent persons in the establishment of the park. The transcript totals 1,094 pages. A copy may be found in the Western History Research Center, University of Wyoming. Those interviewed are:
     Horace M. Albright
     Mrs. Struthers Burt and Nathaniel Burt
     Kenneth Chorley

Jack Dornen

Harold Fabian

Clifford P. Hansen

Harry E. Klissold

W. C. Lawrence

Leslie A. Miller

Homer C. Richards

Laurance C. Richards

Conrad L. Wirth

Mike Yokel

Albright, Horace M. "Reminiscences." Oral History Research Office, Columbia University.

Fry, Amelia Roberts. "Comments on Conservation, 1900 to 1960." Interviews with Horace M. Albright and Newton B. Drury, March 21, 23, 1961. Oral History Office, Bancroft Library, University of California, Berkeley, California.

"Interview with Mr. Horace Albright by Assistant Superintendent of Grand Teton National Park Haraden and Chief Naturalist Dilley at Jackson Lake Lodge, September 12, 1967." Copy in the Horace Albright Collection, Western History Research Center, University of Wyoming, Laramie.

D. GOVERNMENT DOCUMENTS.

Dieterich, Leo H., et al., *Jackson Hole National Monument, Wyoming: A Compendium of Important Papers Covering Negotiation in the Establishment and Administration of the National Monument*. 4 Vols. Washington: Department of the Interior, ca. 1945, 1950. Copy in Western History Research Center, University of Wyoming. This is an invaluable collection of information, articles, reports, and hearings on the park struggle from 1898 to 1950.

State of Wyoming v. Franke, Federal Supplement, LVIII.

U.S., Congress, Senate, *Letter from the Secretary of the Interior*, Sen. Doc. 39, 55th Cong., 3rd sess.

U.S., Congress, House, *Letter from the Secretary of the Interior*, House Doc. 500, 57th Cong., 1st sess.

U.S., Congress, Senate, *Hearings before the Committee on Public Lands and Surveys on S. 3176, S. 3427, S. 3428, S. 3433, S. 4073, S. 4209, S. 4258, and H.R. 9387*, 69th Cong., 1st sess.

U.S., Congress, Senate, *Hearings before the Committee on Public Lands and Surveys on S. 2570, S. 2571, and S. 3071*, 70th Cong., 1st sess.

U.S., Congress, Senate, *Hearings before the Committee on Public Lands and Surveys Pursuant to S. 237*, 70th Cong., 2nd sess, Part 2.

U.S., Congress, Senate, *Hearings before a Subcommittee of the Committee on Public Lands and Surveys . . . Pursuant to S. Res. 226*, 72nd Cong., 2nd sess.

U.S., Congress, Senate, *Hearings before a Subcommittee of the Committee on Public Lands and Surveys . . . Pursuant to S. Res. 226*, 73rd Cong., 2nd sess.

See U.S., Congress, Senate, *Hearings before a Subcommittee of the Committee on Public Lands and Surveys . . . Pursuant to S. Res. 250,* 75th Cong., 3rd sess.

U.S., Congress, House, *Hearings Before the Committee on the Public Lands . . . on H.R. 2241,* 78th Cong., 1st sess.

U.S., Congress, House of Representatives, *Hearings Before a Subcommittee on Public Lands of the Committee on Public Lands . . . Pursuant to H.R. 1330,* 80th Cong., 1st sess.

E. NEWSPAPERS

Denver Post
Grand Teton
Jackson Hole Courier
Jackson Hole Guide
Jackson Hole News
New York Herald Tribune
Rocky Mountain News
Washington Post
Wyoming State Tribune

II Secondary Sources

A. Articles, Pamphlets and Books. The following is a selective list of secondary source materials that have been useful in the preparation of this study. No attempt has been made to be exhaustive with regard to materials on Grand Teton National Park or Jackson Hole.

Albright, Horace M. "The Glory of Jackson Hole." *New York Times Magazine.* January 21, 1945: 22–23.

Anderson, Chester C. *The Elk of Jackson Hole.* Cheyenne, Wyoming: Wyoming Game and Fish Commission, Bulletin 10, 1958.

Bartlett, Richard A. *Nature's Yellowstone.* Albuquerque, New Mexico: University of New Mexico Press, 1974.

Bates, J. Leonard. "Fulfilling American Democracy: The Conservation Movement, 1907–1921." *Mississippi Valley Historical Review* 44 (June, 1957): 29–57.

Betts, Robert B. *Along the Ramparts of the Tetons: The Saga of Jackson Hole, Wyoming.* Boulder: Colorado Associated University Press, 1978.

Blood, Dwight M., Harmston, Floyd K., Rajender, G.R. *A Study of the Resources, People, and Economy of Teton County, Wyoming.* Laramie, Wyoming: University of Wyoming, 1967.

Boyd, Katharine. "Heard About Jackson Hole?" *Atlantic Monthly* 175 (April, 1945): 102–6.

Brant, Irving. "The Fight over Jackson Hole." *The Nation* 161 (July 7, 1945): 13–14.

Burt, Struthers. "The Battle of Jackson Hole." *The Nation* 122 (March 3, 1926): 225–7.

———. *The Delectable Mountains.* New York: Charles Scribner's Sons, 1927.

————. *The Diary of a Dude-Wrangler.* New York: Charles Scribner's Sons, 1938.

————. "The Jackson Hole Plan." *Outdoor America* 9 (November–December, 1944).

Calkins, Frank. *Jackson Hole.* New York: Alfred A. Knopf, 1973.

Carhart, Arthur. "Flank Attack in Jackson Hole." *Sports Afield* (February, 1948).

Clawson, Marion, Held, Burnell. *The Federal Lands: Their Use and Management.* Baltimore, Maryland: Johns Hopkins University Press, 1957.

DeVoto, Bernard. "Sacred Cows and Public Lands." *Harper's Magazine* 197 (July, 1948): 44–55.

————. "The West Against Itself." *Harper's Magazine* 194 (January, 1947): 231–56.

Erwin, Marie H., ed. *Wyoming Historical Blue Book.* Denver: Bradford-Robinson Printing Company, 1946.

Everhart, William C. *The National Park Service.* New York: Praeger Publishers, 1972.

"Harold Pegram Fabian." Pamphlet deposited in the library, Grand Teton National Park, Moose, Wyoming.

Fabian, Josephine C. *Jackson Hole: How to Discover and Enjoy It.* Salt Lake City, 1949.

Fosdick, Raymond B. *John D. Rockefeller, Jr.: A Portrait.* New York: Harper & Brothers, 1956.

Frantz, Joe. *Aspects of the American West: Three Essays.* College Station, Texas: Texas A & M Press, 1976.

Frome, Michael. *Battle for the Wilderness.* New York: Praeger Publishers, 1974.

Fryxell, Fritiof. *The Tetons: Interpretations of a Mountain Landscape.* Berkeley: University of California Press, 1938.

Goetzmann, William H. *Exploration and Empire.* New York: Alfred A. Knopf, 1966.

Gould, Lewis. *Wyoming: A Political History, 1868–1896.* New Haven, Conn.: Yale University Press, 1970.

Gowans, Fred. *Rocky Mountain Rendezvous: A History of the Fur Trade Rendezvous, 1825–1840.* Provo, Utah: Brigham Young University Press, 1976.

Hampton, H. Duane. *How the Calvary Saved Our National Parks.* Bloomington: University of Indiana Press, 1971.

Harmston, Floyd K., Lund, Richard E., Williams, J. Richard. *A Study of the Resources, People, and Economy of Teton County, Wyoming.* Laramie, Wyoming: University of Wyoming, 1959.

Hays, Samuel P. *Conservation As Efficiency.* Cambridge, Massachusetts: Harvard University Press, 1959.

Hibbard, Benjamin. *History of the Public Land Policies.* Madison, Wisconsin: University of Wisconsin Press, 1965 ed., first published in 1924.

Hocker, Jean. "Jackson Hole: Are We Loving It to Death." *Sierra* 64 (July/August, 1979): 14–16.

Hocker, Philip M. "Yellowstone: The Region is Greater Than the Sum of Its Parks." *Sierra* 64 (July/August, 1979): 8–12.

Huntley, Theodore. "Mr. Rockefeller Strikes a Snag." *The Senator* 1 (May 6, 1939): 12–14.

Irland, Frederic. "The Wyoming Game Stronghold." *Scribner's Magazine* 34 (September, 1903): 259–76.

Ise, John. *Our National Park Policy: A Critical History.* Baltimore: Johns Hopkins University Press, 1961.

Jackson, William T. "The Creation of Yellowstone National Park." *Mississippi Valley Historical Review* 29 (September, 1942): 187–206.

Jones, Holway R. *John Muir and the Sierra Club: The Battle for Yosemite.* San Francisco: Sierra Club, 1965.

Kendrick, Gregory D. "An Environmental Spokesman: Olaus J. Murie and a Democratic Defense of Wilderness." *Annals of Wyoming* 50 (Fall, 1978): 213–302.

Larson, T.A. *History of Wyoming.* Lincoln, Nebraska: University of Nebraska Press, 1965.

Leopold, Aldo. *A Sand County Almanac.* New York: Sierra Club/Ballantine Books, 1970.

McCloskey, Michael. "Wilderness Movement at the Crossroads, 1945–1970." *Pacific Historical Review* 41 (August, 1972): 346–61.

Marshall, Robert. *Alaska Wilderness,* edited and with an introduction by George Marshall. Berkeley: University of California Press, 1970 ed.

Mattes, Merrill J. "Jackson Hole, Crossroads of the Western Fur Trade, 1807–1829." *Pacific Northwest Quarterly* 37 (April, 1946): 87–108.

Mr. John D. Rockefeller, Jr.'s Proposed Gift of Land for the National Park System in Wyoming. n.p., n.d.

Murie, Margaret and Olaus. *Wapiti Wilderness.* New York: Alfred A. Knopf, 1966.

Murie, Olaus. *The Elk of North America.* Harrisburg, Penn.: Wildlife Management Institute, 1951.

———. "Fenced Wildlife for Jackson Hole." *National Parks Magazine* 20 (January–March, 1946): 8–11.

———. "The Spirit of Jackson Hole." *National Parks Magazine* (October–December, 1943): 3–7.

Nash, Roderick, ed. *The American Environment: Readings in the History of Conservation.* Reading, Mass.: Addison-Wesley Pub. Co., 1968.

———. "The American Invention of National Parks." *American Quarterly* 22 (1970): 726–35.

———. *Wilderness and the American Mind.* New Haven, Connecticut: Yale University Press, 1967.

Pinchot, Gifford. *The Fight for Conservation.* New York: Doubleday, Page and Company, 1910.

Pinkett, Harold. *Gifford Pinchot: Forester.* Urbana, Illinois: University of Illinois Press, 1974.

Premer, Garnet E., et al. *Recreation and Tourism in the Teton County Economy.* Laramie: University of Wyoming, 1979.

Richardson, Elmo R. *Dams, Parks and Politics.* Lexington, Kentucky: University of Kentucky Press, 1973.

Ross, Alexander. *The Fur Hunters of the Far West,* edited by Kenneth A. Spaulding. Norman: University of Oklahoma Press, 1956, 1st Ed., 1855.

Runte, Alfred. "The National Park Idea: Origins and Paradox of the American Experience." *Journal of Forest History* 21 (April, 1977): 64–75.
———. *National Parks: The American Experience.* Lincoln: University of Nebraska Press, 1979.
———. "Worthless Lands—Our National Parks." *The American West* 10 (May, 1973): 4–11.
Russell, Carl P. *100 Years in Yosemite.* Berkeley: University of California Press, 1947.
Sanborn, Margaret. *The Grand Tetons: The Story of the Men Who Tamed the Western Wilderness.* New York: G.P. Putnam & Son, 1978.
Saylor, David J. *Jackson Hole, Wyoming.* Norman: University of Oklahoma Press, 1970.
Shankland, Robert. *Steve Mather of the National Parks.* New York: Alfred A. Knopf, 1954.
Simon, James R. "When Winter Comes to Jackson Hole Wildlife Park." *Animal Kingdom* (January–February, 1949).
Smythe, William E. *The Conquest of the Arid West.* Seattle: University of Washington Press, 1969 ed., first ed., 1899.
Steen, Harold. *The U.S. Forest Service: A History.* Seattle: University of Washington Press, 1976.
Stegner, Wallace. *The Uneasy Chair: A Biography of Bernard DeVoto.* New York: Doubleday & Co., Inc., 1974.
Stone, Christopher. *Should Trees Have Standing?* New York: Discus Books, 1974.
Swain, Donald. *Wilderness Defender: Horace M. Albright and Conservation.* Chicago: University of Chicago Press, 1970.
Taylor, George Rogers, ed. *The Turner Thesis Concerning the Role of the Frontier in American History.* Lexington, Mass.: D.C. Heath and Co., 1972, 3rd Ed.
Udall, Stewart. *The Quiet Crisis.* New York: Avon Books, 1963.
Vap, Jeanne Robertson. "The Grand Teton: Frontier Newspaper in the Twentieth Century." *Annals of Wyoming* 42 (October, 1970): 149–82.
Webb, Walter Prescott. *The Great Plains.* Boston: Ginn and Company, 1931.
Wood, Harold. "Protecting Nature's Monuments." *Sierra Club Bulletin* 59 (March, 1974): 4–7.
Yard, Robert S. "Jackson Hole National Monument Borrows Its Grandeur From Surrounding Mountains." *The Living Wilderness* 8 (October, 1943): 3–5.

INDEX